Culture and Faith

Und wie von altersher im Stillen
Ein Liebewerk nach eignem Willen
Der Philosoph, der Dichter schuf,
So wirst Du Höchste Gunst erzielen,
Denn edlen Seelen vorzufühlen
Ist wünschenswertester Beruf.

—GOETHE

Culture and Faith

By

RICHARD KRONER

THE UNIVERSITY OF CHICAGO PRESS

THE UNIVERSITY OF CHICAGO PRESS, CHICAGO 37
Cambridge University Press, London, N.W. 1, England
W. J. Gage & Co., Limited, Toronto 2B, Canada

Copyright 1951 by The University of Chicago
All rights reserved. Published 1951
Composed and printed by
THE UNIVERSITY OF CHICAGO PRESS
Chicago, Illinois, U.S.A.

TO

My Students

at Union Theological Seminary
New York

AND AT THE

Theological School of Temple University
Philadelphia

Preface

THE following treatise represents a completely new version of a book I published in 1928 under the title *Die Selbstver-wirklichung des Geistes: Grundriss der Kulturphilosophie.*[1] The outer and inner experience of more than twenty years has changed my views considerably, the more so since these twenty years have brought about a tremendous revolution in political, social, cultural, and spiritual life. Especially did the German catastrophe of 1933, which seemed to destroy in a fortnight the tradition of a thousand years, deeply impress itself upon my mind. The philosopher may sincerely and assiduously aspire to eternal truth; yet he can never escape his own time.

When I wrote the book of 1928 I was little affected by the problems of the time. On the contrary, it was a somewhat romantic mood which made me turn away from the unpleasant aspect of the present to seek refuge in the classical period of German culture. I felt that I lived in the midst of an irresistible decay, the symptoms of which were so unmistakable and deep-rooted that I saw no other remedy than a vigorous renewal of the great upheaval characteristic of the days in which Kant and Herder, Fichte and Schiller, Schelling and Hölderlin, Hegel and Goethe, had disseminated the riches of their ideas. So I fled into that past paradise of the mind and tried as best I could to make use of the harvest I had inherited.

Soon after the publication of my book, my colleague in the Cultural Department of the Technological Institute at Dresden, Dr. Paul Tillich, wrote an article in which he criticized its conservative attitude as well as the way in which I had dealt with the relation between culture and religion. He insisted that religion should not be placed side by side with the other spheres of civilization but should be conceived separately. Not long before this he had written a brilliant pamphlet defending the thesis that it is theology and not philosophy which is able to offer an ultimate

1. Tübingen: J. C. B. Mohr.

understanding of culture. This pamphlet had the significant title: "Ueber die Idee einer Theologie der Kultur."[2] His arguments were elucidating, and subsequent conversations with the author intensified my feeling that he was right. I had already acknowledged in my book that religion is the zenith of the whole cultural trend. Tillich's emphasis only strengthened this opinion, which was further supported by the growing Kierkegaardian movement initiated so powerfully by Karl Barth's commentary on Paul's Epistle to the Romans. Finally, the existentialist philosophy, as expounded by my former colleague at the University of Freiburg in Baden, Martin Heidegger, in his strange but stirring book, *Sein und Zeit*, invited me to rethink my position.[3]

But not until the catastrophe of 1933 came upon Germany did I realize the full weight of all these intellectual and spiritual factors. Only when the storm broke did I recognize how much I had overestimated not only German idealism but the entire power and truth of philosophical idealism. The events of that fateful year illuminated with lightning clarity the frailty of human civilization and of humanism in general. I then found myself obliged to reconsider the relation between thought and faith, between reason and revelation, between culture and religion. I realized that the separation of philosophy and theology as maintained in modern thought had to be revised.

My emigration, first to England and finally to the United States, greatly widened my horizon in many respects. Once more I learned the truth of the theological insight presented by Goethe in his *Faust* through the words of Mephisto, "I am a part of that power which always wants evil, but which always creates the good." In my case at least, evil was turned into good, since my emigration coerced me into enriching my inner experience through learning not only the English language but also the English mode of living, thinking, and acting, in a more intimate way than would ever have been possible without emigration. For the first time I saw from within democracy how democracy works, and I discovered the profound meaning of co-operation in public

2. In *Kantstudien* (Berlin: Pan Verlag, Rolf Heise, 1920).

3. I also owe gratitude to the penetrating discussion of my philosophical views by Siegfried Marck in his book *Die Dialectic in der Philosophie der Gegenwart* (2 vols.; Tübingen: J. C. B. Mohr, Vol. I, 1929; Vol. II, 1931), pp. 56–90.

activities and political life. But it was not only the new spirit and
the new kind of human relationships with which I came in contact
but also the new opportunity of looking at my own country and
at my own culture from outside, which enabled me to correct
prejudices and predilections, thus enlarging my perspectives to
appraise more justly the true values of foreign achievements.

A new man thus developed. He had to write a new book.

I lived in England near Oxford for a few weeks with the late
Bishop Boutflower. One day he gave me a book which immediately fascinated me and elevated my heart as well as my intellect. Its
title was *Beyond Tragedy*. This was exactly the sort of inspiration
and consolation which I needed and which mysteriously agreed
with my own faith. So I became a disciple of the author, Reinhold Niebuhr, whose name I had not known before. I trust that
the new version of my system will show traces of his influence.

However, though modified in the directions intimated, my
thought still preserves much from German idealism, and I am not
willing to repudiate this inheritance. In my book published in
1928 I took a position somewhere between Kant and Hegel. With
Kant I refused to accept any dogmatic or speculative theology,
but with Hegel I refused to be satisfied with ethical idealism as
the highest and ultimate wisdom. With Kant I believed that philosophy approaches the incomprehensible without ever penetrating it, but with Hegel I held that a thing-in-itself cannot express
this self-limitation of thought but that the dialectical method
must vindicate and verify this comprehension of the incomprehensible.

Today I deviate from both Kant and Hegel and, indeed, from
all forms of philosophical idealism in my conviction that the limit
of philosophy is determined and also illuminated by faith and
theology. I no longer consider religion to be a state in the self-
realization of mind or a link in the creative process of culture. I
have come to see that the human mind and the divine mind are
separated from each other by a chasm which is reflected by the
antagonism between culture and faith. Consequently, the new
version of my system emphasizes this antagonism and attempts to
characterize the relation between the two powers in a more subtle
and, I hope, a more adequate fashion.

If I am not mistaken, the philosophy of the future will seek a
better balance among the spheres of world, God, and man than
has been attained so far. Philosophy from the outset has toiled to
bring about the right relation among these three realms of being.
However, in the three epochs of history that lie behind us, this
task was never satisfactorily discharged. In antiquity the idea of
the cosmos was so prevalent that God and man were not recognized with respect to their peculiar mode of existence; both were
regarded as parts or components of the universe, visible and invisible. Christian philosophy based on biblical revelation emphasized the absolute transcendence of God and subordinated the
world and everything within the world to theology. Still man was
regarded as belonging to the world, though created in the image   ·
of God. Only modern thought liberates man from the fetters of
both cosmology and theology and puts him on the highest level of
reality. Indeed, all the outstanding modern books on philosophy
center around man.[4] In Kant this trend reached its climax but also
its critical limitation. Hegel aimed at the synthesis of cosmological, theological, and epistemological thought, thus uniting the
trends of antiquity, Christianity, and modernity. But the modern
strain was too strong in him to allow full acknowledgment of the
weight inherent in faith and Christian theology. The task is therefore yet to be solved.

After having witnessed the brutal forces of a new barbarity in
full sway, we have learned that the trend of modernity has led to
dehumanization. *Man the Measure*—this title of a recently published book was already obsolete when it appeared. Man is by no
means and in no sense the measure either of truth or of virtue or
of any other value. The more he endeavors to make himself the
measure, the more he degenerates into something subhuman.
Nietzsche's arrogant exclamation, which exalts man as the creator
of all values, threatens to destroy all values and man himself. Man
can be human only if he measures himself by standards higher
than his own. This is the truth of theological philosophy.

4. Cf. the titles: *An Essay concerning Human Understanding; Treatise on the
Principles of Human Knowledge; Lectures on the Philosophy of the Human
Mind* (Th. Brown); *Treatise on Human Nature; Discours sur la méthode;* etc.
Spinoza's work is not accidentally entitled *Ethics.* In Leibniz' monadology the
human self is made the model of all existence.

Existentialism, now the "philosophie à la mode," is the last cry of a dying humanistic metaphysics.[5] In its French, atheistic form it sounds a rather hysterical note that no longer rings convincingly. However, by denying the possibility of any speculative knowledge, if detached from the personal and individual subjectivity of the philosopher, it approaches a philosophy of faith. Rather it reapproaches such a philosophy, since Kierkegaard, the initiator of the whole existentialist movement, claimed the thinker to be "existential" only inasmuch as he is a Christian believer. Current existentialism mocks Kierkegaard when it uses his term "existence" in a sense contrary to his own intention.

However, Kierkegaard did not solve the problem of how Christian theology can be reconciled to secular philosophy. He did not even see a legitimate problem in such a reconciliation, although he took his concepts largely from his great adversary Hegel. We are not permitted to shun this problem if we wish to save modern insights about man and yet return to Christian views. I hope my book will contribute to the awareness of the urgency of that problem and to the foundation of a considered solution. The question of how we can philosophize as Christians imperatively demands an answer. The Augustinian position, which presupposes that the thinking mind and the believing heart coincide, was the gift of a blessed hour in the history of Christian thought. We cannot imitate it. We are shaken by outer and inner experiences which have deprived us of the naïveté inherent in such a presupposition. This naïve trust in the harmony between reason and faith was already broken when Anselm set out to demonstrate by means of reason that God exists. It was completely destroyed when Albert and Thomas separated natural and revealed theology. Modern times finally drew the conclusion that philosophy and theology are different sciences, different with respect to their sources of truth, to their methods of procedure, and to their goals.

But this separation ultimately disrupts the consciousness and even the life of man. There cannot be two kinds of truth, unrelated to each other. A new synthesis must be achieved. This task is not confined to the relation between two sciences, philosophy as a secular enterprise and theology as a sacred wisdom; it concerns

5. Cf. Jean-Paul Sartre, *Existentialisme est un humanisme* (1946).

the relation between man's own effort to civilize himself, in all its ramifications, and God's intention and guidance—the relation between culture and faith. The following outline of a system strives after a solution of this supreme problem—an eternal, but also a very actual, one.

The book proceeds from experience, which is the root and the occasion of all cultural activity, through a survey of the cultural realms to faith as the consummation, as well as the limitation, of man's efforts and achievements. Since our whole civilization is endangered today because the modern principle of the division of cultural realms has divided the heart of man, only a radical and fundamental reconsideration and revision of the presuppositions and the ends of the whole enterprise can save and renew the belief in man's striving and working. There cannot be any understanding of the nature of culture without a philosophy of experience, and there cannot be any understanding of the deficiency of culture without a philosophy of faith. Experience originates, faith crowns, culture.

The first part of the book, therefore, deals with the problem of experience as the source not only of knowledge but of the entire human consciousness and of the specifically human task emerging out of unavoidable, but insoluble, contradictions. The second part develops the system of cultural realms, each of which is conceived as a specific solution of those principal contradictions. However, none of these solutions is ultimate, each is limited and deficient in some respect. Thus, finally, the question arises as to whether faith can make good the deficiencies or whether faith also is entangled in, and subject to, contradictions. The third part gives an answer to this question. It tries to construct a bridge from secular philosophy to Christian theology, from the understanding of culture to the understanding of faith, and from the self-comprehension of man to the comprehension of the Word of God.

I wish to thank Harcourt, Brace and Company, for permission to quote the verses from T. S. Eliot's *The Cocktail Party*.

RICHARD KRONER

CUMMINGTON, MASSACHUSETTS
August 1949

Acknowledgments

FIRST, I wish to thank my students for giving me the opportunity to teach them and to answer questions. Only one who has been deprived of this opportunity for many years can fully appraise the great help provided by teaching not only for improving one's knowledge and judgment but also for provoking creative thought.

In the second place, I would like to thank my colleagues for instructive and stimulating conversations in the corridors and offices of Union Theological Seminary. Especially I thank Reinhold Niebuhr, who, despite the great demands made upon his time, took the trouble to read my manuscript and give me some advice.

I have also to thank Mrs. Grace McGraw Smith, a former student of mine, for her careful correction of my English. Not a few Teutonisms were eradicated by her thoughtful and energetic hand. However, I am responsible not only for the content but also for the style of the book; any faults that might be discovered in either should be imputed to me alone. Finally, I am indebted to Dr. Marion Shows for reading the proofs.

R. K.

Table of Contents

III. FAITH

Introduction

A PHILOSOPHIC system may be called an "experiment in thought," since it depends upon experience and tries to interpret the data of experience by means of thought. Whether these means are sufficient or not can be ascertained only by the experiment. We must go on constructing the data out of the experimental conditions, and we must examine whether the construction results in illuminating the account of experience. This procedure, however, does not verify the construction in the way in which the experiment in the natural sciences verifies a theory or a hypothesis, because in philosophy the experiment is itself the theory and the theory the experiment, so that the construction definitely "begs the question." The philosopher cannot step out of his system; whatever he may adduce as testimony to his basic principles is already informed by them. The principles are axioms, and without axioms he can prove nothing. This insight restricts the demonstrability of philosophic knowledge; it prevents the claim of its validity. This should be admitted from the start. In fact, all philosophic systems are restricted; none is tenable forever. Whenever the attempt has been made to maintain a definite system, the result has been philosophic sterility and petrifaction.

The reasons for this continuous revolution and reorganization of philosophic knowledge are deep and cannot be discussed without entering the philosophic realm. In any case they point to the limitations of thought. But they are not so disastrous or destructive as they would be if the philosophic enterprise were of the same type as mathematical and scientific knowledge. Such knowledge provides for steady growth, for ever new steps leading to a goal that is always remote and allows enlargement of the scope of theories and even of principles, while philosophy aims at an understanding of the whole of experience. Such an understanding must be complete in itself; it cannot wait for corrections or for new experiences to be verified or supplemented. It is what it is in a

final sense. Its finite character, therefore, is not manifest in its lack
of completion but in its own intrinsic limitations, which can be
surmounted only by the creation of a new system, which, in its
turn, undergoes the same trial and the same doom. Philosophy
does not proceed as science does, step by step, contribution by
contribution, always growing toward the goal of completion;
rather, it proceeds by means of systems, each of which presents a
picture of the whole of experience and is thereby a totality within
itself. Philosophy, as it were, pays the price for its adventurous
and hazardous enterprise by an ever new start and ever new collapse. Man cannot even wish to obtain exact and demonstrable
knowledge, which is the glory of mathematics and physics, in the
entirely different field of metaphysics.

This inner structure of philosophy is less discouraging and, indeed, less harmful if the philosopher reflects upon it and recognizes the limitations implied in thought. The first to realize this
inner destiny of philosophy was Socrates. He knew that he did
not know and would never know the ultimate substance and
essence of things which his predecessors had assumed to know.
He laid aside speculative metaphysics to make room for the self-
understanding and self-knowledge of man. This is the greatest
revolution that has ever occurred in the realm of thought. Kant
achieved greatness because he pursued the fundamental idea of
Socrates, though in a new fashion, on a new level, and with a new
perspective.

However, the consciousness of the limitations of thought cannot alter the destiny of philosophy because in a certain way even
the critical thinker has to reach out for the ultimate, if not ontologically, then ethically. Self-understanding and self-knowledge
are philosophical only if they answer the question of the ultimate
meaning of life. In this respect the philosopher does not differ
from other men. Whether the ultimate decisions in life are made
on the basis of an explicit consciousness of the ultimate values and
the ultimate goal or merely out of half-conscious and unreflected
instincts, in any case man has to make those decisions and is to that
degree a philosopher, i.e., he is compelled to give an answer to the
ultimate questions concerning the meaning of the human life. The
philosopher only brings the ultimate questions to an issue by re-

flecting upon his actions and his actual decisions in life. Thereby he systematizes his own consciousness, and, inasmuch as his experience has a universal character, his system will be recognized as true.

The contrast and the agreement between the individuality of the thinker and the universality of his mind and thought lead at once to the center of philosophical reflection. Obviously, this contrast and this agreement are rooted in a fundamental experience, the experience of the duality of world and self (or ego). This experience cannot be derived from any higher or more original source. It would be vain to try to deduce the duality of world and self from any phenomenon belonging to the world or belonging to the self. From the beginning of self-conscious experience this polarity has made itself felt. It is an *Urphänomen*, a primordial and primary "datum." It is the most radical opposition we can think of. Ours is a world of oppositions anyway. We confront them in whatever realm of experience or thought we may move. But the opposition between the world and the self that experiences the world and itself is the most fundamental and the most astounding of all oppositions.

Often we talk loosely about the world, as if we knew what we meant and, indeed, as if nothing were better known and more easily knowable. A remarkable thinker of our day begins his system by reflecting upon our "Being-in-the-world." He takes it for granted that one knows what this means. In a certain sense he is right. Everyone knows that he exists "in the world," that his existence is to be characterized that way. And yet no one would be able to say what the term "world" means, and in what way he does exist "in the world." The relation between the self and the world is the most primitive and simplest experience, but it also implies the most formidable problems. Each of us knows himself at least to the point of being able to say "I"; but "the world" is a very vague and indefinite term as long as the philosopher does not try to make its meaning definite. When we start from our "Being-in-the-world," we seem to presuppose that we, in whatever sense, belong to the world, that the world is the whole of our experience, comprising the self which experiences the world as well as everything else. And yet the experiencing self does not belong to the world in the same way that everything else does. The whole of our experience and the world do not seem to be the same. Problems of a very serious and difficult character thus arise out of the duality of world and self—difficulties which are intrinsically connected with our experience.

The "experiment in thought" has to issue from this problem, as we shall see, since it has to issue from experience, and especially from self-experience, if self-understanding is its final goal. As long as self-understanding is the core of philosophic thought, the duality of world and self cannot be abandoned, nor can it be derived from any higher unity, be it the world or the self. Only if the critical method yields to the temptation of a speculative self-understanding, as it did in Fichte and later in Hegel on an even bolder scale, will the basic duality be replaced by the oneness and absoluteness of the universal self or the world-embracing ego. This speculative solution of the ultimate problem ignores the limitations of thought or presumes to have surmounted them by means of a metaphysical intuition and a metaphysical dialectic. It is the basic thesis of the following treatment that such a solution is impossible. It would be possible only if metaphysics could transform faith in the living God, the Creator of heaven and earth, into a system of thought originating from man's mind. In that case metaphysics could supersede sacred theology. Revelation and the action of God would no longer be needed in order to understand how the world emanates or originates from God, and God would be dissolved into an ontological idea or, more correctly, into a system of ideas. Faith would represent a lower stage of the comprehension of truth, a comprehension adapted to that lower stage of intellect which receives it.

If this radical solution is barred; if no logic, no ontology, and no speculative intuition whatever can attain to the knowledge of the living God; if there is a supreme mystery which can be revealed only by the prophetic spirit; if God is not primarily an object to be known, but the head of the community of those who believe in Him; then not metaphysics but sacred theology alone, expounding and explaining the word of God, can deal with the ultimate problem in a logical fashion. But then must not philosophy be altogether discarded? What task can be left to philosophy, if its supreme and most vital problem has to remain unsolved and insoluble? How can a philosophy enervated by such a deprivation preserve its vitality and the impulse which seem to be necessary for its arduous task?

The majority of philosophers would, indeed, answer that such a philosophy cannot preserve its vitality. And the majority of future philosophers will probably share this view. Philosophic thinking seems to be frustrated in advance, if it is impossible to know the nature of things. Such a philosophy runs a great risk of being crushed between two rival forces: the natural sciences, on the one hand, and sacred theology, on the other. And the further consequence of this defeatism and defeat would be that the two victors would try to take over the prerogative and responsibility of the defeated power: the natural sciences would presume to solve the ultimate problem on their part and to perform what the renouncing philosophy admits it cannot perform, and sacred theology would presume to possess the key to the all-embracing understanding of world, man, and God. So we see in the history of thought the Socratic self-restriction already yielding in Plato to a new metaphysics of the real; and in modern thought we observe the deadly struggle between naturalistic and theistic systems, until Kant renews the Socratic self-denial. And in our own time we witness a new naturalism, that claims to solve the riddles of life by the application of the natural sciences, and a new theism, which asserts that it has penetrated into the mystery of existence by means of sacred theology. A. N. Whitehead and William Temple are exponents of these two antagonistic metaphysical possibilities.

But if this danger is imminent and at all times pressing, then the task of philosophy is obviously prescribed. Is it not a worthy and necessary task to avoid the clash of those two contending pretenders to the crown of thought by mediating their respective claims and restricting their universal ambitions? Is not a critical philosophy, precisely because it does not arrogate to itself the right and power of dictating ultimate truth, equipped with the best means of arbitrating the contest of the rival metaphysical fighters? Such a philosophy, by giving up all speculative ambitions, gains insight into the legitimate capacities of the human mind and its inevitable limitations. Such a renunciation might turn out in the end not to relinquish any desirable and reasonable knowledge whatever. If there is a realm beyond the possibilities of human thought, we simply recognize its existence by our renunciation, while it would be foolish and illusory to aim at the conquest of that realm with insufficient and inadequate weapons.

If self-understanding is the highest goal which philosophy can reach, the understanding of the horizon of human experience and thought is of utmost importance. The antagonism between science and wisdom, between reason and revelation, between the secular and the sacred, could best be recognized and interpreted within the scope of such an enlightened self-understanding. The very antagonism of the two rivals in the contest for supreme truth seems to point to the impossibility of reaching it and to the necessity of a mediating discipline which acknowledges the relative right of each and criticizes the unlimited pretensions of both. But does such a philosophic claim not renew the old difficulty, since it unduly enhances the capacity of the human mind by asserting that this mind is able to restrict itself and to arbitrate the conflict? And is this claim not the more repulsive and boastful because one of the contending opponents is the living God himself? Is not sacred theology, if its basis is deemed to be true, perfectly justified in assuming the ascendancy in the whole realm of knowledge, after all? Is it not the only arbiter that is really impartial and sovereign?

But we should not forget that sacred theology is secondary to revelation. The prophet, not the theologian, is the mouthpiece of God. The relation between revelation and theology illuminates the controversy between philosophy and theology to which we shall recur at the end of the inquiry. Sacred theology is based partly on Scripture, partly on Greek metaphysics. Origen wanted a substitute for pre-Christian metaphysics. He rightly realized that pre-Christian metaphysics was obliterated by the new wisdom of God and Christ. He therefore tried to build a new system which would take into account that new wisdom and yet solve the same problem which the pagan systems had endeavored to solve previously. He rightly saw that biblical revelation is relevant to the theological speculations of the pagan philosophers and that these speculations can be deepened and corrected and enriched by reference to the Christian understanding of God, world, and man. Thus the new science of dogmatics arose, which from the beginning was supposed to take the place of the now obsolete systems of the Greek schools.

This step was fateful. It was somewhat questionable, since the character of biblical revelation is incongruous with speculation of any kind—a truth not, or not fully, recognized by Origen. Thus a task arose which could be discharged only with difficulty, if at all. It is still the same task which a contemporary Christian theologian like William Temple tries to tackle. His solution, like that of Origen, presupposes that human and divine, secular and sacred, views can be united without any break or leap from the one to the other sphere; that sacred theology supports the intellectual means by which all scientific knowledge can be arranged as part and parcel of the one sovereign and dominating system which is guided and informed by biblical revelation.

However, the elements of natural knowledge and divine inspiration are not organically reconciled to each other either in Origen or in Temple because they are too divergent in origin, authority, method, and principle to be made links of one great system. The theologian cannot help either secularizing what is divine or speculating on the basis of "doctrines" which are by no means doctrines in the sense of philosophic inquiry but are, rather, articles of faith concerning man's salvation and God's grace. There is a chasm between such a knowledge for the sake of salvation and mathematics or physics, a chasm which sacred theology cannot and should not try to bridge. We cannot and should not think about God and his holy purpose in the way in which we think about the evolution of biological species or the development of the solar system. Plato and Aristotle dealt with all problems in the same fashion and therefore built their systems. But the Christian message—and, indeed, the biblical "doctrine" throughout—makes such unifying and totalitarian thought impossible. This the philosopher should learn from Karl Barth, even if he rejects his dogmatics for other reasons.

But Karl Barth and other theologians do not solve the problem of how the secular and the sacred are related to each other, because they ignore or disregard the task and the function of philosophic thought. They leave the investigation of nature to the natural sciences, but they believe that the philosophical problems, especially the problems of ethics and of man, are far more thoroughly and more truly envisaged from the point of view of sacred theology than they are from the philosophic viewpoint. Although they may be right ultimately, still the philosopher has to say something about the nature of man, his experience, and the meaning of civilization—topics about which the natural sciences know nothing. If the natural sciences are loyal to their own perspectives, they must comprehend man as a specific kind of animal; the specifically human problem lies outside the interest and the method of the natural sciences.

On the other hand, there is a sphere of experience where man understands himself, though neither in a naturalistic nor yet in a prophetic or spiritual sense as biblical "doctrine" does, but in a secular and human way. This is the sphere where philosophic thought has its legitimate rights. The problems of epistemology, ethics, aesthetics, politics—of civilization altogether—have at least one aspect which permits and requires reflection and consideration distinctly separated from all problems belonging to the natural sciences as well as from those of sacred theology. Philosophy in the Socratic sense has its domain in the quest of man. This quest is philosophic only if it is carried through on the basis of man's own understanding of himself unsupported by revelation and faith. Since man experiences not only the world that surrounds him but also himself, he can try to gather self-knowledge by scrutinizing his self-experience apart from all religious and spiritual "doctrines." Such an inquiry has the advantage that it appeals to man as such and that its methods do not presuppose a definite creed or personal devotion and loyalty but are universal, at least in intention and procedure.

Philosophy, understood and carried through in this human and universal fashion, is the true link between the natural sciences and sacred theology. With the sciences it shares universality, and with theology the problem of man. It is secular, and yet it approaches the realm in which the sacred has its legitimate place. It depends upon experience of a nonmystical, nonreligious kind, and yet it ends where this experience ends and where the question of a religious experience unfolds its urgent need. In this manifold way philosophy mediates between the extremes of the natural and the divine science, according to the place which man holds between nature and God.

But, in the end, philosophy has to admit that its task cannot be finally and perfectly discharged within its own territory. The quest of man issues in the quest of God. Philosophy itself learns this truth in the course of its own inquiries and by its own "experiment of thought." Eventually, human thought has to yield to divine instruction. However, this course of philosophic thought prohibits the encroachment of sacred theology upon the realm of secular investigation and theory. Although it is true that human self-understanding must finally appeal to the divine understanding of world and man, this appeal does not obliterate man's own self-understanding but supplements and completes it. This philosophical method has the advantage of being able to acknowledge fully the diversity of the secular and the sacred and to maintain the tension between the spheres while permitting the preservation of the supremacy and sovereignty of the divine. In this form a certain kind of unity between nature, man, and God is established, despite the chasm that separates the realms.

I. Fundamental Reflections

CHAPTER I

Experience, Culture, and Faith

What Is Experience?

EXPERIENCE may be described as the procedure of becoming directly, i.e., by an immediate contact, acquainted with the object of knowledge. It is thus the opposite of learning by means of reason. What we experience is in some way given to us; we do not produce it. Experience is accompanied by the consciousness of certainty, although this certainty may be questioned either by new experiences or by reason. Experience is by no means an absolutely sure method for gaining knowledge, but, even so, it is an indispensable point of departure. We cannot do without experience.

We may distinguish common, or prescientific, and scientific experience. Scientific experience is supposed to answer questions which occur in the context of scientific investigation—investigation itself being the attempt to acquire knowledge by deliberate and regulated methods which produce contact with the object. Scientific experience as the result of that attempt is based on experimentation. Experimental knowledge is, of course, not so direct as prescientific experience; rather, it is guided by reason. The primordial source of knowledge is experience in its prescientific, unguided stage. All knowledge is in some way derived from this source; without an immediate contact with the object, we cannot even reason about it, and we cannot put to it those deliberate and premeditated questions which lead to experimental or scientific experience and knowledge.

It is well known that in the history of epistemology there are two rival schools, the empiricists and the rationalists. The empiricists emphasize the element of experience, sometimes to the point of excluding any other factor as a source of knowledge, while the rationalists insist that reason or intellect is another such source, sometimes exalting it as the sole source of knowledge. I shall not discuss this controversy, since it would require hundreds of pages, with the result that the subject with which I would deal could not be treated at all. But I will nevertheless say a few words in defense of the import of experience in its direct and prescientific stage. Such a defense, however, must necessarily reject empiricism in its best-known historical form, that form which the English classical thinkers of the eighteenth century have given it.

These empiricists take it for granted that all experience originates from impressions. Consequently, they study the connection of impressions and show how the complex tissue of knowledge springs from them. They are so fascinated by this question that they disregard the more fundamental one as to how, out of impressions and ideas, feelings, and habits, a knowledge worthy of that name, i.e., valid propositions concerning the nature of the object, can arise. Or, in other terms, they are engrossed in the investigation of the facts of knowledge but not in the investigation of that special factor which gives knowledge its proper value and without which knowledge is an empty word, a mere connection or separation of psychic contents. They deal with experience in a manner similar to mechanics or chemistry. They are blind to the most significant and most wondrous quality attached to it: the claim that it is true, i.e., that it mediates between object and mind so that the mind comes to know the object. Berkeley is the deepest among the empiricists: he appeals to theology and faith in order to break the vicious circle of a merely psychological analysis. Hume is the most consistent among them, and therefore his thought issues in skepticism.

The rationalists, on the other hand, aim at a speculative metaphysics, sacrificing the epistemological problem to their special interest. This is true with respect to the rationalists before as well as after Kant. All of them believe in the power of reason to penetrate into the core of the object. Experience is only the occasion, not the source, of knowledge, according to their rationalistic theory. Even Kant is not altogether free from this prejudice, although he more than any other thinker tried to reconcile the opponents and to discover a middle ground on which they could meet. The empiricists are, at bottom, psychologists who vainly attempt to understand knowledge; the rationalists are, at bottom, metaphysicians who are eager to justify their claim that knowledge is able to comprehend the universe. Both fail to respect the real problem of epistemology; both fail to answer the question: What is experience?

Kant discovered the real meaning of this question, and he answered it by combining, but also transforming, the psychological method of the empiricists and the metaphysical method of the rationalists, creating in that way a new philosophical discipline, a "metaphysics of experience."[1] He discovered that experience itself raises a question which can no longer be answered by means analogous to those of mechanics and chemistry—or, indeed, to any of the natural sciences—but only by a reflection upon the logical function of knowledge, i.e., its claim to be true. However, Kant was interested only in the truth of scientific knowledge. Therefore, he fashioned his inquiry so that, from the outset, experience was understood as the source of scientific knowledge. Or, to put it differently, he presupposed that science alone, namely, mathematics and physics, is truly knowledge and has objective value; and he set out to inquire how this is possible in spite of the fact that science is based on experience and that the truth-value of experience as contrasted with rational proof is questionable.

Kant's answer was that the same highest principles which reason assumes or, more correctly, which constitute the very essence of reason in its theoretical use also precondition the experience from which science proceeds and that no experience whatever is possible which does not presuppose those highest principles. Thus we can perfectly understand that experience, though it is not derived from reason and cannot be proved by reason alone, nevertheless conforms to reason and can therefore serve as the basis for scientific knowledge. Impressions and reason col-

1. Cf. the excellent work of Professor Paton, *Kant's Metaphysics of Experience*.

laborate not only in scientific reasoning—in analysis, calculus, and theory issuing from experience—but even within experience itself, which thus is to be identified not with impression but with propositions or statements about objects. As objects are composed not only of elements corresponding to our impressions but also of elements corresponding to the principles of theoretical reason, so experience is composed of both impressions and forms and is therefore well suited to "give" us the material which science needs to comprehend the objects and to build up objective knowledge, i.e., knowledge which corresponds with the objects themselves.

This profound and ingenious theory of experience and scientific knowledge, however, does not explain why we can trust experience. To be sure, the theory does guarantee that no experience whatever can disagree with the rational principles of scientific knowledge, since these principles, according to the theory, constitute the objects themselves of that knowledge. But this guaranty is not enough to assure us that we may trust experience, for experience represents a synthesis of those rational forms with an empirical content not to be derived from the forms. Kant himself admits in the Introduction to the *Critique of Judgement* that the synthesis of those two divergent elements is a "happy accident" that cannot be deduced. Indeed, no theory whatever could succeed in demonstrating that two elements belong to each other which are alien to each other in such a way that neither can be derived from the other. The combination of empiricism and rationalism meets its limitation at this point. The two one-sided epistemological schools did not, of course, struggle with this problem for the simple reason that they were one-sided. The new difficulty arises from the two-sidedness of the Kantian theory, it arises from its very strength and depth. Unless we assert with the empiricists that knowledge completely depends upon impressions or with the rationalists that it completely depends upon reason, we cannot arrive at the problem of its inner unity.

I can well understand that experience is a synthesis of material and form (or of impressions and principles); but, if experience is such a synthesis, then I cannot understand that experience should give me true knowledge, since the truth of experience is not guaranteed by the presence of forms in statements about the objects but depends upon the true synthesis of material and forms in every actual instance; it depends upon the inner unity of the two elements in every act of perception, a unity which is supposed to agree with the unity of the very same elements within the object itself. Only if I can be sure that this unity, this agreement, this synthesis, is "objective," i.e., true, can I rely upon experience as the point of departure in scientific knowledge.

Perhaps one might oppose this argument by saying that science does not rely upon immediate, prescientific experience but examines it by means of experimental devices and thereby reaches results which often repudiate immediate experience. Take, for instance, the Copernican theory: it directly negates the impression which leads to the view that the sun turns around the earth, and it arrives at the contrary proposition that the earth revolves around the sun. Reason thus has to mistrust the direct finding of experience; reason can trust its own "eyes" alone. This objection, however, misses the decisive point. Although it is true that the evidence of the senses is rejectd by the Copernican theory, nevertheless this evidence is the starting point even of that theory. Without it the Copernican theory could never have been established. This theory, after all, does not reject the whole content of immediate experience; it only corrects it, thereby reversing the relation between sun and earth but not denying that there is circular movement and that one of the two bodies involved moves around the other. This is the basic fact and can be learned only by the direct contact of the mind, through the instrumentality of the corporeal eyes, with the two bodies. There is some truth in the evidence of prescientific experience. This truth can be stated in the following way: *I see* that the sun moves around the earth. This statement is perfectly true. It indicates the change in the mutual position of earth and sun as I perceive it from my own point of view. If this statement were not true, science could never have proceeded to its theory. This theory presupposes the truth of the direct observation, although it partly abandons it in the end.

We have to trust immediate experience, i.e., the synthesis of sense-impression and rational form, although we cannot prove that this synthesis is true or that experience deserves to be trusted. Science can never become a substitute for direct experience; it can use experience only as an instance for its theories and hypotheses.[2] Science has to return to direct experience over and over again to check and to verify its knowledge. Trust in pre-scientific experience is indispensable to the operation of reason. This trust implies a kind of belief. We may assume with Kant that reason begins its operation on the very lowest stage of experience and that contact with the object would be impossible without the activity of the mind. Even so, this initial activity would be impossible without the initial belief that sense-experience, however fragmentary and in need of supplementation and correction, opens the door to the knowledge of the surrounding world and leads eventually to the acquisition of truth.

The contrast and rivalry of empiricism and rationalism mirror the duality of world and ego which experience discloses but also tries to transcend. Science only continues and resumes what has its beginning in immediate experience. Science only elaborates the contents of sense-perception; these contents are given; they are, as it were, revealed. This impression is not merely metaphorical. It points to the true character of "givenness" as implying that there is something outside the receiving mind which impresses itself upon the self and that we are not deceived by the object that "gives" itself to us and makes itself known. In the last analysis it is a mysterious process which thus mediates object and mind, mysterious in spite of the operation of reason within it and in spite of the rational character of scientific elaboration, mysterious inasmuch as no physical—indeed, no knowable—contact takes place when we come to know the truth about the object. There seems to be an original unity or harmony between world and self which is re-established in the act of experiencing. Revelation on the part of the world and belief on the part of the self are involved in that process. Only further discussion can shed more light upon this mystery.

2. Cf. Albert Einstein: "The whole of science is nothing more than a refinement of every day thinking" (*Out of My Later Years* [New York: Philosophical Library, 1950], p. 59).

Kinds of Experience

MOST modern philosophers, including Kant, have used the word "experience" in a very narrow sense, namely, in the sense of that knowledge which is fulfilled in science. Scientific experience, however, is only one of a variety of activities, all of which can equally well be called "experience" and, indeed, are so called in ordinary language. Even when mystical or religious experience is excluded, philosophy should not ignore other important kinds of experience which nourish our minds with indispensable and trustworthy knowledge. Scientific knowledge, currently overrated, is but an infinitesimal fraction of the store of knowledge we need, acquire, and use in daily life. Our age often forgets or ignores this simple fact and tends to regard all nonscientific knowledge as unreliable and even contemptible. And yet the scientist himself cannot help trusting sources of knowledge other than the scientific one. Like all of us, he depends upon the immediate experience of the surrounding world, of the persons with whom he lives, of the circumstances under which he lives, of the nation to which he belongs, of his country, and so on. Man lives by experiences of many sorts.

The philosophers of modern times have singled out sense-experience as the prototype of all experience and have analyzed sense-perception almost exclusively when they have inquired into the nature of experience.[3] Not until the rise of romanticism was the full significance of immediate awareness and acquaintance detected and honored. Hegel was the first to call attention to the wide scope of experience and to its momentous meaning, not only for the sake of scientific investigation but for all spheres of human activity. In his *Phenomenology of Mind* he takes the reader through all the worlds of experience, personal and impersonal, individual and generic, intellectual and emotional, moral and political, aesthetic and religious, until in the end he arrives at that kind of knowledge which gathers together the fruit of all previous stages and to which he gives the title "Absolute Knowl-

3. Cf. the carefully written account of Otis Lee, *Existence and Inquiry* (Chicago: University of Chicago Press, 1949).

edge."[4] Hegel describes his book as "The Science of the Experience of Consciousness"; he believes that consciousness experiences itself and nothing but itself in all spheres and worlds, but it does not know this fundamental truth; therefore, it has to go through all the different stages until at the end it learns that it is itself the Absolute. Although this conclusion is too rash, nevertheless Hegel's enlarged conception of experience is valid.

Scientific experience is impersonal in a twofold sense: it is neither an experience of persons, personal relations, personal institutions, and so forth nor an experience of personal relevancy and significance. It is objective precisely because of the lack of this personal element. Usually we attach the idea of objectivity to the idea of truth, because we are inclined to think of truth in terms of scientific knowledge. The greatest portion of knowledge, however, is personal, and so is its foundation, experience. Now it is undeniable that personal experience does not possess the same kind of validity as scientific or experimental experience has; its validity is qualified by the consciousness of the person or persons who are interested in this sphere of knowledge. But this restriction does not diminish the value of personal experience, which is inevitably connected with the needs and values of that sphere. What a person means to me I cannot learn from any scientific account, and no scientific observation or examination, no scientific experiment or theory, could possibly supersede or improve personal experience. The very truth concerning that meaning actually demands personal acquaintance and concern. How could an objective statement be made about the friendship I feel toward another person or about the love with which I cherish my mother, my wife, my children? I have to be engaged, I have to be moved, in order to experience those feelings and relations. But they constitute the very stuff out of which the tissue of life is woven, out of which destiny and happiness or misery arise. Error might be fateful. It is this kind of experience which produces the dramatic tensions with which every life abounds.

Sense-experience is only a small fraction of total experience; there is no type of experience such as that which the empiricists

<hr/>

4. Cf. the commentary by Jean Hyppolite, *Génèse et structure de la phénoménologie de l'esprit de Hegel* (Paris: Aubier, 1946), pp. 14 ff.

select for their study and theory. So-called sense-experience is never a real, i.e., an independently existing, kind; rather it is always imbedded in the stream of real experience; it is, in other words, merely an abstract constituent of real or actual experience. The scientist may isolate a particular sensuous phenomenon by means of experimental arrangement; even so, as experienced, the phenomenon always has properties or aspects or relations which cannot be described as being sensuous. Scientific or experimental experience is itself always imbedded in a wider and fuller stream, and it is only artificially isolated and cut off from actual experience, which always has a personal reference because the experiencing subject is not an abstract intellect supported by abstract sense-perception but a living person. Total experience embraces all kinds within the totality of human life, which is always personal.

This living experience is at the root not only of all branches of experience but of life itself. What we call "life" in the human sense is by no means a biological process, as some philosophers consider it; it is an interplay of experience and action (including reaction) which mutually influence each other and inform each other. "Experience," however, is the wider term because action itself (in the human sense) is accompanied by self-experience; it would not be human action or reaction if the person were not conscious of it. Self-experience is inseparable from the self and therefore from will and action, by means of which the self realizes itself. Human life is this self-realization of persons who are interrelated by mutual experience of themselves and of one another. In the concrete stream of life all kinds of experience penetrate and permeate one another and are connected and interconnected in a living and personal fashion. The so-called "philosophy of life" in Germany tried to comprehend this complex experience without recognizing its true character; therefore, it was not protected against the danger of a biological interpretation of life. The whole depth which is essential to the problem of experience is likewise essential to the problem of life and existence.

As experience accompanies action, so action begins in experience. As we shall see, the activity which produces works and institutions—cultural activity in all its forms and differentiations—

originates from the depth of experience. In turn, the various kinds of experience—scientific, economic, artistic, political, and the rest—originate from the various branches of cultural activity. There is a continuous interplay between immediate and mediated cultural experiences in the life of individuals as well as in that of groups and, finally, of mankind.

Ultimate knowledge—knowledge of ultimate truth and reality, if there is such a knowledge—cannot be achieved without the co-operation of all kinds of experience, impersonal and personal, individual and social, private and public, immediate and mediated. How could ultimate truth relinquish any of these sources of knowledge? How could ultimate reality exist without being tinged by the contents of total experience?

Experience and Culture

EXPERIENCE and culture or civilization[5] are not two different modes of human life, they are intrinsically interwoven as stages in a development. Culture is an outcome of experience, and experience issues in cultural activity, in man's self-civilizing exertions and performances. This intrinsic relation, however, is not only, as the description might suggest, that of cause and effect; rather, it is also that of motivation and operation. Experience motivates cultural activity, it contains the task or sets the purpose which is carried through in the multiplicity of activities unfolded in civilization. Experience is incomplete and unsatisfying if it does not lead to civilized and civilizing industry and production; it aims, as it were, at this production and finds in it its fulfilment.

But is not civilization simply a biological process? Is it not true that this process begins in the animal realm and that the same impulses, needs, and desires which prompt the ants to build their hills and the bees to construct their ingenious hives are also at work when man builds his cities with their universities and

5. The two terms are used here and throughout without distinction. The Germans, especially since Spengler, use the word "culture" for the intellectual and spiritual spheres, the word "civilization" for the technical and economic. The English word "civilization" seems to have a wider scope than the word "culture," embracing all spheres (cf. pp. 14 and 30).

theaters and museums, when artists design paintings and statues, and engineers construct machines? Is not the song of birds the first stage of the development that finally results in the compositions of a Bach, a Beethoven, a Verdi? Certainly, there are analogies to human invention and skill, to human craft and art, in the kingdom of the irrational, uncivilized beasts; there are, especially, analogies to human behavior, to human virtues and vices, among the domesticated brutes which imitate man's behavior or are themselves treated by men in a quasi-human fashion.

All of these and other analogies should not mislead us, however. What we call "culture" or "civilization" is confined, as far as we know, to the human realm. The beast can be understood as acting out of necessity alone, out of those needs which concern the preservation of individual and generic life, out of instincts which drive the organic being to the fulfilment of those needs. Although we find final causality or the operation of ends in the organic world, still we do not find consciousness of the ends and the capacity for pursuing the ends by means of deliberation and debate. We do not find will and intellect. Therefore, we do not find science and art, politics and morality. We do not find freedom and struggle for freedom, development and decay, in the cultural sense. We do not find what we call "history," which is more than change and temporal succession of changes. Man alone is concerned with the meaning of his life—a phrase which points to the end of all ends, the purpose of all purposes.

In some respects the animals are more perfect than men precisely because at their level they do not seek such a meaning and are not able to direct their will toward an ultimate end but are content with the existing state of affairs; precisely because they do not deliberate and debate but are securely guided by their instincts and impulses, by just those "final" causes which are not final in the human consciousness. The beasts never leave their prescribed areas of life; with unfailing certainty and determination or, more correctly, determinateness and with a fixed direction they fulfil the needs of their vital ends and thus may impress us by their inner balance.

The ants or bees seem to exhibit greater social virtues than men. They never desert their "duties"; they never act against the

esprit de corps; strict obedience, self-sacrificial deeds, and selfless
co-operation are certainly better exercised by them than by men
—if we allow ourselves to speak of their habits and usages in
terms of moral norms and virtues, which we should not do precisely because the beasts do not act on the basis of deliberation
and because they cannot refuse to practice those "virtues." We
might say the "blind" animals represent in the state of nature
what man is called upon to represent in the state of morality. The
coincidence of desire and duty, of impulse and final end, is a kind
of pattern which man strives to imitate on his own level with the
means of his intellect and will. In that sense we may say that animal life is an ideal to be restored on the stage of conscious life.
However, this is only a figure of speech, since it is not actually
the animal mode of life which we have in mind when we take it
as an ideal.

The beasts do not need science because their creator, or nature,
has provided them with all the knowledge they instinctively
apply. They do not need money and markets, for the exchange
of goods is regulated in an organic fashion. They do not need
courts and parliaments, for their way of life is foreordained and
is modified only by the consequences of the struggle for bare
existence. They do not need museums and historical societies because they have no history and they do not remember deeds or
works of their past. No doubt we men are animals like them. We
also have vital needs, and a good deal of our own energy and
skill serves the pursuit and fulfilment of our animal desires. But,
even so, human life does not consist solely in this; it is not human
if it is nothing else than this; it is less stable, less "secure" in the
intellectual and spiritual sense, less well-ordered, and consequently less "natural."

Man is both less and more than the animal. He is more, for he
lives in the hope of a better future; he is less, for he suffers present deficiencies and insufficiencies which the beasts do not suffer.
Man is more, for he can change his status, he can revolt against
existing conditions in the political or moral world, he can improve his knowledge and overcome his ignorance, he can aspire
to heights and depths which completely transcend all animal
needs and lusts. But precisely because he is thus infinitely supe-

rior to the conditions and limitations of organic existence, he is also infinitely more miserable than, and inferior to, the unconscious, unrevolting, unaspiring, and intellectually untroubled beast. Man is more than an animal because he has a rank never to be reached as long as the natural equilibrium between desire and deed is not interrupted and replaced by the uneasiness and ambiguity of the cultural state; his specific human dignity and nobility have no equivalent on the organic plane of necessity. Man is more than the brute; human brutality is the loss of humanity, while in the brute it is simply the natural. But man can sink below the level of the "innocent" beast. Man alone acts, while the beast simply behaves according to his nature. Behaviorism ignores the very humanity in man; it ignores man's specific dignity, his "inner" life, his intellectual, emotional, and spiritual aims and ends, his freedom and self-determination, his specific human experience and civilization. If the brute were able to observe itself, it would arrive at a behavioristic psychology; but, to arrive at this theory, the beast would have to take the step from animal experience to scientific experience and knowledge—a step which man can do just because his life is more than "behavior." Man builds up civilization because he has an inner life originating from an experience which itself has an inner meaning and asks for meaning—for a meaningful life, for a meaningful activity which would solve the task inherent in his experience.

It is dangerous to exaggerate the superiority of man and to forget that this superiority is also the source of man's misery and depravity. Man is as exalted as he is, only because he has to realize himself, because he has to act in order to be what he should be; he has to civilize himself in order to correspond with the noble image which his aspirations depict of him. But this high goal may discourage him, he may feel frustrated and wretched if he fails to reach it. "Idealism," which tends toward an undue exaggeration of man's dignity and nobility, may contribute to man's failure by generating expectations which life and destiny do not redeem. Such an idealism is dangerous because it underrates man's frailty and his inability to make himself what humanity postulates. Eventually it leads to disappointment and despair. But it is even more dangerous to forget or completely ignore the rank of man and to conceive of him as if he were nothing but a beast. The modern ideologies of bolshevism, fascism, and naziism are, or should be, warnings, if we look at the practice ensuing from them. "Idealism" may produce despair; naturalistic or biological philosophy produces barbarity and brutality.

Culture is bound up with human experience. It is the specifically human response to experience. Man hovers between unconscious nature and the ideal of a natural consciousness that would also be cultural; or, if we personify that ideal, we may say that man hovers between animal and angel, nature and heaven. He is man for the very reason that he outgrows nature and he is engaged in creating civilization; but he never succeeds in conquering heaven. By his animal nature he is prevented from becoming an angel; by his angelic vocation he is not permitted to fall back to the animal status. This is his highly problematic and precarious, though also potentially glorious, condition.

The most obvious difference between man and beast is language. Although psychologists speak of the language of the animals and have inquired into their sounds and conversations, here, as before, the human is more than the animal language. Man expresses not only desire and passion, satisfaction and dissatisfaction, but the meanings of his impressions, feelings, perceptions, thoughts, and so on. Since his life is meaningful and aims at the fulfilment of its meaning, man's language is expressive not only of his organic needs and fulfilments but also of his human experience and activities. Language is both natural and cultural, not only because it communicates human contents but also because it has a physical, physiological, biological, and psychological aspect as well as an intellectual, volitional or moral, and spiritual one. Therefore, language is more than sounds, it is uttered life itself. Man cannot live without such utterance and communication. Language springs directly from experience, but it is also the first step toward cultural production and creation. It is itself the product of man's cultural capacity. Human experience, though it is not always expressed, presupposes the potentiality of expression nonetheless, and it is this potentiality which makes human experience human.

Inasmuch as human experience is a kind of comprehension and

cognition and inasmuch as cognition rests upon general or universal notions and notions are attached to words, the word is the entrance to the human realm. Culture begins with speech. Culture might be conceived as language itself in a wider sense. All culture sets forth that communication of meaning and meanings which is the task of speech and conversation. All cultural works serve this very same task, though in different forms, on different levels, and with different intentions. Science and art elaborate immediate experience, thereby communicating meanings which spring from the final end to make the fragmentary and discontinuous meanings of immediate experience complete and coherent. For this purpose they create their proper and special languages. Experience of a richer and culturally interpreted sort— mediated and directed experience—is thus made possible. In immediate experience all the ramifications of cultural languages are already prepared and predisposed; from the start they tinge and inform the materials out of which the riches of cultural expression grow.

Experience and Faith

AS HUMAN experience motivates and produces civilization, so it also contains the rudiments and roots of spiritual faith. Plato and Aristotle have both remarked that philosophy begins in wonder; it does begin in wonder because it begins in experience, which is itself a wonder. We are so accustomed to this wonder that we, especially in maturity, completely forget its wondrous character, so deeply felt and so well known in childhood. In a way we mature by becoming increasingly deaf and blind to that primordial experience, the experience of the ignorance from which we start, and to the fact that it is a kind of revelation which helps us to overcome that ignorance and to enter research and productive work. Later in life we are so engrossed in doing that work in some special field that we are no longer aware of the wondrous character of the begining, a character which nevertheless perseveres throughout our enterprise. We may thus say that nature reveals itself to man or, more generally, that reality reveals itself.

Indeed, that there is a world which I can experience is the most astounding primary revelation; that this world is as it is, is the next revelation. We take it for granted that there are earth and sky, that there are stars in the sky and land and oceans on the earth; but all this, as well as all the detail which we come to know by immediate contact with the world, does not derive from reason, it is evident by no logical standard but is knowable only because and in so far as we experience it. It is surprising in all its data and reveals the concrete nature of things. Faith is thus suggested by experience, at least with respect to the feeling of mystery which is an inherent and indispensable element of both experience and faith.

This feeling of mystery, however, is not specifically religious. It is not yet faith itself but tends toward its unfolding. In receiving the data of the world, we trust not a "giver" but the "given," not a sender of the message but the message. We have faith in the account which our perception conveys to us, but this faith is incomplete and fragmentary as long as the account itself is incomplete and fragmentary or while it remains nothing but an account of perception. When we say it is the world which reveals itself in the data we perceive, we suggest that behind the data a complete and perfect whole exists, and it is this whole which we would finally trust if we could perceive it or if it revealed itself in its fulness. "Experience" thus refers to something which we do not immediately experience.

The term "trust" is not quite adequate so long as we do not turn to a person whom we trust. To be sure, we can also trust an impersonal power or energy, but then we use the word in a derivative sense. In the last analysis only a person deserves trust because only a person is morally reliable, and it is moral reliability which alone can evoke trust in an ultimate sense, including the certainty that our moral purpose will be sustained and that the moral meaning of our personality and our life will be guaranteed. However, experience does not grant that the whole represents or incloses or implies personality. On the contrary, the contrast between the world which we experience and ourselves seems to exclude such a possibility.

As long as religious experience does not modify this exclusion, experience remains inconclusive and unsatisfactory. This very lack of completeness and self-sufficiency pushes experience forward to action. We cannot stand on the ground of immediate experience. We must proceed to its elaboration, to cultural production and creation in all their varieties. Culture in this deepest sense is an attempt to find the "giver" of the given, the sender of the message, that we trust. But culture seeks him in vain. Man cannot produce or create him. The data of experience do not suffice to construct him. Neither science nor art, neither political nor moral action, can ever reach him. If we confine culture to these productivities and creations, we will end in the same state of bewilderment as that in which we began. Experience as such—nonreligious, secular experience—does not offer that satisfaction and completion which are demanded. Culture based on this experience does not change this situation in principle. The decisive answer has to come from the "giver" himself; only then can it be the satisfactory answer needed.

From the point of view of a metaphysics of experience, this result is inevitable because the duality of world and self cannot be transcended if no third entity exists which unites within itself the two poles of secular experience, an entity which is both world and self—the world as a self or a self being the world. Secular experience, by its very nature, excludes this solution. A "world-soul" (Plato) or a "world-mind" (Heraclitos, Anaxagoras, Aristotle) cannot be experienced; they are products of philosophical speculation, of highly fanciful and easily refutable concepts. All philosophical ideas of god share the same unlucky destiny; they give neither what the heart demands nor what logic and reason require; they are unhappy mongrels of heart and reason, of speculative and mythological imagination.

Faith is latent in experience, but experience does not produce faith. Cultural gods are subterfuges of an errant mind that believes only in its own creatures and yet longs for a being that would be more than its own product. The cultural mind is strangely imprisoned within its own horizon but feels that there is something outside, a light which does not shine within its own compass. Faith alone can provide man with that light, because it must shine in from outside the cultural walls if it is to be genuine

and fulfil the task we expect from it. This light already shines
dimly on the scene of immediate experience, since we would not
trust the account of that experience at all without feeling its
rays. Moreover, actual experience is at no time merely immediate; it is at all times affected by the mediation of some cultural activity and by some kind of religious, though superstitious,
faith. The distinctions among immediate experience, culture, and
faith do not correspond to temporal stages, although it is true, of
course, that culture and faith develop so that immediate experience gradually loses its character of immediacy. Even so, the
three stages of man's attitude toward reality can be distinguished;
immediacy never disappears completely, culture and faith never
coincide absolutely.

Religious experience is bound up with cultural development,
but nevertheless it has its own character, even at the most highly
developed stage of culture. Schleiermacher's description of religion, in his "speeches on religion to the cultivated among its
repudiators," has been called[6] the description of a "culture-reli-
gion," i.e., a religion which is itself the product or reflex of culture; but this description recognizes the existence of something
beyond the horizon of culture and of man's own intellectual
productivity and makes this existence the very cornerstone of
religion.

The distinctions here maintained among experience, culture,
and faith abstract, as far as possible, from the mutual interrelation
among the three realms for the sake of clarification. They deal
with experience in the nonreligious sense, with culture as the human activity which issues from this experience, and with faith as
not being produced by cultural activity alone.

6. By Friedrich Gundolf.

CHAPTER II

Antinomies of Experience

Ego and the World

THE duality of ego (or self) and world is the most fundamental factor in experience, permeating and molding all its contents. I belong and yet I do not belong to the world. In so far as the world comprises all things and all beings, I do belong to the world. But in so far as I cannot even speak of the world without making the world the content of my thought, I do not belong to that content; indeed, the content of my thought would no longer be that content if my thought did not separate the world as its content from myself as the subject who thinks. It is not important to conclude from the fact that I think, as Descartes did, that I exist; but it is important to conclude that I exist in distinction from whatever is the content of my thought. This basic distinction makes experience fundamentally possible and meaningful. To be sure, in the growth of the child the distinction develops slowly. But only when the child knows himself, does his experience take on this specifically human characteristic.

From the outset, an inevitable contradiction therefore encumbers our experience of the contrast between world and self. The child first feels this contradiction when he longs for the breast of his mother. In this experience the child learns that he cannot exist without the outer world, although his ego does not belong to it; that he depends upon the world, although as a self he does not. I am an infinitesimal part of the world, and yet I embrace the whole world in knowing just this fact. Pascal has given lively expression to this basic and astounding riddle of man, which constitutes at once his infinite smallness and his infinite greatness.

And long before Pascal the term "microcosm" pointed to the fact that man is not merely a part but also the world itself, though in a contracted form. Aristotle first alluded to this truth when he said that the soul is in some way the All.[1] It is more correct, however, to call the self a counterpart of the world.

World and ego need each other; they supplement each other, but they are also opposed to each other, so that a permanent tension exists between them because in one perspective the ego is nothing but a tiny speck in the universe—indeed, less than a speck, since it has no spatial extension whatever—while from the other perspective the world is nothing but a content of my consciousness. It would not even be sufficient to say that my consciousness contains a picture or a vision of the world, since I cannot make such a statement without comparing my world picture with the world at large, which implies that I also embrace, in whatever sense, the world at large—how else could I compare my picture and the original? Thus from one perspective I am totally embraced and, as it were, swallowed up by the world, while from the other perspective the world is embraced by myself and has no self-dependent existence of its own.

The world cannot exist except as the content of an ego, although it is no less true that the ego does not exist except as contained within the scope of the world. This is a puzzling contradiction, by no means easy to resolve. Indeed, its resolution is, as we shall see, altogether impossible. It is as pervasive and enduring as it is inescapable and basic. It is the root of many other contradictions.

One might think it possible to avoid the contradiction by distinguishing the body and the mind of the ego and by distributing the two so that my body is that constituent of myself which belongs to the world, while my mind does not. Such a distribution, however, is all too cheap. Clearly, my mind is also imbedded in the stream of the world process, although not in the same way as my body. My mind, in a certain sense, even depends upon my body, and in another sense my body depends upon my mind, so that the dilemma which we tried to evade only returns when we take refuge in the duality of body and mind. This duality is as

1. *De anima* Book iii.

puzzling as the former duality of ego and world; it is simply a corollary of the latter.

Since we know both world and ego only by and from experience, it is admissible to separate them. I may think of the world as if it could exist without an ego, but then I forget that the world exists in my thought precisely when I conceive of it as independent of myself. I can never get rid of myself. To assert that the world could exist independently of an ego purports that I am forgetful of the way in which I experience the world, i.e., as related to myself in many ways. If the world is the world of my experience (and how else should I know anything about the world?), it can never be severed from its tie with me, who experience it. It is true that, in experiencing the world (and the things within the world, including myself), I do experience the world's own existence independent from my existence. But again it is I who thus experience the world, and, if I cancel that I, I cancel at the same time the character of the world as being the world of my experience. Both are true: the world as I experience it exists for and in itself, independently of myself, and it does not exist independently of my experience. The antagonistic views of epistemological immanentism (or idealism) and epistemological transcendentism (or realism) are equally well grounded in experience.

But it is not this epistemological antagonism which interests us here; it is a deeper contradiction which only reappears in epistemology. The contradiction within the account of direct experience is presupposed by all theories of knowledge and therefore is basic. Before we proceed to any theory of knowledge, we experience the puzzling duality of world and self, each striving within our thought for absolute sovereignty. No theory of knowledge can get rid of this rivalry; we must simply acknowledge that it puzzles the thinking mind and that also it is actual and splits our consciousness in a way which endangers the very unity of the self. For in the last analysis it is the very self which is split by this rivalry between itself and the world.

In a way, however, it seems as if the contest could be settled in favor of the self. It is the self which experiences the world, while the world does not experience the self. Experience is a prerogative of man. It is man who, among all beings, is endowed with that peculiar kind of consciousness which is attached to his self-hood and which alone makes his experience possible. Experience rests upon self-experience, which, in turn, is the counterpart of world-experience. Thus the contrast between world and self is descriptive of experience, but it is the self which has the primacy in this relation because it experiences both the world and itself. Indeed, what we mean by "world" is nothing but the totality of all things in contrast to the ego.

It would be more correct to describe the basic contrast not as that of world and ego but as that of the world and myself, since the term "ego" seems already to be a "term," while I myself am not a term but myself. The word spoken by God, "I am who I am," can also be put into the mouth of every human being, since I am not anything that could be predicated of me, but precisely I myself, the speaking subject. I can never speak about myself, as I can speak about everything else and even about everyone else. I can never make myself the object of my thought or of my experience in the same sense as I make anything else such an object.[2]

2. Cf. the words of the "unidentified guest" in *The Cocktail Party* of T. S. Eliot, spoken to Edward, who is embarrassed because his wife has left him and because he does not understand why:

"But there's more to it than that. There's a loss of personality;
Or rather, you've lost touch with the person
You thought you were. You no longer feel quite human.
You're suddenly reduced to the status of an object
—A living object, but no longer a person.
It's always happening, because one is an object
As well as a person. But we forget about it
As quickly as we can. When you've dressed for a party
And are going downstairs, with everything about you
Arranged to support you in the role you have chosen,
Then sometimes, when you come to the bottom step
There is one step more than your feet expected
And you come down with a jolt. Just for a moment
You have the experience of being an object
At the mercy of a malevolent staircase.
Or take a surgical operation.
In consultation with the doctor and the surgeon
In going to bed in the nursing home,
In talking to the matron, you are still the subject,
The centre of reality. But stretched on the table
You are a piece of furniture in a repair shop
For those who surround you, the masked doctors:

I cannot entirely objectify myself, because, even when I try to do so, I am still the objectifying subject. Thus the ego-world relation is unique because the ego itself is unique in so far as it is the subject of experience. In other words, the experience relation to all things and to their totality, the world, is unique in that it is not a relation between things belonging to the world alone. No relation of that kind could possibly reveal the world to the subject of experience, for the world can be revealed as world only to a subject which stands over against the world and which by virtue of this privilege, its world-transcendence, can enjoy world-perspective. We would never understand the world-transcendence of the living God as ascribed to him in the Bible if our own human ego did not enjoy this transcendence analogously. This analogy is probably one of the roots of the dictum that man is created in the image of God. Of course, man is not so transcendent as the creator God is supposed to be, because man also belongs, in spite of his world-transcendence, to the world and is interconnected with all other things in the world, dependent upon them and, like them, a possible object of experience. This is the puzzling contradiction of man's self.

The first philosopher to emphasize this truth in all its embarrassing significance was Kant (although Augustine, Eckehart, Cusanus, Descartes, and Leibniz had touched upon it before him). Even Kant did not quite realize the abyss of contradiction manifested in this truth. He evaded the full consequence by dividing the ego into two constituents—one universal, the other individual. Only the universal ego—reason or understanding as such or, in his terminology, the transcendental self or subject— underlies all experience, while the individual ego is mingled in the stream of world affairs and, in that sense, is immanent in the world. As we shall see later on, this evasion is inadmissible.

The world which I experience, the only world of which I

All there is of you is your body
And the 'you' is withdrawn."

(From *The Cocktail Party*, copyright, 1950, by T. S. Eliot. Reprinted by permission of Harcourt, Brace and Company, Inc.) This whole speech illustrates precisely the ideas developed in the text; whether the words spoken by the "unidentified guest" are especially poetical, I will not decide. But in any case they are philosophical (perhaps too much so to be poetical).

have and can have any knowledge, is bound up with the ego that experiences it. I need not develop here all the important consequences of this truth. The only consequence I wish to point out is that the experiencing ego is a focus from which all the lines of the world proceed, as it were, and toward which they all return. Such a statement does not sound upsetting when I think of the ego in terms of scientific or philosophic reason instead of in terms of concrete and total experience. Its abysmal truth is fully recognized only when I understand that the world of experience needs the individual and concrete ego in order to be the world of experience. In me—in my own self—the world of my experience has its focal point, and without this point it is not even *a* world or, better, *the* world, the totality of all things and all events that I can possibly experience.

The world needs the embracing and unifying function of the experiencing ego to be the world, to be itself, i.e., the unity which I mean when I say "world"; this unity is an essential element in the concept of totality. The world needs to be comprehended—com-prehended—in order to be the unity and totality of all things. My own self is therefore at once my own and the self of the world; it is the self of the only world I know and can know, the self of my world, which is to me, however, the actual world, since I have no access to any other world or ever will have. The ancient conception of a world-soul probably originated from this inner experience, although Plato, its initiator, did not realize its full meaning. Every human soul is indeed a world-soul, and only as a world-soul is the human soul human.

The human soul animates the world. Animistic religion was a primitive expression of this fundamental truth. The world which is not centered in myself, which is not animated by myself, is not even a world in the full sense of this word; it is a chaos, a mass of impressions and feelings, an incoherent and incomprehensible manifold of contents. Only in the experiencing self does the world find its unity and its totality, its own self and soul. World and self are bound up with each other in a fateful and singular sense.

But this insight only aggravates the antinomy. How can I myself, who am a small part of the universe, be at the same time the soul and the self, the very center, of the universe? How can I bear the whole world upon my shoulders? How can I, mortal as I am, coming so late into the world and leaving it so soon, be the animating and unifying principle of the whole world? Should I not be eternal myself if that were true? Or at least as old and as lasting as the totality of all things? And yet experience speaks loudly enough and with an irrefutable certainty. The totality of all things is, precisely because I embrace them all, actually or potentially, the world.

I say that experience speaks an irrefutable language. Is it not true that the world, as Shakespeare says, is mirrored differently in every head? This truth is just what makes conversation and communication difficult. One can easily and quickly come to terms with every man, so long as one does not touch upon those issues which make up one's Weltanschauung; but, at the moment when those deeper perspectives are touched upon, one is forced to recognize that the whole world, the totality of all the little things which surround us, converges in the other self as much as in one's own because it participates in selfhood as such. It is just this seemingly remote and extremely general outlook which is most emphatically one's own center and focus, as it is also the center and focus of one's world.

In this world-significance of the human self we meet the innermost riddle of its nature. Man is what he is because of the way in which he is the center of his world. But man is also what he is because of the way in which he acts, is acted upon, and reacts in the world, by the way in which he is interwoven into the manifold of world affairs of all kinds, natural and cultural, personal and impersonal, and private and public. How can the two divergent poles of man's nature be reconciled to each other? How do they exist together within man's own experience and inner life? It is evident that the contradiction is bound to provoke all sorts of conflicts and controversies not only between different persons but in the very soul of each person; that a split in the human self seems to be the inevitable outcome of this basic self-contradiction.

Indeed, I cannot abstain from making myself the center of my world (because otherwise the world would not have any center at all and thus would not be a world, and I myself would not be a self), but also I cannot abstain from making myself an object of my experience, in the sense in which I experience other persons (although I can never completely succeed in objectifying myself). This inner duplicity creates the irony of experience. I see myself in all the weakness and mediocrity which I feel obliged to admit, and yet I have to take this ego much more seriously than any other ego precisely because I am myself the center of my world, upon which the very panorama of the world depends. I am simply not allowed to consider myself as someone who is legion and who will soon die as all beings do, as someone who has certain insurmountable limitations which inhibit his seeing things as they are. I am not allowed to persevere in this view (although I cannot help taking it from time to time) because, as a self, I am responsible for my limitations and because my limitations hamper my selfhood and independence from the world, upon which my dignity as a man hinges.

The irony of self-experience is most evident in those cases in which the extremes of man's inner independence and dependence meet in one and the same incident, e.g., in passionate love. The lover who "adores" the beloved and for whom the beloved person represents the whole world and who therefore projects his own center into the self of the beloved feels this irony with pain when he discovers that the object of his love is nevertheless dependent upon the world, not only physically but also morally; that vanity and selfishness of all sorts disgrace the beloved; or when he discovers within his own love symptoms of his own weakness and lack of dignity, worldly features which deny the quasi-religious height of his "adoration." Then suddenly the veil of his double nature tears, and he descries the split within his selfhood and the contradictions of his self-experience which produce its ironical ambiguity. When this happens, the need of a deeper adoration which cannot be stained by man's dependence upon the world is clearly felt.

The antinomy of the world-ego relation develops, in the course of experience, into many contradictions, some of which are worth careful study. In the first place, the contrast of individuality and universality, or of the self- and the world-significance of the human person, ensues from that of self and world. In the second place, the contrast of oneness and manifold develops; it is evidently contradictory that the self should be the self of the one world and that nevertheless many persons exist, each of whom is a self which claims to be its own world-center.

Individuality and Universality

THE individuality and universality of the human self cannot be so simply separated that man's individual character and disposition could be reckoned among his purely worldly traits while his universal selfhood alone could be regarded as non-worldly, conditioning world and experience. This Kantian solution is a Solomonic judgment which destroys the very self-hood of the self. For this tension between the two antagonistic constituents of the self permeates human life completely, and to recognize it grants the only true understanding of all the struggles, accomplishments, and failures of this life. Only when we understand that there is such an inner contradiction within man can we understand why man undertakes the work of civilization.

Only because man as an individual is nevertheless also a universal ego (the ego of the world which he experiences) is this experience concrete and total and not merely intellectual or rational, scientific or speculative. Only because of its double nature and its ambiguity is the self full of inner tensions and anxieties. It is man's very individuality which claims world-significance, and it is his very universality which exalts man to the level of moral dignity, entitling him to determine himself in moral freedom. The moral agent is not an exclusively universal will, as Kant conceives it, but is at the same time man's individual will, because this will alone is real and active. However, this individual will is entangled in a net of natural and moral threads which make its universality highly problematic, which, indeed, seem to deny outright such a claim, since those threads originate from worldly sources.

It is not difficult to prove that individuality and universality co-operate with and also contend against each other in every self. Moral life gives abundant illustrations of both tendencies.

The very virtues which make a man morally outstanding impair the development of other virtues. Determination means limitation; *determinatio est negatio*, as Spinoza says. Individuality excludes totality, even when it unfolds within the confines of its determinateness its own universality. This is most obvious in the case of the creative artist. No poet, composer, painter, or sculptor reveals in his work the totality of world-intuition and world-interpretation. Even the greatest are circumscribed in their creativity by their individuality and by the conditions and peculiarities of the period to which they belong.

Individuality and universality are so closely interwoven that greatness implies as much a strong and pronounced individuality as it does an equally strong and pronounced universality. The greater a creative artist is, the more have his individual manner and style incorporated within themselves universal significance. It is his individuality which is universal, and his universality appears in the form of his individuality. The great personality in all performances unites those extremes so that it is impossible to separate them. Not only do many Germans regard Goethe as the greatest of all German personalities, but, in fact, many consider him the model of a man who would unite within himself all human excellencies, so that his individuality would embrace humanity as such. These are certainly exaggerations, but they show that the two divergent elements of the human personality cannot be divorced. The unoriginal, shadowy, and indefinite personality, though it is less individual, is for this reason not more but, on the contrary, less universally outstanding.

As world and ego are inseparably united and thereby contradict each other, so also universality (derived from the world-function of the ego) and individuality (representing the ego-function of the ego) supplement and yet contradict each other. Goethe in all his universality is an individual, after all, with many deficiencies, one-sided virtues, gifts, and inclinations; he is by no means a model man. And yet no one can deny that these individual features are inseparably connected with his greatness. He would be less universally remarkable if he were less individually limited. Only by working out the individual form of his mind could he make himself a universal mind.

The first to understand this intrinsic unity and duality of the two extremes was probably Michel de Montaigne. He was aware that his extremely individual opinions, leanings, passions, estimates, and habits nevertheless had a universal meaning and interest; in that respect he is the first "existentialist" and perhaps among all philosophers of existentialism the only one who took this principle seriously and therefore wrote his philosophy in the form of essays about himself. Of course, the *uomo universale* in the Italian Renaissance had preceded him, but without deriving a philosophy from himself. The permanent bond between the extremes is not confined to the human personality, it extends to man's works. The world which is depicted in the plays of Shakespeare may be regarded as the world "itself"; indeed, many enthusiastic admirers of these plays would insist that Shakespeare depicts the world as it "really" is. And yet they could not deny that this world has peculiar features, to be traced back to the individuality of the great poet. Caesar was regarded by his friends and followers as the model of an emperor, and his very name was identified in the course of history with that office. Compared with other statesmen, he was universal in his outlook and intentions. But his individuality is as clear-cut and incomparable as is his universality. Hegel compared Napoleon with the world-soul, but at the same time he was fully aware of his individual limitations.

Since there is a world in each of us, even in the smallest and most insignificant of human beings, there is also a universality in each of us which cannot be taken from us as long as our humanity is not completely crushed. One might dare to say definitely that man as such is logos incarnate: he is an individual world-ego, an individual world-soul; the world's universality is individualized in him, as his individuality embraces within its often narrow confines the entire world. It is this truth which ultimately vindicates the democratic principle that every person in the state has the inalienable right to make his opinions articulate and of consequence. This right is rooted in the metaphysical nature of selfhood.

The great question which arises out of this metaphysical situation concerns the synthesis of the opposites. If it is true that human individuality cannot be divorced from universality, is there any individual who would be so universal as to reconcile the two opposites within selfhood? Is there any individual who rightly deserves the title of a model man? If every individual legitimately claims universality, such an idea seems to be excluded. Individuality by its nature means determination. If any individual were to be the absolutely universal self, would such an individual not necessarily cease to be an individual? Would he not be so universal as to exclude any boundaries, that is, any individuality? Logic seems to lead to such a conclusion. But if it is true that the more individualized individual is at the same time the more universal one and vice versa, as the examples of Goethe, Shakespeare, and Caesar seem to demonstrate, is it not possible that the most individualized individual would also be the most, the absolutely, universal one?

Oneness and Manifoldness

THE contrast of individuality and universality can be reduced to the more abstract contrast of manifoldness and oneness. All individuals face the same world, each in his individual way, so that the one world is reflected in a manifold of individual worlds, each of which nevertheless signifies the one world to each individual. How can the manifold of worlds be reconciled to the one world? The puzzling thing is that each individual is convinced that there is only one world and that the world as comprehended by him is this very world, while he at the same time has to recognize that there are as many worlds as individuals, at least in so far as concrete, immediate, total experience is concerned. This experience therefore confronts each individual with the contradiction springing from this contrast, an unavoidable, irreducible contradiction which threatens the reliability of our own world-consciousness as much as it threatens communication with other individuals. This contradiction is, of course, a consequence of the inseparable connection of self- and world-consciousness, which makes each individual self the self of his world, and the world as experienced by the individual the world of his self.

Each self believes himself to be the one self on which the world hinges, though this belief may not assume the form of conscious reflection. I cannot help believing it, since I have no other means of experiencing the world; I have to rely upon the presupposition that my world is the one world, though I may know only fragments of the world intimately. But I could not even know that I know fragments if I did not also know that they are fragments of the one world, which again I do not know except in the form of my experience, that is, in the form of my world. I cannot leave this magic circle; I am inclosed in it; but at the same time I cannot dwell within it without meeting the contradictions which ensue from my imprisonment and which do not permit me to rest in it. The contradictions do not even allow me to feel imprisoned, for they indicate that the prisoner transcends the wall of his prison and can look at his prison from without, a situation which can never take place in the world of space.

Each individual is the self of his world, but this world is also the one world, and thus the self of each individual is the one self of the world, even though this self is only his individual self. The oneness of this self contradicts the plurality of individuals, and this contradiction is only another form of the contradiction of oneness and manifoldness. It is a contradiction that there are as many selves as there are individuals, for each of those selves is at the same time the one self of the world. Oneness of the world contradicts the many worlds in the individuals, and oneness of the self contradicts the many selves belonging to the many worlds.

One might think that these contradictions can be resolved by a simple logical operation which separates the one and the many according to the contrast of individuality and universality of self as well as of world. But we know already that such a resolution is impossible. I am myself precisely because I am not only an individual but also a universal self. I am, therefore, at the same time the one self and one of many selves, each of which has the same right and the same obligation to believe itself to be the one self. It is precisely this inner tension which exalts me over the sphere of spatial existence and which nevertheless threatens to destroy me. I am legion, and I am who I am, the ego of the world, the one self of the one world.

The contradiction is serious, because I cannot objectify myself. If I could, it would be possible to distinguish different aspects or constituents of myself. I could, for instance, plead that the oneness of myself is that aspect of myself which is related to the one world, while the manifold of selves is related to the many individual worlds. But such a distinction ignores the radical and fundamental fact that I am one and the same self in both relations and that I would not be a self at all if this sameness did not exist.

Another resolution seems to open when I distinguish myself as the thinking self from myself as the self of total experience. But this distinction ignores the fact that total experience is the very ground on which I stand, the primary source of all my thought. In thought I may abstract from those contents of my total experience which characterize myself in difference from the other selves; but this abstraction does not solve the contradiction implied in the selfhood of total experience, since the abstract self embraces only an abstract world, while the actual world is not abstract but concrete, not a world of thought merely but a world of feeling and sensing, of will and action, of actual conflicts, victory, and defeat. This is the actual world of experience, and it is related to myself in totality.

The contradiction of the One and the Many is peculiar to the experience of the contrast between world and ego. Parmenides solved the contradiction by his majestic dictum: The One alone really exists, while the Many is an illusion. Plato showed that this dictum, majestic though it is, nevertheless cannot be maintained, since the One dissolved from the Many could not even be the One. In fact, even Parmenides needed the Many to demonstrate that the One alone is truly real. But Plato, correcting his great teacher, did not realize that Parmenides, in spite of his logical contradiction in demonstrating the Oneness of the real, nevertheless had deep reasons for his paradoxical statement. Parmenides tried to solve the contradiction of the One and the Many as it is involved in the world-ego experience. He saw clearly that the ultimately real, be it the world or the self of the world, is endangered by this contradiction, and he decided to solve it by proclaiming that the one world alone is the truth, while the many worlds or aspects of the world as they are real in individual experience are illusions.

Of course, this solution is as magnificent as it is violent. Plato was by far the more moderate and more considerate thinker when he demonstrated that oneness and manifoldness are compatible—indeed, that they demand each other and supplement each other so that neither can be dismissed. This is certainly true with respect to the contents of thought. Each concept is both a unity and a plurality—a unity because of its form, a plurality because of its contents. And the same can be said about everything that we experience. A thing is both itself and the manifold of its properties, aspects, relations, and attributes. It is therefore one and many; and these two categories, though contrasting with each other, nevertheless do not contradict each other. Each number is both a unit and a manifold of numbers; each line or figure is both one in its wholeness and many in its parts.

But this neat solution of the Parmenidean problem loses its strength the moment I try to apply it to the contrast of ego and world. Although one might say that the ego is the unit or unity of the world-multiplicity and that the two in this way can be compared with the contrast of form and contents or of the thing and its properties or of the numerical unit and its numerical elements, this analogy is not complete, because the ego is not an object of thought or experience but the unobjectifiable experiencing subject, and, as this subject, it is not only the form, the substance, or the numerical unit of the world-multiplicity but rather it is both this form and also a multiplicity of selves and thus, as it were, contaminated itself by the manifold of the world, involved in the contradiction of ego and world. It is both form and content, and these two aspects are only abstract categories which presuppose the concrete wholeness of experience.

In the last analysis, even the poles of objective thoughts or things, though united in thinking and experiencing, lead to the same ultimate contradictions in which the ego-world polarity is steeped. For it is this polarity which underlies even the polarity of oneness and manifoldness in objects. In a definite way each thing or thought is one only in so far as I who think or see it am one and the same ego, and it is a manifold in so far as I can think or see it from different points of view or in different situations, i.e., in so far as I myself am not only one and the same ego but also subject to the manifold of impressions and relations which characterize myself as conditioned by the world. The contradiction between universality and individuality, between the oneness and the manifoldness of myself, is thus conferred on the contents of world and thought.

It is not my intention to carry through this thesis in a system of categories. The discussion so far has shown that the contrast of oneness and manifoldness is cognate with that of identity and diversity, and this more abstract contrast might be basic from the position of a logical and ontological analysis. But such an analysis is not the proper problem of my central theme in this book.

Freedom and Necessity

THE most bewildering contrast which follows from that of ego and world is the contrast between freedom, the characteristic feature of man in his opposition to nature, and natural necessity. Man as a self does not belong to nature, and therefore he is exempt from that necessity which binds all natural existence. Freedom in this widest sense is almost identical with consciousness, selfhood, humanity, and personality. All these terms point to one common denominator—the position of man in contrast to the position of subhuman beings and entities—and freedom is the very means by which man holds that position and acts as man. He is free inasmuch as he is not subject to the nexus of cause and effect which is the order of the succession of events in nature. Man as an ego is not a link in that nexus; he is not a mere event or the result of forces which generate him and which work in him so that his actions are determined by those forces. On the contrary, he acts in the only true sense of the word, he is the author of his actions, the agent of his deeds. Man alone is that agent, man alone performs deeds in the proper sense, that is, in the sense of free acts. His deeds originate from his self, which in this respect is manifested as will. The will is free because the will is the very self, the person, the individual ego as the author of actions.

The meaning of this freedom, however, is not yet sufficiently described and comprehended, for not only does it contrast with the nexus of subhuman events, of natural processes (including organic life), but it also contrasts with the nexus that connects facts as facts. Man as an animal is subject to natural causality, but as man he is woven into the tissue of historical causes and effects. His will is determined by circumstances and conditions, situations and surroundings. It is the outcome of a manifold of forces and influences which often can be traced back to more remote causes. His feelings and opinions, his purposes and intentions, depend upon those causes, even when they seem to originate from his will alone. Not only is causality the order of nature as the subhuman sphere of the world, but it dominates the world in all its spheres and realms, including the realm of human life. What we call "character" in the moral sense is evidently the result not only of moral efforts, i.e., of the conscious deliberation of the individual self, but also of the inheritance from one's parents, of the way in which one is educated or misdirected, of the good conduct or the misdemeanors, the good or bad habits, of one's fellow-men, of the demoralization brought about by historical fortune or misfortune, and a thousand other factors which mold a man in his childhood and youth. Man seems to be as much the product of outer forces and events as he is the product of his own will and moral energy. Historians and biographers try, therefore, to "explain" all the deeds and works of their figures out of previous conditions and dispositions.

But this is only one side of the total experience. The other side reverses all these evidences and persists in showing that man is not the result of factors other than himself; that his will is the only responsible and actual source of his actions; that he is the builder and the master of his will and the author of his character, even the creator of his self. If we were permitted or obliged to explain self and will by other sources, the moral dignity and nobility of man would be destroyed. His selfhood would turn out to be an illusion, an arrogant self-deception. For selfhood is bound up with the contrast of world and ego; it rests upon the impossibility of self-objectification; it implies the transcendence which alone makes the self the center and pivot of its world and which makes the world dependent upon the self.

Thus an unavoidable contradiction arises. Both are irrefutably true: man's independence and his dependence, his freedom and his lack of freedom, his being a self and his being a thing. One cannot cancel either of the conflicting statements without doing harm to the full truth about man. And one cannot mitigate or eliminate the contradiction by dividing the totality of the person into one half that would be free and one half that would be determined, as wise men might think. This again would be the judgment of Solomon; man would be killed by such a division. He is alive just in so far as he lives in the tension between the two aspects, ever feeling himself responsible for his decisions and yet also driven to decide as he does. He actually lives within and outside the world, and this contradictory situation generates the consciousness of the bottomless abyss which opens underneath the surface of his existence.[3]

Freedom does not seem to tolerate any restriction: either it is absolute, or it is not freedom at all. Freedom means that man does not belong to the context of causes and effects which we experience as being the order of the world; he is not ordered by this order but stands outside it. Only thus is he able to observe

3. A recent attempt to solve the contradiction pleads for the primacy of determinism, reducing freedom to a principle of moral judgment which has no ontological truth (Erich Fromm, *Man for Himself* [New York: Rinehart & Co., 1947]). Moral judgments, the author argues, make us believe that man is free because they presuppose that man knows what he is doing and knows that he takes an active part in his actions. If we identify this activity with freedom, man is free indeed. But this freedom does not differ from the capacity to change and influence forces outside and inside ourselves "and to control, at least to some extent, the conditions which play upon us." "The structure of our total personality" is operative in our decisions and actions, but so is the structure of all things which change and influence the forces outside themselves. What deceives us into believing that we are more free than all things are, is the value which we attribute to moral actions. But this value is not different in principle from the value of paintings or even of shoes (p. 236). We should not attribute freedom to our actions any more than we attach freedom to those valuable things. This comparison shows how completely the author fails to recognize the uniqueness of moral values and the uniqueness of the moral agent. He does not go beyond the concept of freedom criticized by Kant as "the freedom of an automaton," which Leibniz had confused with the freedom of the self.

this order, to observe even himself in relation to it and entangled in its net. Only thus is he able to order himself, not as an organic being, subject to the specific causality of organic development, self-defense, and self-propagation, but as a moral agent who knows not only what he is doing but also that his very selfhood is at stake in choosing the good or the bad and that in choosing the good he chooses himself, while in choosing the bad he allows himself to be deprived of his selfhood. This metaphysical meaning of morality is the key to the concept of freedom; it is, at the same time, the root of the metaphysical contradiction of freedom and necessity.

It is true that the organism is a transition between the mechanical necessity of the suborganic and the moral freedom of the human sphere. The organism is not subject to the same kind of "blind" necessity to which the atom and the molecule are liable. It is a kind of self, though in a material form, and therefore it has the capacity of acting according to the end or ends of its organic existence. But this capacity should not be mistaken for freedom in the human sense. The beast does not act in a moral sense; it is not its selfhood as such but only the material existence of its self which is at stake. The beast can act so that its ends are not fulfilled, i.e., in a direction opposite to its own advantage, but it cannot act in a morally bad direction. A utilitarian ethics takes man as if he were nothing but an intelligent beast; this is the metaphysical blunder of all utilitarianism and pragmatism.

Organic causality is a precondition of freedom, but it is not freedom itself, since often enough it even prevents man from acting as a self and subjugates him to the yoke of his animal desires and impulses. Man governed entirely by organic necessity would not act as a morally free self, although his actions would not be prompted by mere physical necessity, in the sense of physics or chemistry. Selfhood elevates man over the whole sphere of nature and even over the level of world-existence. Kant was the first to recognize and elucidate this deepest significance of moral freedom. But he thought that the contradiction between world-causality and moral freedom could be solved by the distinction between man as an "empirical" and man as an "intelligible" being or as a "phenomenal" and a "noumenal" being. He did not see that this distinction does not help, because it is just the identity of the self in both spheres that creates the problem and because this identity is lost by the distinction.

The riddle of man consists in this identity of the self or the person which shows two antagonistic, incompatible aspects, both of which are "true," i.e., have their basis in experience, the one in world-, the other in self-experience; the contrast of world and ego generates that of necessity and freedom. Of course, in actual life the superiority of freedom over necessity is not doubted. No man can escape the uneasiness of his conscience by considering himself the product of forces and circumstances; by so doing he would give up his selfhood and even the possibility of reaching any truth at all, for this possibility is bound up with his being a thinking self and not merely a determined thing. But nevertheless the tension between the two views is not solved by the superiority of freedom. It leads to the ultimate questions: What am I? What is my relation to the world? Is there any third power or reality which reconciles the two views? Such metaphysical questions and their religious answers are the inevitable consequence of the contradiction.

Time and Eternity

THE contradiction of freedom and necessity with respect to the self and the will shows that I am woven into the tissue of world-events and subject to the principle of causality, while I am also the free agent of my own deeds and in this respect not subject to that principle. It is only a consequence of this insight which leads to the further contradiction of my being both involved in the temporal succession of events and exempt from it. As a self I am enmeshed in the nexus of cause and effect, and yet precisely as a self I am the observer of that nexus outside and within myself, and as such an observer I cannot be immersed in it. I must have a vantage point from which I look at the flux of time and the succession of events. In the act of the will I am the self which is able and obliged to examine and to foresee the concatenation of cause and effect; I have to consider the means leading to my ends and the motives moving me to different ends; my final decision is built upon these observations and considerations which circumscribe the deliberation of the mind prior to the action of the will. Before I act, time is, as it were, suspended; I am free from its urge and drive. For a little while I live above time, looking at the stream but not yet swimming in its waters. Only when my decision is made, when my deliberation is finished, do I jump into the whirlpool and produce a new beginning in the chain of causes and effects.

As I belong to the sphere of necessity, so also do I belong to the rule of time. But, in so far as I am free, I belong not only to that sphere but also to another one which I call "eternity." The connotation of this term does not yet have a religious or spiritual touch but is confined to the moral will and its action. A being entirely submerged in the stream of time can certainly not be conscious of the sequence of events. Time-consciousness is conditioned by a certain distance from the rush of time. I may be pressed, by the advance of certain circumstances, to act before I have come to a quiet consideration of all the factors involved; I may be interrupted in my deliberation by a message which prompts me to intervene at once, in order to prevent some deed of another person or to help someone in an emergency. Even then, deliberation and action can be distinguished. When I am pressed, I am not simply driven or physically pushed or thrown into action; in that case my action would no longer be mine at all but an accident, something that happens to my body and so to myself. As long as I have the opportunity and the duty to act, I also can deliberate concerning what I should do; and for that "period" I am not determined, but I determine myself; I "make up my mind," in the telling English phrase, which suggests that my mind is closed during this "period," not open to the influences of ongoing time but closed within itself, in the balance of indecision (*libra* means "balance").

To be sure, from the point of view of an objective observation, I may regard all my deliberation and consideration as a temporal process in which certain thoughts come and go, certain emotions accompany them, certain impulses rise and subside. But such an observation is totally different from the actual meaning of the deliberation itself, in which I am weighing the pro and con of reasons and the goodness or badness of motives. In the first case I am an object of observation, in the second case I am the observer and the actor. In weighing and deciding not only am I a sequence of states of mind or a succession of thoughts, emotions, and impulses, but I am the self which thinks, feels, and wants, and only thus am I able to determine the weight of reasons and motives and to arrive finally at the decision.

Not only is my decision a temporal event, but it also has a meaning; in deciding, I decide not merely for or against the end of my action and the means to bring it about but also for or against the moral value of my end, and thereby I determine the moral value of my action and of myself in determining myself. This value has a meaning that surpasses the hour of decision and action; it concerns the eternal worth or worthlessness of myself. I have to stand for my action, regardless of how much time passes; its significance belongs to an order resembling the order of truth and beauty, which also is independent of the flux of time. A true proposition remains true whenever it may be found; the length of time does not change its truth in the least. The realm of the morally good likewise exists independently of the transitoriness of events, even of actions themselves which are good or bad. In so far as I relate myself to that realm, I participate in its timelessness; and I am an ego only inasmuch as I do participate in it.

The organism is already relatively independent of time, in so far as organic causality no longer agrees with the direction of the temporal succession but reverses its course. "The end is in the begining" is already true on the level of organic life. The mutual relation between organic ends and means in the unity of the organism shows that this unity defeats the direction of time. The organism is not, like the atom or the molecule, subject to the order of succession; it partly governs this order, it makes itself the master of time by choosing the right means to its ends. But, even so, this triumph over time is still not a participation in the eternal realm of truth, beauty, and moral goodness. Only the human ego enjoys this privilege and confronts this challenge and obligation.

Therefore, all philosophical systems in our time which regard the organic realm as the crest of existence, like the system of Bergson or that of Whitehead, fail in understanding the human self. All biological metaphysics stops short of the problem of man. Bergson has analyzed the difference between mechanical and organic time, but he has not seen that even biological time is still not the actual time in which we as human beings live. Therefore, he ignores the contrast between time and eternity, replacing it by that of *temps-espace* and *durée*, i.e., of a spatialized time to be illustrated by the movement of a point on a line, and of organic time, which penetrates into an unknown future like a flying arrow. This description, graphic and fascinating though it is, does not even do full justice to the reversal of the time direction as it appears in the operation of final causes. An organism is not an arrow; it is able to anticipate the future by means of instinct and to bring about what it anticipates.

This anticipation is, to be sure, unconscious in the organic realm, while it is conscious and voluntary in man. The final cause is less than a purpose; only the ability to intend the end and carry through the intention by choosing the right means can elevate man above the enslavement to time, because this ability is connected with the power of judging the moral value of the purpose, i.e., its eternal significance. Therefore, man alone lives in a sphere which is modified by the contrast of time and eternity.

This modification is manifest in the consciousness of the time dimensions—past, present, and future. Augustine first had this important insight, which has not been fully regained by the philosophy of our own period, in spite of its interest in the riddle of time. Augustine recognized the significance of the time dimensions because he was aware that only a being who is conscious of eternity can be conscious of these dimensions. Aristotle defined time as "the number of motion in respect of before and after," i.e., he knew only physical time and did not know that the time dimensions of before and after are transformed into past and future by the consciousness of the present which separates them. His concept of the present as the "Now" means merely the gliding point on the line which represents the boundary between the before and the after. But it is man's consciousness of eternity which alone enables him to divide time into past and future; a point outside time is necessary to transform the objective and relative relation between before and after into the subjective and absolute relation of past and future.

It is by recollecting what has been and by anticipating what will be that man lives in the actual dimension of the present. Remembrance and expectation meet in his consciousness, inasmuch as he disposes of time and is not merely subject to it. By remembering the past, he saves it from the destruction which transitoriness inflicts upon everything present; he reactualizes, he re-presents it, he makes it present again, although as something that is no longer present. And, by expecting the future, he makes present what is not yet present as something that will be. In that way he masters the flux of time, standing himself outside the on-rushing and disappearing stream; he is able to dispose of the future, to divide it and fill it according to his intentions and duties. He is no longer the subject of time but makes time his subject. To dispose of time, man needs a place which is both inside and outside the course of time. The present is this peculiar place.

To use an image, time may be compared with a train which passes a certain station. Man awaits its arrival in the station, he sees it as it approaches, as it stops for a few minutes, and as it starts and disappears again in the opposite direction. He himself arranges the station, the track, and the direction of the train. But the wonder is that he also sits in the train while it moves. For man is not the absolute master of time, he is also mastered by it; he lives in this tension between time and eternity, belonging perfectly to neither realm but torn this way or that way, now directing the stream, now whirled in its vortex. Thus he experiences his power over time and his surrender to time, as he also experiences his superiority over the necessity of natural processes by using them for his purposes and his utter inferiority when he is crushed by an accident, illness, or age. This contradiction characterizes human life. It tinges all man's aspirations and frustrations, all his accords and conflicts, all his triumphs and defeats.

Most moral virtues reflect this state of man. They concern the way in which he overpowers time by holding to the past or by molding the future. Loyalty, veracity, sincerity, steadfastness, endurance, patience, industry, and carefulness are related to the struggle between the fleeting and the permanent self. Neither is ever absolutely victorious, neither ever absolutely subjugated.

This contradiction postulates a solution. At the horizon there looms the idea of an eternity which, rather than being in contrast with time, embraces the totality of time itself, all time and all times. This idea is not simply the opposite of time—timelessness; instead, it conquers its opponent, it is a synthesis of the opposites, an eternity which unifies itself and time, thereby reconciling the antagonistic poles and solving the contradiction which tears man's consciousness. Such an eternity would also solve another problem which threatens the thinking mind—the problem of temporal infinity.

Time has no beginning and no end. It is infinite in both directions. Even a beginning of time would presuppose time, and so would an end of time. This infinity obstructs the capacity of the thinking mind and threatens to destroy its unity. We can neither grasp an endless time nor understand how time should begin and end. Mind confronts an abysmal alternative. If it yields to the infinity inherent in time, it destroys itself, it ends in despair. If it insists on its self-preservation, it violates the character of time. Thus the thinking mind oscillates between suicidal recognition of infinity and preservation of its own integrity at the expense of infinity. Evidently the human mind cannot escape this alternative; it finds itself on the horns of a dilemma. The idea of a synthesis of time and eternity previously outlined may rescue the mind from this dangerous oscillation.

In a way, the idea of an end suggests a certain solution. An end is an ambiguous term. It means both purpose and the last link of a series of actions. This idea first emerges in the organic process, where the end of growth or of a series of self-preserving actions satisfies both meanings: purpose in the form of the final cause and the last link in the form of the operation which carries the final cause to its self-realization. Psychologically, the desire comes to its end in the fulfilment. But, of course, this end in time is not the end of time.

In the realm of human aspiration the idea of an absolute purpose might be helpful. If there is an absolute purpose and if man should ever be able to pursue it to the very end, then time should be fulfilled. The absolute values of truth, beauty, and goodness point to such an absolute end. Man pursues it in civilizing himself. But he never reaches it. The only way in which man reaches an absolute end of time is by death. Indeed, death is both an empirical and a transcendent or eschatological event; therefore, it challenges the human mind. He feels that death means something that can neither be denied nor understood. Experience in its nonreligious sense reaches its own end in confronting the postulate of a time-embracing eternity in the event of death.

The labor of civilization, as well as the mortality of the individual, demands a solution of the contradiction between time and eternity. But neither civilization nor the experience of death grants such a solution; both confront the abyss of the contradiction. Faith alone shows a way. The idea of an eternity which contains the beginning and the end of time and thus rounds time into a totality finds its only realization in the revelation of an infinite God who creates time and world and directs both to the consummation of man's aspirations.

Character and System of the Antinomies

THE contradictions of experience can be called "antinomies," if we understand by this term contradictions which can be neither avoided nor solved. The contradiction of world and ego and all the contradictions derived from it are neither avoidable nor soluble; they are genuine antinomies or metaphysical contradictions inherent in experience and in self-understanding. That I confront a world is my basic experience; in this statement the word "I" (or "my") means both the individual and the universal ego or, in other words, myself and every self. So-called "solipsism" insists that every self knows only itself and can be certain only of its own existence, while the existence of every other self may be doubted and must be demonstrated in order to be certain. This theory brings to mind the uniqueness of self-experience. It is true that I know only myself in an immediate and direct way and that I can never know the other person with that same immediacy and directness. But it is not true that I need a proof for the existence of another person, for in another sense my experience of other persons is also immediate and direct; in fact, I could never know myself without knowing other persons, because the I presupposes the thou, as the thou presupposes the I. I cannot know myself without knowing that there are other selves, because my individuality implies the distinction from other individuals: the term "individuality" has meaning only if there are many individuals, i.e., if I am not absolutely isolated, not a *solus ipse* but one among others.

World, as experienced, has no clear and distinct meaning; it is not yet a concept but a problem to be analyzed and discussed. But one feature of what we mean is clear and distinct from the outset: world comprises everything except myself. Fichte called the basic concepts "ego" and "nonego," in order to be sure that this distinction would exhaust the all of existence and also in order to leave it open as to what nonego means. But Fichte's system was deductive, it departed from a supreme thesis, while the system here offered rests upon experience and advances toward principles by a procedure of discussing the content of experience. Even so, it might be underlined that experience gives us more light with respect to the meaning of the ego than with respect to the totality of those contents which stand over against the ego and which we call "world." Although I myself am a riddle to myself, just because I confront a world to which I belong and yet do not belong, still, in ordinary experience and in daily life, I know very well what I mean by the term "I," while I do not so well know what I mean by the term "world."

So far we have seen that this term includes more than the visible universe, more than nature as the object of the natural sciences (the subhuman world-sphere); it includes also myself and all the other persons, indeed, the whole human world-sphere as it expands in history, in all the works and institutions of man's civilization. But it does not contain the human world-sphere in the same sense as it contains the subhuman one because of the antinomy between world and ego or because the human selves and their works and institutions are involved in that basic contrast and contradiction which is the essential feature of human

experience and life. "World" in the wider sense is tinged by the
ego-world relation. Therefore, the term will be elucidated to the
same degree as this relation can be understood.

A beginning of such understanding, which has to be a self-
understanding, since only the self can offer the key to the relation, has been made by the discussion of the contradictions implied in the basic antinomy. This antinomy unfolds into more abstract and less immediate concepts which clarify the opposition
between ego and world and which make their contrast more distinct. Of course, this method cannot arrive at an understanding
of the origin of the contrast itself from a higher unity or an original common ground. Experience puts us in this world of ours
and gives us no hint as to how the duality of world and ego is
rooted in "the nature of all things," if this notion has any meaning at all. Especially, experience does not disclose whether one of
the contrasting sides may represent an ultimate unity of both
world and ego; whether perhaps an absolute ego (as Fichte ac-
cepts it from the outset) may "set" itself and its opposite by
affirming and negating itself or whether, instead, world may ultimately embrace both the ego and the nonego. Experience gives
us no hint in either direction, and, as long as we rely upon experience alone (in the nonreligious sense), we may oscillate endless-
ly between a system which stresses the primacy of the ego (as
German idealism does) and a system which, on the contrary,
makes the world independent of the ego and regards it as the all-
embracing whole. I say that experience gives us no hint in either
direction and therefore it does not support either system; on the
contrary, experience shows us that there is this duality.

But this is not all. Experience also shows us that this duality
cannot be ultimate, since it entangles us in a net of contradictions; and, furthermore, experience shows us that, of the two opposites, the ego has a certain ascendancy, since only the ego experiences world and itself and since only the ego experiences the
contradiction between the two. Thus we may conclude that, if
there is any solution at all of the basic antinomy, if either world
or ego represents ultimately this solution (though in a way which
surpasses all experience and, indeed, all understanding based upon
the ego-world experience), then the ego has at least a preroga-

tive in the competition between ego and world. The ego deserves the higher position.

It is strange that the discovery by philosophy of the basic antinomy has come so late in history. If it is true that the contrast of world and ego is at the very bottom of all experience, why did the Greeks not see it? Why did the world have to wait until Kant for the basic character of this opposition to be philosophically recognized and made the cornerstone of the whole building? This puzzling question can be answered only in a psychological and historical fashion. Man depends on nature to such a degree that he forgets that he himself is also independent of nature. So the first Greek thinkers turned first to the visible universe as the proper object of investigation and speculation and thought of man only as the inhabitant of this majestic cosmos. The experience of this universe was so overwhelming and powerful that the self-experience of man seemed to be of a secondary rank. We can notice that even today this rank-order impresses itself upon thinkers, so that many tend toward naturalism and cosmology simply because of the psychological weight of world-experience.

The first to understand that self-experience is of a higher rank was Socrates. "Understand yourself" was the oracle which he thought was most important and informative. He turned from cosmological speculation to ethical considerations as the most basic in the whole realm of philosophy. Indeed, he identified the ethical and philosophical attitudes. But still the mind of man was too much impressed by the experience of the cosmos, and so Plato returned to cosmological speculation, though with the Socratic awareness that the inner experience should guide the philosopher. But not until the religion of inwardness had exalted the worth of the human soul more than had ever been done before was man able to concentrate upon self-experience. However, when the Christian Fathers began to philosophize, they were suppressed by the enormous weight of Greek thought, and they were not strong enough to throw off this inheritance and make a completely new beginning. Augustine did move in a new direction; he did recognize that the soul should be the center of philosophical interest. But he was not philosopher enough to destroy the cosmological inheritance; and the young Germanic peoples in the Middle Ages were even less able to withstand the temptation issuing from the studies of the greatest master of thought.

Descartes saw the preponderance of the ego-world relation, but he spoiled his own insight by his ambition to understand the universe with the means of the new science, which was so successful in analyzing the mathematical relations within the processes of nature; thus he succumbed anew to the cosmological problem. It was Kant alone, strengthened and fortified by Hume's penetrating but skeptical analysis of man, who succeeded in victoriously carrying through the hints of Socrates, Augustine, and Descartes. But Kant thought that he could accomplish the task of solving the antinomies of experience by a critical distinction between the things which we experience and the things-in-themselves which we cannot experience, while the real difficulty arises from experience itself, from the experiential contradiction between self and world.

As the split of the atom in our period generates a constant threat to the welfare and security of mankind, so the split of the human consciousness into the poles of man's experience generates a constant threat to his spiritual welfare and peace. For this split permeates and invades all spheres of his life and thought, and no distinction between things and things-in-themselves can deceive us about the deadly danger which we confront. The system of antinomies is the most obvious proof of this danger. Hegel, in trying to unfold this system out of the original opposition of being and nonbeing, was certainly on the right track, although it might be doubted whether it is or ever will be possible to derive all categories from one opposition and whether any system at all of antinomies can be given in which one great inner movement of thought generates the sequence of antagonistic concepts.

That there is an inner trend toward a system, no one who has studied this most intricate problem in earnest would easily deny. I have confined myself to the discussion of some antinomies which seem to me of central significance. The categories which were operative in those antinomies are parallel to the basic contrast between world and ego. Universality represents the unity which turns the manifold of entities and events into one entity, the universe; individuality represents the uniqueness of each ego which makes it an individual. But the world is also itself individual, in so far as it is my world, and I am also universal, in so far as I am the ego of the world. Universality and individuality are more abstract and conceptual than world and ego; they are no longer contents of experience but "categories," which apply to all things and to all beings. Every stone is both the universal "stone" and this individual stone. Aristotle thought that this polarity does not lead to contradictions but to the synthesis of matter and form in one and the same substance. He did not realize that such a synthesis would be conceivable only if matter and form had a common denominator or if they were one and the same; otherwise, the identity implied in the concept of substance can never be explained or understood.

Oneness and manifoldness are even more abstract and conceptual than are universality and individuality. Not only every entity or being but even every concept and every category are subject to this opposition. It can be derived from the original polarity between world and ego, since world is a manifold united in the ego, so that oneness and manifoldness are elements corresponding to the basic contrast.

The opposites of freedom and necessity, as well as those of time and eternity, do not emerge in quite the same way. It is true, of course, that necessity is a category which governs the order of all processes in the world, while freedom is the special excellence of the self. But the two polar concepts are not so conceptual and abstract as are the preceding ones; freedom is exclusively attached to the ego, although analogies of freedom exist in the organic realm. Eternity, too, is peculiar to self-experience, though again it has antecedents in organic life. However, both freedom and eternity have significance beyond their immediate sphere of experience. Both point to a synthesis of world and ego which transcends self-experience.

Contradiction and Self-contradiction

THE antinomies of experience are not experienced as logical antinomies, but rather they are brought into that form by the thinking mind, which, of course, is directly active in experience, though not in a philosophical fashion. This philosophical approach results from the need of self-understanding. In "pre-philo-sophical," unreflective experience the antinomies appear in the form of emotional tensions and passions, like grief and despair, anxiety and longing, unrest and agitation, embarrassment and perplexity. All these emotions, which move the soul in its depths, are evidence and symptom not only of individual and specific difficulties which the self undergoes but also of the universal situation in which man finds himself, of his metaphysical status. The definite occasions and objects of such emotions as they occur in life are only the peculiar manifestations of that status. But sometimes this status announces itself in the form of unspeci-fied emotions; then we no longer feel a definite grief, longing, or perplexity, but rather we feel the entirety of the conditions of life. These indefinite feelings are, as it were, the emotional mes-sengers or representatives of the antinomies of experience. What is emotionally experienced in this indefinite, vague way is clearly and distinctly thought out and expressed in the logical form of contradictions which we cannot evade, dissolve, or dismiss.

Thought does not create the antinomies, but it does create the logical form in which we think them. In actual life the antinomies betray the underlying discord of the self, the inner split between contradictory motivations, the antagonism of opposite dimen-sions which tear the unity of selfhood. We feel the finitude, the fallibility, the imperfection of our human status. We feel that we cannot arrive at that perfect peace which would correspond to the unity and totality of the self. Instead of being a unity, we are divided within ourselves. Instead of determining ourselves in per-fect freedom, we are pressed and driven. Instead of enjoying the vision of "all times and all being," we are fragments of the waves which the stream of time carries and into which it transforms and dissolves itself in an endless change. Thus we can never grasp and we can never be the whole of experience. We are tossed about between the world and ourselves, now crushed by the onslaught of events, now able to withstand them, to command ourselves, and thereby to create a dominion over the world.

Thought does not generate experience, which is, rather, the presupposition of thought. Thought only comprehends it, thus formulating contradictions which render what we find in life in the language and logic of the thinking mind. It thus reflects what is lived through. Experience is primary, thought secondary. This distance between life and thought, which does not hinder their being in agreement with each other, can be expressed by the two terms of "self-contradiction" and "contradiction." Indeed, in life it is the very self that contradicts itself emotionally and thereby feels perplexity and anxiety, while in thought the mind formulates propositions which are mutually exclusive, the one being the positive, the other being the negative, of one and the same logical statement.

The antinomy expresses, in a logical form, the emotional strain produced by an immediate self-contradiction which, as such, has no logical form. But contradiction presupposes self-contradiction. If the self did not feel the contradictions, the mind would not discover them; but they have to be stated, in order to contradict each other logically, and only the mind can and does state them. Only the mind unites (or rather tries to unite) the divergent directions, the positive and the negative ones, and thus makes their divergence explicit. The mind finds itself torn by contradictions when it renders the pre-logical disunity in a logical fashion. Contradiction rests on self-contradiction, as thought rests on experience and philosophy on life.

The original meaning of "contradiction" is an expression of disagreement between two persons or their utterances. I contradict what has been said by someone else. I deny the statement made by another person. This personal contradiction is the archetype of that inner contradiction which occurs in the "self-conversation of the soul with the soul" which the Platonic Socrates holds to be the origin of philosophy, as it is certainly the origin of self-understanding and self-comprehension. This inner self-contradiction is the beginning of logical discussion and discourse.

Self-contradiction is possible only because I am a self and wish to be in agreement with myself, since my very self is at stake when I disagree with myself. The logical antinomies reflect this inner situation, this metaphysical experience. By formulating them, I clarify my perplexity and anxiety and thus begin to understand myself. Logic as a whole is an outcome of selfhood. It is the mode in which the self tries to defend itself against the danger of being lacerated and given over to the manifold, the necessity, the temporal change of the world. The ego asserts itself; it expresses its sovereignty in thought.

Self-contradiction is at the root of contradiction, just as experience is at the root of thought. I always contradict myself if two propositions contradict each other. A proposition is a kind of depersonalized statement, but behind the statement there is the person stating it, and without that person no statement and no proposition would be possible. Indeed, only a self torn between world and ego, between itself and what is not itself, between antagonistic voices within itself, can think. Only a self in danger of losing itself sets up propositions, theses, theories. Only such a self philosophizes. The infinite mind, which is not torn and divided against itself, does not need philosophizing. The very idea of such a mind, therefore, transcends all categories and, indeed, all possibilities of human thought, as it also transcends the entire structure of human experience.

Identity is the logical category which corresponds to selfhood. Therefore, it is the sole guardian of truth. If I lose the identity of my concept, I must necessarily err. Self-contradiction is the opposite of identity; it denies the identity, i.e., the selfhood of myself. Only because we find ourselves in the state of an inner struggle for identity do we set out to think, hoping that we will discover the means of self-unification, thus establishing selfhood by means of thought. Whether or not we can succeed depends upon the character of our thought. Dogmatic philosophy asserts the possibility of success; skepticism denies it. A critical philosophy, which finally comes to understand why it must end in faith, stands between those extremes, mediating between them and establishing the relative right and the relative wrong of each.

The Antinomies of Experience and the Task of Civilization

THE task of civilization is set by the antinomies of experience. Man cannot remain in the state of immediate experience because this state is unsettled and explosive. Man cannot be at rest as long as his consciousness is divided against itself as it is in the state of immediate experience. He has to save the unity, identity, and totality of his self. He has to overcome the basic opposition within his mind and heart. He tries to overcome it by the labor of civilization. Of course, civilization does not solve this task by a merely logical effort; but, just as thought has to formulate the inner tension of the human soul in a logical way, so also it has to understand the activity of civilization as the solution of those antinomies which correspond to the perplexities and anxieties of life. Only in such a way is thought able to understand the plurality of cultural spheres and realms in a logical fashion, in the fashion of a philosophy of culture.

Human experience and human culture complement each other. The directions and ends of cultural activity and creativity are preconditioned by immediate experience. And, on the other hand, immediate experience, informed by language, is permeated by culture. Human experience can never be absolutely uncivilized. As Genesis narrates, God brought the animals unto Adam "to see what he would call them: and whatsoever Adam called every living creature, that was the name thereof." Adam, or man as such, begins his experience by naming the creatures of the earth, thereby gaining power over them. Thus language is the first action by which man builds a bridge between himself and nature and begins to overcome the duality of world and ego. The name is more than a conventional sign; it is the conquest of the world by the mind. The names which man gives to the creatures are their true and real names; the conquest is achieved by the capacity for knowing, which penetrates into the essence of things.

Cultural activity takes up what is inherent in experience. From the outset, experience is not merely a passive receptivity but rather an active receptivity or a receptive spontaneity in which two opposite attitudes are united, representing the opposites of world and ego. Cultural activity elaborates the element of activity innate in experience; it pursues the attitude of spontaneity and unfolds it, so that the gulf between world and ego may be overcome and their opposite claims reconciled to each other.

But is not this philosophy of culture too "idealistic"? Does it not interpret man's efforts in civilizing himself too exclusively from the point of view of his metaphysical nature, thereby neglecting the fact that man is also an animal and that a goodly number of his cultural aims and ends are determined by his very animal nature? I do not deny, of course, that many aspects of civilization derive from this nature, at least in part. When we assume that civilization began with the plow, we certainly can understand this step as a means of producing more fruit and perhaps more satisfactory fruit than uncultivated trees and grasses would yield. Was not this first impulse determined exclusively by man's animal needs and wants? Nevertheless, as I have said above,[4] man is, on every level of his activity, more than an animal because he is always guided by his total experience. He can devise tools and machines just because he is not prompted solely by his animal nature, i.e., his instinct and impulse, to satisfy his needs and wants but, rather, is free to determine the means by which he may satisfy them; only this high gift enables him to invent new and civilized means of feeding himself.

In seeking for these new means and ways, man manifests his metaphysical nature. He becomes a fisherman, a hunter, a farmer, or an engineer because he is the unsettled being that aims at his self-unification and self-reconciliation. He aims at this end in all the fields and activities of civilization, even when he is also prompted by his animal nature to seek food, shelter, weapons, and luxury goods. Altogether, culture is man's adventure, and man is an adventurer because he is unsettled and longs for an indefinite good which would definitively satisfy his supreme need, the need to solve the antinomies of experience.

Man is unsettled—indeed, he is not quite himself—as long as this need is unsatisfied. Man is, as it were, unfinished as he finds himself in his self-experience. He is in an untenable, unstable state in which he is not what he really is and in which he is what he really is not, i.e., in a state of self-contradiction from which he must save himself. Culture is the supreme, intellectual way in which he tries to perform this work of self-salvation. He has no choice. Although he is free in choosing the means of this self-salvation, the task is nevertheless prescribed to him by his un-

4. Part I, pp. 21 ff.

finished, imperfect state. Of course, this compulsion is not a physiological necessity but a spiritual or metaphysical one, manifesting itself as purpose and voluntary activity.

Man is the only being that has to apply spiritual energy in order to fulfil his end, in order to become what he is supposed to be. Man, therefore, is both real and ideal; his reality is the state of unrest and imperfection, his ideal is the completion of his selfhood by the eradication of his self-contradiction. In civilizing himself he realizes himself, i.e., he makes the ideal real. This is the goal and meaning of culture.

There is no human experience which is not informed by some culture, be it ever so primitive and fragmentary. Man is a cultural as well as a natural being. It is, as it were, his nature to face a task which transcends nature altogether, which even transforms nature according to the call of his metaphysical goal. The ancient myth of Prometheus illuminates this situation in which man is imprisoned and from which he strives to escape. Prometheus discovers man's spiritual misery and tries to help him by bringing the fire from heaven, the symbol of all the arts and sciences which would civilize him. Zeus punishes Prometheus severely for this act of charity because Prometheus thereby violates the eternal order, that is, the order of the cosmos which determines for every being his state of existence. Man is the only being that cannot dwell in his own state but finds it necessary to transcend the cosmic order by using divine power (the fire) supported by a friendly being, half-human and half-divine.

The biblical story of paradise and the Fall serves a similar end, but it is more subtle and mysterious. Here also man is depicted as longing for some perfection which is denied him, in spite of his happy status of harmony with all creatures and with his Creator. The serpent, half-divine and half-bestial, awakens this longing and seduces Eve to fulfil it by transgressing the order of the Creator who has placed them in the garden. Man and serpent are punished by God, but out of man's punishment grows the human civilization which causes both misery and satisfaction.

In both stories it is hinted that the work of civilization is something extraordinary that is not in agreement with the original plan of the universe, something of doubtful value.

Indeed, if this work does not reach its goal, if it is not able to fulfil man's spiritual need, it really is a doubtful undertaking. As we will see, this is man's tragic destiny. Although his cultural energy performs glorious deeds and succeeds in approaching the highest goal, it can never fully achieve its end. It never succeeds absolutely in reconciling ego and world, and therefore it never succeeds in bringing about that equilibrium which alone would make man perfect. Man never regains paradise by his own effort.

II. Culture

CHAPTER III
Preliminary Considerations

System and Reality of Culture

THE culture which man builds is experienced not as a system but as an actual reality which dominates his life and in which he participates by his conduct and attitude through active contribution and creativity. Culture is a presupposition of human life as well as a product of it; it is both an outcome of human experience and part and parcel of that experience. Man experiences everything in the light of his culture, which stamps and molds his experience by generating the conceptions which inform him, when he perceives the world and himself or his fellow-man. The child of the twentieth century does not have the same experience as that of the child of the tenth century or that of the centuries before Christ. The peculiar trend and style, the form and the content, of his culture influence the form and the content of his experience from birth to death. He is unable to throw off these cultural fetters or, one might say, this cultural armor; every individual has only the opportunities which his own period offers, not only with respect to his labor and enjoyment, but even with respect to his experience. In this sense, experience is never immediate but always mediated by the historical background of civilization, although the relative difference between immediate and mediated experience has to be maintained in the abstract.

It is not language alone which forms and informs the contents of experience, but it is also all the habits and manners, traditions and remembrances, aspirations and results, of a living culture which more or less determine the modes of daily experience. The

71

empiricists are indeed blind to insist that experience is originated by the impression of external things upon a *tabula rasa*. External things are always apprehended according to the way in which a living culture comprehends and shapes them. This is the case not only because each culture produces tools and also transforms the external things but also because it presents even those things which it does not shape according to the standards of its own understanding, in the widest sense of this word. Oscar Wilde has said, "Nature imitates art"; this is perfectly true. If one travels through Italy studying the paintings in the churches and palaces, museums and public houses, one's eyes are schooled to look at the actual landscape in the manner in which the painters have seen and portrayed it. And this extends, in an analogous pattern, to the relation between experience and all the fine arts, including poetry. We live in agreement with the images which surround us and fascinate us. We behold people through the imagination of poets; we experience love, friendship, work, and destiny as the theater and the novel teach us to experience them; of course, out of these experiences new artistic conceptions and interpretations of life arise, slowly changing the course of cultural life and therefore of experience from year to year and from decade to decade—at least in our own quickly moving and changing period.

Although culture and experience stand in the close relationship of mutual exchange and although culture, therefore, is as alive as experience, a certain logical division unfolds within this stream of moving life, just as the logical division of world and ego and all the other categories implied in it or derived from it are also already present in immediate experience. Thought, if thought is loyal to its task and solves it rightly, produces nothing which is not preconceived and pre-existent in experience. Thus the main classes and types of cultural activity unfold even at the level of pre-philosophical life. This life displays itself in different cultural manifestations by producing cultural works and cultural institutions. Craft, science, and art separate; economic, social, and political life unfolds. These distinctions pertain to the immediacy of life, and language reflects them long before thought tries to classify and systematize the manifold of culture. Thought only follows a path already discovered and paved by experience.

In so far as culture lives and changes, it has a historical character; it is bound up with the peculiar spirit of particular epochs and periods. Thought, therefore, in building a systematic comprehension of the unity and diversity of cultural realms and activities, must be aware of this historical fluidity and relativity of culture or cultures. Indeed, a philosophy of culture is incomplete if it is not simultaneously a philosophy of history or if it fails at least to include such a philosophy.

However, awareness of this should not lead us to conclude that a philosophy of culture has to be reduced to, or dissolved into, a philosophy of history, as contemporary thinkers are prone to do. On the contrary, a sound and tenable philosophy of history can be built only upon the ground of a philosophy of culture; otherwise it would easily degenerate into a kind of historicism, i.e., into a philosophy which is essentially historical. Historicism is no more adequate than that naturalism based on the sciences.[1] Both commit, in principle, the same mistake; they apply the methods and categories of a special science to the problems of philosophy, whereas, instead, a true philosophy would make those methods and categories the objects of its inquiry and try to understand the special task and contribution of each science.

The history of culture shows that the divisions within cultural life proliferate and harden while they develop. In ancient cultures the divisions are less developed and pronounced than they are today. In Asiatic civilizations all the cultural divisions are still imbedded in the total stream of life, so that one cannot speak about art as if it were detached from religion; about religion as if it were detached from speculative thought; about this thought as if it were detached from mystical feelings; or about these feelings as if they were detached from moral and political wisdom. In the great culture of Athens these various aspects begin to separate; for the first time art is recognized in its own right; philoso-

1. Frequently both blend, as in Spengler's biological "morphology" of historical cultures, which denies the very character of world history—its continuity and universality. Toynbee, the English Spengler, is more historical, but, lacking a philosophy of culture, he also sometimes applies biological thought-forms (cf. *A Study of History*, abridgment by D. C. Somervell [London: Oxford University Press, 1947], pp. 253, 261, 277, 327 ff.).

phy separates itself from religion; mystery cults arise apart from the official state religion, and even morality begins to make its own demands. "Reason," severed from tradition and convention, awakens. But even in this culture the various directions still have one focus; they converge toward one point in which they are united. Greek art never cuts the tie with religion; philosophy never turns absolutely away from religion; morality never emancipates itself completely, as it does in Kant's idea of the categorical imperative of reason; and the state always remains a center which gathers all the realms together. The state itself is the religion (as Jacob Burckhardt has stressed in his book *The Culture of the Greeks,* and as Werner Jaeger and Julius Stenzel have discussed in detail). The gods are the gods of the state, but they are also the gods of the poets and of the sculptors; tragedy has a religious significance; and philosophy vies with the tragedians, as Plato is proud to say. Science and philosophy are still in the closest contact with each other.

In the Middle Ages the all-embracing church unifies culture. Science, philosophy, and theology are one *summa;* the arts serve ecclesiastical ideas and realities almost exclusively; the state is, at least according to the papal theory, subject to the church; and morality is entirely determined by the standards of the Roman Catholic code. However, we can observe severe tensions in this union of culture: the state never fully acknowledges the supremacy of the Holy See; science and philosophy slowly develop their own methods and principles; and finally even the fine arts claim autonomy.[2] In Galileo mathematical physics brusquely destroys the bond between itself and philosophy and sternly rejects all intervention by poetical imagination and myth. Modern times are characterized by this ever increasing separation and autonomy, until at last the danger of complete dissolution and cultural chaos appears imminent in our own period. It is high time that the inner unity and totality of culture be rediscovered. The so-called "totalitarian" states have felt the necessity, but they have turned to despotism and the police-state, in order to enforce externally a unity which does not exist internally.

2. Cf. the excellent new account by Christopher Dawson, *Religion and the Rise of Western Culture* (Gifford Lectures [New York: Sheed & Ward, 1950]).

The problem is great, and a solution is not yet in sight. In the meantime, philosophy is called upon to seek the inner bond of all the divergent cultural activities and aspirations. Perhaps the discharge of this task will illuminate the greater task of bringing about a new unity of culture in the reality of life. In any case, it is important to understand the way in which the divisions cut up the whole of culture, and it is this understanding to which the following system will lead.

Contemplation and Action

CULTURE is divisible into spheres. But, as a whole, it is also one answer to the self-contradiction of experience; it is one attempt at a self-reconciliation and self-unification which would produce the reality of a self victorious over the split into world and ego. All the spheres of culture aim at one and the same end: the solution of the antinomies. Culture strives to generate a consciousness within which the contemplation of the world is compatible with the self-dependence of the ego and the action of persons is compatible with the existence of a self-dependent world. Only contemplation can unite the many worlds which live in the many selves; only action can unite the manifold of persons so that they can live together peacefully.

Thought can schematize a solution of the cultural task in an abstract way. The basic contradiction of world and ego may be formulated for this purpose as a contradiction which endangers either the unity of the world or that of the ego. The unity of the world is endangered by the plurality of worlds among the many selves; the unity of the ego is endangered by the plurality of many selves, each of which claims to be the center of the world. The unity of the world can be recovered or saved by a contemplation which either suppresses the manifold of worlds or exalts one world above all the others as the only true one. The unity of the ego can be recovered or saved by the action of one self which either suppresses all the other selves or declares itself as absolute and sovereign. All these ways have been tried in the history of civilization in many forms and on various levels. But the unification of the world was always the object of contemplation, while the unification of the ego was always the object of action.

World is, in actual experience, the object of a cognitive attitude which aims at knowledge, while the ego is, from the outset, not an object at all but the feeling, sensing, desiring, willing, and acting subject. This basic and consequential difference provokes the differences of cultural attitudes. The contradiction between the oneness and the manifoldness of world and worlds can be removed only by contemplation; the contradiction between the oneness and the manifoldness of self and selves only by action. In both cases oneness is victorious, bringing about the cultural unity of ego and world, a unity in which either the world or the ego prevails. If the many worlds are united by contemplation, either the ego is completely eliminated, or the manifold selves are made a part, though primarily the central part, of the one world. If the many selves are united by action, the world is not eliminated, but the many worlds are united together with the many selves as their worlds, since the world of the sovereign ego determines them.

This very abstract and schematic division underlies the system of cultural realms. The cognitive and contemplative attitude is at the bottom of science and art, while the volitional and active attitude dominates the political, the moral, and, as we shall see later on, the religious areas of civilization. At once I would like to add that art and religion represent less one-sided attitudes than do science and politics. The feeling, desiring, and willing subject is more concerned with artistic creation than it is with scientific investigation and production, nor is the cognitive attitude completely absent in the religious sphere. Furthermore, religion does not belong to culture in the same sense as that in which the other branches do. All these points must be thoroughly elaborated in the course of the discussion.

Although all these divisions exist potentially on the level of immediate experience, they are not yet clearly divided. In this respect infantile experience resembles the dawn of civilization. And the development of the child resembles the development of mankind. The child's experience is more immediate than is the adult's; even immediate experience is less immediate in the age of maturity, because the person is cultivated and culture encroaches upon experience on an increasing scale. The child that sucks at his mother's breast does not yet distinguish between the object of his perception and the object of his desire, between his cognitive and his active attitudes; they are still fused as the leaves in the bud, while the attitudes of the scientist and the politician are clearly and evidently distinguished and even separated in the reality of life.

The contrast between contemplation (or cognition, intuition, speculation) and action, however, has to be qualified. The ego is always in the ascendancy because it is the contemplating as well as the acting subject, because it is that which contemplates the world while the world is merely contemplated, and because it acts upon itself (or upon the other selves). This primacy of the ego corresponds with the primacy of action over contemplation. In a way, contemplation itself is action, or—to avoid the disturbing ambiguity of this term—it is an activity. Indeed, without an activity of some kind, culture is impossible. All culture is activity, be it contemplative or active, cognitive or volitional. Activity, in the cultural sense, is always productive and sometimes creative. Nevertheless, activity, productivity, and creativity in the sphere of contemplation are clearly distinguishable from the activity, productivity, and creativity in that of action.

Accordingly, unification of ego and world, even when the ego is suppressed altogether or treated as a part of the world, is always self-unification of the ego. It is always man who builds up culture, even when he neglects humanity in the picture of the world which he works out or when he gives himself only an insignificant place within that picture. Nevertheless, by contemplating the world, man tries to unify world and ego within his own consciousness, for even the world which he productively contemplates is his world and, by producing a picture of the world, he indirectly unites all the selves, in that he obliges them to acknowledge his picture of the world as authoritative. Every scientist must acknowledge the authority of science and of the world-picture dictated by scientific cognition. Science and art contribute no less than politics and religion to the goal of self-unification and self-reconciliation of the ego. All branches join in mitigating the self-contradiction of the experiencing subject and in solving the basic antinomies of experience.

Both contemplation and action are activities, but the activity of contemplation is no action because it is not dominated by the will but by intellect and knowledge, observation and intuition, inquiry and vision. One may call the element of will "active" and the element of intellect "passive." Indeed, in impression and sense-perception passivity prevails; only through the elaboration of these primitive foundations by scientific and artistic endeavor does the element of activity appear and unfold in the production of theories and in the creation of works of art. On the other hand, in impulse and desire the element of activity is strong, and it is even stronger in political and moral action; but in this latter the element of intellectual insight also has a certain part. The division of culture into contemplative and active realms by no means excludes the relative significance of activity for the field of contemplation, or of contemplation for that of action, although the activity of scientific production and artistic creation is not action in the proper sense and although that kind of knowledge and intuition or intellectual insight which is operative within political or moral action is neither scientific nor artistic, and therefore not contemplative in the first place. Activity serves contemplation in science and art; contemplation serves action in politics and moral life. In religion the most perfect balance between the contemplative and the active spheres is attained, but, even so, the aim of action prevails: the aim at a unity of all selves.

Thus the question arises as to whether culture, even if we include religion in its system, can ever attain its goal. If it is true that the original opposition of ego and world persists in the diversification of cultural activities and that either world or ego, contemplation or action, is in the ascendancy, then it seems that the very multiplicity of cultural branches implies a frustration of all cultural striving and working. If it is true that the contrast of world and ego splits the human mind even in the very endeavor of overcoming its original split, how can we ever hope to reach the goal of perfect self-reconciliation? The antinomies of experience seem to persist to the end. Man seems to arrive at merely fragmentary and one-sided solutions which serve only to perpetuate the inner strife.

But, before the last word can be said on this crucial matter, we should analyze the structure and mutual relationship of the realms of culture in greater detail.

Primacy of World versus Primacy of Ego

ONE question concerning the competition of cultural activities may be raised at once: the question whether, perhaps, outright action is more comprehensive and therefore superior to the activity of contemplation or, in other words, whether, perhaps, the attempt to unify world and ego by directly reconciling the manifold of selves is superior to the attempt made by reconciling the worlds to each other; that is, to put it simply, whether, perhaps, the ego has the primacy not only in experience and because of its cultural activity but also within culture. That the ego is primary in experience and in the activity of civilization may be the reason for its primacy in the competition of cultural directions and achievements. If the world is the world of an ego, the ego cannot be subject to the world in the ultimate solution of the antinomies; therefore, the "world-solution" must be inferior to the "ego-solution." The definitive unity of world and ego, the definitive decision about the contest between oneness and manifoldness, universality and individuality, freedom and necessity, and between time and eternity can be found not by seeking it in the world but by seeking it in the ego, in that ego which would embrace the world as it also would embrace all the individual selves and all the worlds belonging to them.

The logical conclusion from the fact of the experiential and metaphysical predominance of selfhood is, therefore, that the "ego-solution" has the best chance of gaining the ultimate victory. If cultural creativity (including religion) could arrive at the foundation of a community of all persons under the guidance and command of an absolutely universal, and yet also individual, Self which would be the pattern and the ideal for every other self and embrace within its scope all reality, such an achievement would be supreme indeed. There can be no doubt that the biblical God comes nearest to this "ego-solution." He commands absolute obedience and reverence when he makes his covenant with man. He demands the totality of man's devotion: absolute surrender of all man's ambitions and aspirations. And his promise is that on this ground all men shall be inwardly united and work together. It is characteristic of the Old Testament to treat religion as the sum total of civilization. There is no competition of spheres, ends, methods, or ideals because the one overwhelming religious solution absorbs all other cultural tasks and results. There is only one culture, and this is the outcome of the obedience and loyalty of man to God. Culture in this uniform and monistic sense is neither scientific nor aesthetic but fundamentally moral and spiritual and secondarily political, while science and art serve solely that supreme end of establishing a peaceful and pious community. It is not a picture of the world but rather the actual life of wisely organized human beings which is the guiding star.

However, this "ego-solution" is not the solution of culturally striving man in the sense in which scientific, technical, and artistic production and creation are such an achievement. It is not a solution to be placed even on the same level as that on which man strives after political justice and moral order. Rather, this solution transcends all the ends and activities of man. If it is valid, it cannot be man's own achievement; indeed, it cannot be a cultural achievement at all. We have to delay the considerations which arise in this context. But it may be said at this point that the cultural mind, if it understands itself, would be most satisfied with this transcultural solution. The philosophy of culture has to evince this truth by transforming itself into a philosophy of faith. But, before this can be done, the cultural realms must be examined in detail.

The primacy of the "ego-solution" may be doubted, however, for several reasons. One may think that the antinomy of world and ego would be solved by contemplation rather than by action, because contemplation alone is able to discern reality in an impartial way, unblinded by the aims and ends of man; that such a solution alone would correspond to the eternal truth, while all human actions are concerned with temporal intentions and results; that contemplation alone penetrates into true reality, whereas action is the result of opinion and purpose; that, finally, even experience points to the "world-solution," since the primacy of universality over individuality originates from the primacy of the world over the ego—in short, that the universe, not man, should be regarded as ultimate.

All these reasons have weight, indeed. Time and time again in the history of thought they have led to the primacy of cosmological ideas; they have supported the ontological claim that being as such, not the ego or the self, is the central and the absolute principle of philosophy; they have tempted modern thinkers like Descartes to abandon the thinking ego as the real and true ground of reality and to replace it with nature, a nature in which the thinking ego is degraded to a thinking thing and paralleled in metaphysical dignity with the extended thing. This whole vision has a mighty ally in the senses, which loudly proclaim that the earth and the sky are realities more impressive than man not only because they are bigger and surround man's life, forming the stage on which his actions take place, but also because they are more permanent than man, who passes away while they abide.

The transcendental philosopher will smile at the naïveté of the naturalistic arguments; but he should not merely smile, for the arguments, taken together with those reasons previously mentioned, are strong and have influenced human thought even at its highest levels. Ancient philosophy never freed itself of this influence, even in the most sublime and profound speculations of Plato and Aristotle. The Greeks never gave up the idea that the cosmos is the real reality, although they acknowledged that the noetic sphere is "beyond" the visible universe. Therefore, they never abandoned the belief that the stars have souls and that God moves the stars primarily and human affairs only secondarily. In other words, they never overcame the fundamental paganism which is at bottom identical with the primacy of the "world-solution" because the gods belong to the cosmos and even Aristotle's Prime Mover belongs to the greater whole, since, although he transcends the realm of nature, he is a part of the cosmos. The

Bible alone teaches that there is an absolutely transcendent God, who cannot be contemplated or comprehended without being obeyed. The Bible demolishes the cosmos.

What can be said against the reasons pleading for the "world-solution"? The necessary counterreasons have already been given. They may be repeated for this special purpose. First, contemplation alone is able to look at reality impartially. It is perfectly true that man is not impartial when he puts himself in the center of reality and thought; indeed, he is obviously partial in this appraisal. But is it an appraisal? Are terms like "partiality" and "impartiality" rightly applied in this discussion? Are man's aims and ends indifferent when we ask which attitude, which activity of man, is supreme? After all, the scientist and the artist are men, too; they have special aims and ends like the man of action, although these do not directly concern the well-being of the human community.

Man is involved not only in the realm of political and moral action but also in that of scientific and artistic production. Certainly, it is not man whom science and art want to organize and whose needs they want to control. But, even so, scientific truth and artistic beauty are discovered and expressed by men for men. They satisfy an essential need of man. But is not truth true whether man cares for it or not? Does not the scientist discover an "objective" truth which has a validity independent of both man's work for it and his comprehension of it, and, therefore, is not scientific knowledge more impartial than any other cultural achievement? I will deal with science in particular later. Here I would like to say only that scientific truth is not so absolute as the objection suggests; rather, it is bound up with man's understanding and with the human duality of understanding and sense-experience, which, in turn, represents the contrast within his mind, and the truth he discovers in science is conditioned by this interest.

It is true that this interest is not partial in the sense in which individual wants and desires are partial. But exactly the same is true with respect to political and moral action. The very term "partiality" is taken from this realm of active self-unification. Justice as the highest goal of political striving and self-control as that of moral endeavor are themselves impartial; they are the very archetypes of impartiality, and without moral self-control even scientific work cannot be done. As truth in science and beauty in art point to eternal values, so do justice and virtue. Socrates labored to show that morality is not merely a matter of opinion but of reason as well, as is the case with truth and beauty, and that universality is as much the predicate of moral reason as it is a predicate of the universe. He called himself the "best politician."

Therefore, primacy of contemplation over action cannot be defended by those arguments. Culture, as a whole, aims at the self-realization of man, at his self-reconciliation through his self-unification. This aim is impartial and of eternal value, whether its light is broken into the rays of scientific truth, artistic perfection, or social and moral goodness. But if, on this level, no primacy either of contemplation or of action can be established, nevertheless action is more directly and intentionally concerned with man's self-unification. In so far as the goal of self-unification embraces all cultural activities, that activity which explicitly and exclusively aims at this end can rightly claim the ascendancy. If action could reach its own goal absolutely, science and art would be satisfied thereby.

The primacy of the "ego-solution" was indirectly recognized even by the ancient thinkers. Not only did they think of ethics and politics as important branches of philosophical thought (Plato dedicated most of his discussions to this problem), but they crowned their system by the idea of a world-soul or a world-mind, indicating thereby that the self, though in a cosmic and divine fashion, has the primacy; that the cosmos owes its harmony and unity only to the moving and governing power of itself. Philosophy has had to learn from theology what man is; only by the recognition of God as the ruler of the world could man begin to understand his own soul and selfhood. The history of philosophy from Plato and Aristotle through Philo and Plotinos to Augustine, Descartes, and Kant teaches precisely this. Socrates is a lonely figure, anticipating later insight. Today the position of man has almost reached the dimensions of God. Indeed, Nietzsche thought himself to be Dionysos, and the existentialists have placed themselves on the throne of the highest; they are not atheists but polytheists. The time has come for the philosopher to go back via the primacy of the ego to the primacy of God—the Living God, who rules the world, indifferent to the changing views of the philosophers.

Subordination and Co-ordination

CULTURE, like nature, is a hierarchy containing lower and higher realms. There are numerous differences in the way in which the goal of civilization is approached. We have seen that the difference between contemplation and action, derived from the antagonism between world and ego, is fundamental. It remains to analyze the character of the differences among the various activities and realms as they unfold within the scope of that fundamental division. In this section, however, I will confine myself to reflection upon the distinction between the main types of contemplation, i.e., between science and art. A similar distinction exists on the level of action (that between politics and religion), but discussion of this duality can be postponed.

It is evident that science and art, although both aim at an understanding of the world as it presents itself in experience, are nevertheless of a very different structure; that their immediate goals are not the same; that they also vary in rank and in their respective achievements. It is not so evident in what manner this difference can be conceived and what the reasons are for this division and variance. There is a certain rivalry between them. There is also a mutual influence. In ancient Greece, science was guided by the artistic instinct; the very idea of the cosmos had an aesthetic tone and meant harmony. This aesthetic influence blended with the religious one, since religion was mythological, i.e., poetical. In modern times science has emancipated itself from this domination and recently has begun to take the lead, as is manifested by naturalism in poetry, cubism in painting, and many other contemporary movements.

Both science and art are concerned with the existing world, trying to grasp it in an intellectual way and to transform its immediate impressions by means of signs, symbols, and images. Both aim at an eventual understanding and description of the world. How are they related to each other?

In one respect science seems to be superior; in another, art. Science, it seems, is more loyal to experience; it tries to render the world of experience as it "really" is, while art transmutes it, thoroughly and perhaps arbitrarily. Therefore, science alone seems to have that kind of validity which we conjoin with the term "truth," while the work of the poets, painters, and sculptors may be of great value but fails to give us a true account of the "real" world. Or, in other words, science alone seems to result in knowledge, while the arts delight us. There is no "glamour" about physics or chemistry; instead, they deliver reliable formulas, representing laws which the actual processes in nature obey. The equations of mechanics or electrodynamics may be "elegant," but they cannot compare with the beauty of a masterpiece. The natural sciences contribute only fragments to the panorama of the world, but this panorama is supposed to copy the world in its totality; the arts produce images which are perfect wholes, like the world itself, but the images are restricted to mere fragments of the real world which we experience.

None of these assessments is false, but all are vague and need elaboration. The most obvious difference between scientific knowledge and artistic creation concerns the fact that knowledge does not give a picture—i.e., a concrete, sensuous image—but rather an abstract, intellectual, or rational description or explanation. The arts are the work of creative imagination, the sciences the work of the analyzing and comprehending intellect. To be sure, the artist is also a thinker, and the intellect has an important part in his creation. The scientist, on the other hand, is an observer; he starts from sense-perception and verifies his results by returning to the source of his knowledge, the experience of the senses. But, even so, the result itself is abstract and has no similarity to the reality of immediate experience. The work of art, on the contrary, is concrete in that it resembles the world of sense and "imitates" that world, as the ancient thinkers insisted. This remains true in spite of the necessary qualification that the usual sense of the word "imitation" certainly does not apply to the arts (least of all to music, but also to poetry and even painting and sculpture) except in a superficial sense. And yet there is a truth in the ancient theory that the arts do present things in a fashion which more closely resembles their appearance than do the natural sciences.

This difference points to the various methods of uniting the opposite poles of oneness and manifoldness or of universality and individuality in scientific and artistic work. The sciences do not unite those poles in their extremity; rather, they transform them so that the intellect can subordinate the vast variety of individual phenomena to principles, categories, laws, or generic rules, thereby uniting them as specific cases or examples of general notions. Thus they interpolate between the absolute opposites of the universal and the individual a mediating polarity: that of the general and the particular, which, as Aristotle has shown, dominates all logical thinking. The metaphysical contrast is transformed into a contrast which permits the intellect to submit all contents of experience to its own logical procedure.

Or, to put it differently, the absolute totality of the world, in which every single datum has its unique and definite place, function, and significance, is replaced by the relative totality of general laws or classes, which embrace all the data but in an abstract manner; and the absolute individuality of the experienced data is transformed into a relative individuality which itself is also abstract and devoid of its original uniqueness and definiteness. The thoroughly individual world of experience is thereby reduced to a schematic multiplicity of events or "occasions" which can be subordinated or, more correctly, are essentially subordinated to patterns of general rules. Henri Bergson's philosophy rests upon this insight. He opposes to this scientific method which breaks up the world an intuition which he claims can grasp directly the full concrete stream of individual life and depict the totality of the world as a universal *élan vital*.

Bergson, of course, does not fulfil his promises because only the artist can do so (though Bergson's language has artistic qualities indeed, his whole philosophy being tinged by artistic intuition and imagination). But Bergson is right in his analysis. The sciences (including biology, which is misused by him for metaphysical intentions) do abstract from the actual world; they do build a second world which does not resemble "our" world but consists of elements which are creations of the intellect made for the purpose of subordinating the world to intellectual concepts and symbols. This is not to say that these creations are arbitrary or, as a certain group of philosophers of science would have it, merely conventional; they correspond to the actual world, but they do not depict that world in the fulness of its actuality, nor do they comprehend the whole of its scope. Instead, they merely touch upon the abstract features inherent in the phenomena of circumscribed classes and construe the relation between them in the way in which they really are related to one another, though only as reduced particulars. The real world does not consist of atoms, particles of atoms, electrical fields, or mechanical motions but of oceans and mountains, stones and trees, flowers and birds, vermin and weeds, and human beings, plus all the things they have designed and erected.

The world of the sciences is not sensuous. It is deprived of its colorful garment, its sounds and its tastes, at least in the "ideal" scheme which science hopes to work out eventually. The layman may easily mistake this scheme for the actual world and may believe that the scientist comprehends the real nature of things better than he; and not infrequently the scientist himself may fall victim to such a heretical interpretation. I will later discuss this kind of scientific superstition, the most popular and most dangerous superstition in our period. Mechanical laws and equations do regulate the locomotions of all bodies everywhere, including those of organic beings, even of man. Chemical affinity does govern the composition and dissolution of all materials, including those organized in an animal, even the human flesh and bones. Biological necessities and regularities do expand upon the life of our race and that of every individual, be he an ordinary man, a hero, or a saint. But, true as all this is, it says not the slightest word about the world as a whole or about the individual fulness of any man or about humankind as such.

The work of art, on the contrary, is as universal as it is individual. It reaches out to the extremes of world-polarity. It em-

braces, though in an image only, the totality of experience. The
world is not broken up but is depicted in that image, even when
the objective content is only as small as a single flower painted by
Dürer or a tree etched by Rembrandt. The world is depicted by
means of its individual content, in all the fulness of its most
definite manifestations. Because of this tremendous difference between science and art, science can be seen to deprive the world
not only of its universality and individuality but also of the
meanings it has in experience. These meanings are related to
man's life, his needs and aspirations, his longings and wishes, and
to his cultural goal and work. Man as man cannot figure in the
world-picture of science; he can only figure as a particular species of nature, exhibiting certain biological and psychological
properties and functions, as he does in so many pseudo-philosophical accounts inspired by the natural sciences (including
psychology and sociology, when treated according to the fashion
of the natural sciences).

The sciences can interpret the world only as "nature," i.e., as
the subhuman sphere of the visible universe. The arts portray the
true whole, even when they deal with the subhuman sphere only.
The world of the artist is the world of experience, and for that
reason it is always animated by the human soul. It is the world of
the human self in all dimensions of experience. Art unites the
polar opposites of oneness and manifoldness, of universality and
individuality (as world-features), not by the method of subordination but by fusing the extremes, by co-ordinating and merging
them so that in every image the whole world appears, and in such
a manner that the world is always individualized and made manifest in a sensuous fashion. The image of the arts is not only sensuous but, at the same time, intellectual; it is both, within one inseparable synthesis. We call this synthesis "spiritual," for the
reason that it is not merely logical and intellectual; the logical
method of subordination is not applied here but, instead, the
superlogical method of co-ordination, of creative intuition and
imagination, which makes the intellectual sensuous and the sensuous intellectual and thus both spiritual.

In the work of art the world in its wholeness is imaged. This is
the wonder of art; the key to its fascination; the reason why it

not only attracts our senses but satisfies our mind; and the explanation of its greatness and its power to reconcile and even to redeem the human soul. This is, in a word, the reason why the metaphysical dignity of the arts outshines that of the sciences. The work of art harbors the whole world in an image, in the form of a microcosm, which is why it is so precious, if it is a masterpiece. The tension between the opposite poles of experience is solved, in so far as this can be done, within the framework of the "world-solution." It is for this reason that so many philosophical systems are enamored of the idea of the world as a whole conceived in terms of aesthetic intuition. Indeed, if we were able to forget that the microcosm cannot be extended to the macrocosm, because of the gulf separating the sphere of artistic images from the actual scene of life, we might believe that the artist is the best and only guide to truth and that he solves the antinomy of experience absolutely.

Although the artistic solution of the antinomy of experience is not absolute, it is definitely superior to that of the sciences. The world-image of great art is more universal and more individual than that of the sciences; it is in that sense more "true." Actually, the contrast of truth and beauty as distributed to science and art is untenable. Beauty is not opposed to truth, it is the higher stage of truth itself. It mediates a fuller and broader truth, a truth more comprehensive and more penetrating, than that achieved by the sciences. A work of art is beautiful only if it is also true and only inasmuch as it is true. Of course, this truth is not mathematical or physical, it is spiritual and human (how this statement is compatible with the fact that the artist is an individual will be discussed in a later chapter).

Beauty, if it is not also truth, is a shallow and sentimental thing, resembling the real value of the work of art only in a formal sense, deceiving the mind and not solving the task of its reconciliation—a counterfeit instead of the genuine pearl, generating the illusion of that synthesis which is achieved in a masterpiece. Artistic truth is truth on a higher level than that of scientific truth because it reveals the world-significance of the phenomena, the universal within the individual, the way in which the manifold contains within itself the oneness of all things. The great poet compares everything with everything, certain that there is an underlying unity which makes all things akin to one another and connects them on a spiritual level. The single and empirical facts are thus illuminated by the artistic imagination; they are no longer single and empirical facts alone but are, at the same time, manifestations of the all-embracing context to which they belong. Science offers general, art offers universal, truth.

In the work of art the opposition between essence and existence, between surface and depth, between substance and accident, is overcome; every detail is as important as the whole. Such is the effect of co-ordination. Beauty without truth does not truly co-ordinate the poles but plays upon the surface, using the means by which the genuine synthesis is produced, but not producing it. It is therefore merely sensuous and only pseudo-spiritual. Rationalism mistook this beauty for the original and thus came to the conclusion that the arts generate a truth dimmed and veiled by the senses, in contrast to science, which reveals and expresses the supersensuous, i.e., the rational truth itself. But the truth is not rational in its ultimate aspect, because it "saves" the phenomena: it does not abstract from them, but it shines through them, and the great artist is the master of this illumination.

The difference between subordination and co-ordination leads to a characteristic difference in the way in which science and art accomplish their respective tasks. Since the sciences never touch upon the extreme poles of universality and individuality but proceed by means of a compromise, they never reach their goal in any single work. Indeed, there are no works in science comparable to the works of art. There are only contributions to the one work which science is ever going to build. The work of science can be compared with a great cathedral which is never finished, but to which every epoch carries some new stones, slightly changing the plan and style of the fragmentary whole, there adding a turret or here modifying the ornaments, slowly transmuting the appearance and function of the parts. Of course, this metaphor is not quite correct, since the architecture of the sciences is not even so much of a whole as the cathedral is at any given time of its growth. The sciences represent a multiplicity of approaches toward a common goal, divided by the variety of phenomena to be studied. The theories and hypotheses in the various sciences are more or less in agreement with one another, but they are not a system, not even in the logical sense of subordination, as Plato thought science should be. This more or less coherent manifold of principles and theories, of equations and descriptions, never displays one comprehensive picture of the universe.

The arts, on the other hand, consist of works each of which is such a picture, in spite of its special content, style, and method, which is determined by the genus to which it belongs, the period in which it is created, and the individuality of the genius who has fashioned it. The sciences never conquer eternity; they march like an army in closed ranks to meet the obstacles which hamper the conquest of truth. The arts achieve in every masterpiece the very end of artistic aspiration and thus reach eternity. The sciences, in other words, are satisfied to grow in the course of time, while the arts aim at perfection in every single work. This far-reaching difference springs from that of subordination and co-ordination. Subordination, in accordance with its avoidance of the extremities of the antinomy and thus also of the extremity of a solution, slowly and solidly proceeds; co-ordination hastens to the absolute reconciliation of the absolute opposition.

Lower and Higher Levels

SUBORDINATION accomplishes the task of civilization on a level lower than that of co-ordination. This thesis is as valid in the sphere of contemplative culture as in that of active culture, although we have discussed it only in reference to science and art. In each sphere subordination works with the tool of logical or rational methods, while co-ordination uses intuition and imagination. The man of genius in the realm of artistic creation rises vertically to the lofty height of perfection, while the scientist moves in a pedestrian way along the horizontal line of gradual progress. We shall find an analogous difference on the side of active culture when we compare the statesman and the prophet (sometimes combined, as in Mahomet). The division of lower and higher levels, however, concerns not merely the rank of achievement, it is also connected with the manner in which cultural activity is related to both man the animal and man the cultural worker and creator. On the lower levels man the animal is more vitally interested in cultural achievement than he is on the higher ones. Intellect or reason is not so superior to the animal level as are intuition and imagination; indeed, we may even suppose that the "higher" beasts are endowed with a kind of intellect, although it does not strive after eternal truth, but they are certainly not endowed with artistic or religious intuition and imagination.

Bergson has asserted that intuition is nearer to the animal instinct than is the intellect, and this theory has given him the opportunity of building up his metaphysical biology. It would be more correct to say that man on the level of intuition combines both intellect and instinct or that he reconciles this opposition as much as he does that of freedom and necessity or time and eternity. His intellect works like an instinct, and his instinct works out what the intellect wishes to perform but never can perform. The genius, so Kant and Schelling teach, produces as nature does, but consciously and deliberately. This is the glory of the genius and of his imagination.

But, just because the genius thus reconciles nature and mind and body and soul, he is more remote from the merely natural and physical than is the scientist. Although the definition of truth proposed by the pragmatists certainly does not do justice to its majesty and sovereignty, yet on the level of science this definition is not altogether wrong, as the close connection between science and technology, between technology and economics, and between economics and man's physiological or animal needs and wants demonstrates. Of course, science in its pure form is not technology and does not intend merely to serve the practical purposes of man; rather, it aims at truth for the sake of truth. Science investigates nature in order to find out how nature proceeds, what order exists, and why things are as they are. Physics, like mathematics, deals not with questions concerning welfare and prosperity but exclusively with those concerning the structure of the world, the causes of its change, and so forth. It deals with purely "theoretical," i.e., contemplative, questions; it wishes simply to know the truth.

Nonetheless, science in the modern sense was, from the outset, occupied with practical problems. It arose from technical needs, and it was supposed to improve the material, hygienic, and mechanical conditions of life, often understood and praised as the only objectives of civilization, as its core and substance. The distinction between civilization and culture as it is made in some languages (especially emphasized by Spengler) concerns precisely this point. "Civilization," according to this usage of the word, means improvement of the conditions of life, while "culture" means the higher level on which truth and beauty are sought on their own behalf, regardless of what profit or comfort they may bring to man.

Science is the result of careful and methodical investigation, analysis, and theoretical synthesis. Both man's physical needs and the split into sense-perception and intellectual comprehension, which is characteristic of our experience and rests upon the split between world and self, urge man to investigate intellectually the world that surrounds him, supports him, and threatens him. Scientific (purely theoretical) and technological (practical) interests are thus closely connected with each other. The combination of the two interests is the most powerful factor in modern civilization; indeed, it is this combination which first comes to mind when we talk about civilization today. From the purely theoretical point of view the combination is too close today; it endangers the cultural rank of science by making it the "handmaid" of technology. A scientist recently complained that science is now exposed to "prostitution," since it is tempted to abandon theoretical purity and submit to the demands and exigencies of commercial or military purposes.

Such a danger can arise only because of this close connection between the two aspects of science—its quest for truth and its pragmatic usefulness—or because science stands between the highest cultural level of art and the lowest level, on which man works to satisfy his physical needs (which, of course, are not purely physical needs because man satisfies them not in a merely physical but also in an intellectual, that is to say, a cultural, way). How is the combination of the two aspects possible at all? In what sense does man satisfy his animal needs by means of civili-

zation? Or, more correctly, what is the cultural value of the
lower stages? Is there any cultural value in the intellectual and
scientific satisfaction of physical needs? Is there any contribution made by this stage to the solution of the ultimate goal of
culture—the solution of the antinomies of experience?

One point is clear at once: if science is completely absorbed by
technical intentions, its cultural value vanishes, and the civilization which indulges in such a degeneration is itself on the verge
of decay. Our own civilization certainly tends toward this decay.
The absolute separation of science from art at the beginning of
modern times already contained the seed of such a ruin. In men
like Leonardo da Vinci science and art were still inwardly
united; even in Kepler the tie was not yet broken. But the trend
toward the idea of technical application as the main motive of
research was destructive. This trend already existed in Leonardo;
it was raised to the level of a "philosophy" by men like Francis
Bacon, whose slogan "Scientia est potentia" ("science is power,"
namely, technical power) expressed accurately the victory of
the idea of applicability over the idea of pure truth, which Bacon
slandered outright.

What, then, is the cultural value (in the precise sense) of the
lower levels, if there is any? It would be foolish to deny that
civilization comprises these levels or that they have a legitimate,
though lower, place in the entire building of culture. If man
should continue to live as his ancestors lived in the primordial
jungles and on the steppes, devoid of all technical facilities like
the beasts, we would not call him civilized, even if he (of course,
a fantastic possibility, though somewhat approached by hermits
and monks) were able to pursue the end of theoretical investigation, artistic creation, and religious meditation. The subject of
experience—the metaphysical being that man is—ceases to be a
mere animal, even in his animal state. He would not be able to
serve the highest, the genuine, goal of culture if he did not also
feed and clothe and shelter himself in a human, which is to say, a
civilized, way. Even the hermit and the monk apply their intellect and their knowledge to this purpose, though in a manner
which stresses the lower rank of this quasi-cultural sphere.

The contrast between man as animal and man as cultural being reflects the original split within experience between world and ego. It is the ego in man which leads to civilization, while as an animal he belongs to the world. This original duplicity reappears in the duality of man's physical and metaphysical vocation, in the duality of natural and cultural aims and ends. It is an integral part of his self-civilization to civilize his animal life, to make himself a self even in those realms of his existence which are conditioned by the fact that he is not merely a self but also a biological organism whose needs and ends are necessitated by nature.

Thus civilization, in the narrower and degraded sense of the word, i.e., technical civilization, does belong to the total structure of culture, though on a lower level. Civilization in this sense is both the culturally necessary presupposition and the consequence of man's higher vocation. The shepherd, the smith, the hunter and farmer, the industrialist and merchant, the craftsman and engineer, all work in the service of the highest end of culture, though on a level lower than the scientist and the artist because their work is auxiliary only. It prepares and accompanies the real work of culture. It is, after all, the same task which is to be solved on all levels: unifying the self. This task is most directly and most effectively solved on the highest level of art because here the opposite poles of experience are brought into a complete synthesis. Science interpolates intermediary opposites which can be united by means of intellectual or rational operations. Technology unites not the poles themselves but the nature and culture of man, for the sake of satisfying his natural needs.

Technical civilization is on a lower level, because here man subordinates culture to nature, while on the higher level of science he subordinates the element of nature (the sense data), to the element of ego (intellect); and on the highest level he coordinates world and ego, so that the world is totally impregnated by the ego and appears in the image of art as the ego-world, which it actually is in experience. Of course, the spheres are not so neatly and distinctly separated in reality as they are in thought. It is always the same being which works now for his vital physical wants, now for his intellectual wants, and now for his spiritual self-unification. And this sameness expresses itself and even comes to the fore in the collaboration of workers on all levels, as we see it in social life. There is a sliding scale between pure and applied science, as we have mentioned already; there is also a sliding scale between technology and the fine arts, as architecture, the movies, and the application of the sense of beauty in practical life show. The painter seeks for rooms and walls where he can exhibit his art; the sculptor for occasions to adorn the places of labor and business life. Festivals and ceremonies demand a display of music, rhetoric, and so forth. Human life is not to be divided into tight compartments; it is fluid, and all the levels of culture permeate and interpenetrate one another. Even so, the thinker has the duty of distinguishing the stages and conceiving of the peculiar task and performance of each level and each branch. Only so can he understand the complexity and disrupted unity of culture. The differences and distinctions are not his arbitrary contrivances, since they exist in reality, after all.

So far I have discussed only the spheres of contemplative culture. If we now turn briefly to the active realm, we discover an analogous structure. The very term "social life" touches upon the political in the broader sense. Indeed, the word "life," if not confined to biological thought, comprises all cultural activities, but especially those of the active realms.

As technology is related to science, so is the economy to the state. Technology designs the tools, machines, and instruments; the economy produces them and, with their help, the materials and merchandise which are necessary for the sustenance and comfort of society. Economy cannot exist except in a community which is ordered and governed by law, since it rests upon collaboration and exchange of products, i.e., upon a market. The political organization represents a lower level than the religious community, since the former corresponds, as we will see, with the principle of subordination, while the latter corresponds with that of co-ordination. The state, however, is a lower stage of active culture not only for this reason but also because it is more closely connected with the economic sphere than is the religious community. In both cases the active sphere of culture is perfectly analogous to the contemplative one.

As the sciences have to precede their application, so the state or some kind of political organization must precede the exchange of products. The sciences furnish technology with the intellectual knowledge needed for its special purpose; the state furnishes the security and order needed for economic activity. As the sciences are in danger of succumbing to the dictates of practical ends, so is the state in danger of becoming enslaved by the demands of economy. Both dangers are actual in a similar way today. Indeed, they are one and the same danger: the reversal of the hierarchical order of culture so that the lower levels make themselves the superior ones. Or, in the terms mentioned above, culture is endangered today by civilization. We witness an invasion by technology and economics into the higher realms of culture, a kind of technical and economic dictatorship which threatens to empty the heart of culture and to frustrate the whole meaning and value of cultural life.

CHAPTER IV

Science—Art—State

Science: (a) The Intelligible Universe
or Nature

HEINRICH RICKERT, my teacher at the University of Freiburg in Baden, used to say that nature is a product of culture. This bon mot hits an important truth. Nature, as we conceive it today in the light of the natural sciences, is a product of the intellect, which makes the world intelligible by comprehending it in accordance with its own rules and principles. These rules and principles are not merely conventional or capricious; rather, they constitute the order of the world which we experience and in which we live or, more correctly, the order of that province which exists as the natural subhuman background of human life and history. Of course, this order is intellectual and therefore intelligible because it answers the question of the intellect or because it is produced by the subordination of sense data to the unity of the understanding, which investigates and reasons about the natural phenomena. In this definite sense nature is intelligible: it is ordered in the way man's intellect finds it ordered. In another sense nature is much more than this intelligible world. It reveals a deeper order to the intuition of the artist and of everyone who views it with the eyes and the heart of the artist, and it is perfectly true to say that, at bottom, nature is a work of art, beautifully shaped, the harmonious cosmos of the ancients.

As there is a mathematical order in music, though only as its skeleton; as there is a kind of arithmetic in verse meter; as there is geometry in the plastic arts and especially in architecture, so nature, too, is fundamentally mathematical. Plato proclaimed this truth in his old age; the Pythagoreans had seen it earlier; but not until the dawn of modern times was it methodically applied and carried through in the various fields of natural knowledge. The new mathematics of nature marks the beginning of the modern era in the contemplative sphere of civilization. Man confronts the world with a new kind of courage and curiosity. He feels sure that his intellect is able to read the writing of nature, if he builds his theories on the ground of careful and specific observation and analysis with the help of mathematics; he discovers that the language in which nature speaks is not the language of speculation or philosophic thought, as Aristotle believed, but rather the language of geometry and arithmetic. The former attempt to unseal the book of nature by means of general concepts which were supposed to rule physical change and growth was abandoned, and the place of those concepts or "substantial forms" was taken by equations expressing quantitative relations between the main factors involved in the facts under investigation.

This method turned out to be not only much more reliable but also better adapted to the ultimate goal of science: the subordination of the facts to the intellect. The reduction of natural science to a mathematics of nature was not merely a gain, however, it was also an abandonment and eventually evoked the temptation to replace the old Platonic and Aristotelian metaphysics by a new one based upon mathematics and physics. To the eternal glory of Galileo, it must be said that he recognized at once all these aspects of the Nuova Scientia. He protested again and again that the method which he devised and applied would not lead to a knowledge of the "nature of things," as had been the aim of the ancient systems; that the exactitude of experimental results was bought at a high price—the price of restricting the scope of opposites to be united. Greek speculation had tried to depict a panorama of the world comprising its uttermost extremes, the poles of its absolute unity and absolute manifoldness, its universality and its individuality, its material and its spiritual structure. Modern physics gave up this gigantic task; it abandoned metaphysics.

Whereas Galileo had warned that the mathematical method cannot penetrate into the ultimate constitution and the ultimate fulness of things, his philosophical successors—Descartes, Spinoza, Leibniz, and others—disregarded this warning and aimed at a new metaphysics, either directly based upon the mathematical method or imitating this method and transforming it into a "geometry of God." Only Hume and Kant renewed the warning of Galileo, making his restriction the principle of their own philosophies (with the difference that Hume doubted even the empirical truth of physics, whereas Kant confirmed this truth in the spirit of Galileo). Kant showed that the intellect is able to spell the language of nature, if it confines itself to the phenomenal realm, i.e., if it does not pretend to give a world-picture—to solve the absolute task of contemplation.[1] He showed that the natural sciences do reach an empirical truth by subordinating the phenomena to a general unity—the unity of a general understanding —and to general concepts and principles of knowledge, thereby uniting all the empirical data under general rules or laws. But he also showed that they can never reach a speculative truth which could rival the intuitive and imaginative work of art in uniting the extreme poles of experience, thereby presenting the "things-in-themselves."

Science does achieve its task by reconciling oneness and manifoldness in a limited way. The mathematical method can discharge this task better than any other logical procedure, e.g., classification, can because it permits more thoroughly and more effectively the subordination of the particular to the general. If the complexity and impermeability of individual occasions and events are left behind and if, in their stead, quantitative relations are investigated, then it is possible to dominate the facts by means of symbols which can be replaced by definite numbers, in order to describe their "individual" reality. This individuality is then no longer, on the one hand, sensuous and, on the other, meaningful in a human sense; rather, it is made intelligible, transparent to the intellect. Numbers are themselves products of intellectual operation. They represent, unlike the species in a classificatory system, concepts which cannot be derived from higher, more abstract and generic concepts because they have specific attri-

1. The term "phenomenal" as used by Kant is frequently misinterpreted as meaning what appears psychologically in the human consciousness, whereas Kant means what is finite and fragmentary, corresponding to the ever finite and fragmentary status of the intellect.

butes (*differentiae specificae*); numbers are, rather, as much generic as they are specific because they are produced in accordance with general rules which underlie the whole system of numbers. In this way the facts are completely subordinated to the intellect; nothing incomprehensible, nothing irreducible, no irrational, individual residuum remains. This is the "magic wand" of
modern physics.[2]

   But it is evident that this ingenious method does not really
solve the problem of individuality. It neglects and suppresses the
fulness of the individual features of the world, paying attention
only to the generality of its quantitative relations. Now these
relations do exist; they are an intelligible and rational element
within the individual world of experience. Science has been successful because mathematics is inherent—as it were, in nature. To
deny the metaphysical ambition of science does not mean to deny
its empirical truth, which, on the contrary, can be understood
and appreciated only if its empirical restriction, as stated by Galileo and interpreted by Kant, be acknowledged.

   The picture of the world as science sees it is correct as far as it
goes, but it is fragmentary and abstract. The "higher" truth of
art is not reached; yet it is not precluded. Science's interpretation
of the world on the lower level of subordination is most brilliantly carried through by the mathematical method. This method
has still another advantage. By eliminating the full individuality
and the absolute universality of the world of experience, science
also eliminates the individuality of the ego more successfully and
more thoroughly than speculative physics and metaphysics have
ever done and can ever do. Mathematics has a kind of universal
validity which can never be attained by speculation. No one
would deny the conclusiveness of Euclidean geometry (though
modern geometry has made it the special form of a more general
geometry). There was never a Euclidean "school" concerning
geometry as there were philosophic schools. Euclid's individuality is completely absorbed and, as it were, annihilated by his own
system. And today mechanics is no longer tinged by the person-

   2. Cf. the brilliant discussion of this point by Ernst Cassirer in *Substanzbegriff
und Functionsbegriff: Untersuchungen über die Grundfragen der Erkenntnis
Kritik* (Berlin: B. Cassirer, 1910).

ality of the founders. If the modern physics of Einstein is correct, his individuality is of no significance (though, of course, it will be remembered and will be of great interest to the biographer). It is effaced to the degree to which his theory is true, i.e., generally valid.

In this way the antinomy between oneness and manifoldness, between individuality and universality, is solved by modern science; this is its contribution to the task of culture. This contribution is restricted, of course, and so is the truth of science. The antinomies are not absolutely solved. What has been said about the polarity of oneness and manifoldness, of universality and individuality, is also valid with respect to the polarity of freedom and necessity, as well as of time and eternity. It is even more obvious here because these antinomies are concerned with oppositions within the self and not with oppositions within the world. In so far as science eliminates the ego from its world-contemplation, science cannot solve the antinomies of the self; it does not even recognize and acknowledge them. In the view of science, freedom and eternity, in their proper sense, simply do not exist.

However, in a certain sense they do exist. Although science intends to find out the necessity in the processes of nature and although it succeeds, inasmuch as it subordinates what seems to be accidental to laws and rules, the very existence of laws points to a court higher than the necessity of those natural processes. The laws themselves cannot be so necessary as the facts subordinated to them. The facts, as it were, "obey" the laws, and this "obedience" is the source of their necessity. The facts are necessary just because they occur in agreement with the content of the laws. But the laws themselves cannot be necessary in the same way. They do not "obey" higher laws; they "command" the facts; they (or Nature through them) determine the course of events. Nature as the lawgiver of the natural processes is not coerced by the laws but is free. Science here encounters the problem of freedom on its own ground or, more correctly, at the fringe of its territory, for science as such is not interested in solving this problem; its task is circumscribed by the investigation of the facts and their necessity.

The antinomy between time and eternity is touched upon in a

similarly indirect way. The facts exist in time; the events occur according to the temporal succession of cause and effect. But the laws do not exist in the same fashion. They do not "exist" at all, if existence is understood in a scientific sense, just because they do not exist in time. They are not "facts" or "events" in the way that natural phenomena and processes are. They belong to the Platonic realm of eternal Ideas; indeed, they partly fulfil the mission which the ideas in the system of Plato were supposed to fulfil. But, again, the scientist is not interested in raising the question of how and where the laws exist. The scientist is interested only in the investigation of temporal processes, although he claims timeless validity for the truth he finds. The antinomy of time and eternity enters the realm of science not directly but only indirectly, at the fringe of its realm.

Science: (b) The Scientist

THE scientist does not figure within science and its world. He is the tacit, hidden actor behind the scene. The world he investigates and presents is the world of facts and events; in this world he himself has no place, for he is neither a fact nor an event but the author of the play and the stage manager of its performance. Science may succeed in explaining everything that happens in the world; it will never succeed in explaining the scientist and his work in terms of science. The problem of science is not a scientific problem, nor is the problem of the scientist such a problem. Neither science nor scientist belongs to nature (in the sense of the natural sciences); they are presupposed by the sciences, just as the ego is presupposed by experience. The world of science consists of objects and objective events, but the scientist is a subject, namely, that subject for whom objects exist and who investigates and explains them. This subject must necessarily exist outside the scientific world, as its bearer and constructor. The scientist belongs to the cultural world in which he actively participates, which he helps to build up, and in which science is one of the realms.

It is not science but the philosophy of culture which alone can solve the problem of the scientist. I have already mentioned that the individuality of the scientist must not encroach upon his work; it does not enter the truth he seeks. This truth is as "objective" as is the object about which it is the truth. In both cases objectivity means subordination of the particular to the general. Objects are objects of science only in so far as they can be subordinated to general laws or rules, and the truth of science is objective only if it is discovered by that general intellect to which the particular scientist submits his individual subjectivity. The general intellect must therefore control the scientific experience of the individual scientist. And the scientist, in turn, has to train and discipline himself in order to reach "objectivity."

This means that the scientist has to eliminate all the sources of knowledge which are not controlled by the intellect, because they may become sources of error. His senses may deceive him, since they are always exposed to all kinds of illusion; he has to submit their message to the examination of the intellect. For this purpose the intellect devises special methods, capable of eliminating all "subjective" aberrations. The main device concerns the means of observation. The experiment supplants individual judgment with instruments which register the data of observation in an impersonal and objective way. Another device is the continuous collaboration of a manifold of scientists, who mutually check their findings and thereby exclude merely individual influences. This collaboration is not confined to observation, of course, but extends also to theories and hypotheses. Whereas the artist is the only critic of his work as long as he is creating it, the scientist is permanently criticized and controlled by the community of scientists, so that the manifoldness of their worlds is permanently reduced to the oneness of that world which is recognized to be accurate by all of them. The idea of a "national" or "political" difference of scientific theories is therefore a challenge to the very principle of science as such.

"Hypotheses non fingo" is the often quoted catchword of Newton. The same is expressed by Laplace when he dismisses every theory which is not the "résultat de l'observation ou du calcul."[3] The scientist must therefore regard an unbridled imagination as his greatest enemy, to be defeated at all costs. This does

3. In *Exposition du système de monde* (1796).

not imply that imagination has absolutely no part in scientific discovery or the creation of theories. A certain scientific imagination is even indispensable, in order to anticipate insights and to set forth hypotheses which later experimental experience might or might not verify. But this imagination should not be mistaken for her sister in the realm of poetry, and even less for mere fancy or caprice; neither should it be confused with what the rationalists of the seventeenth century called "imagination," by which they meant sense-perception as over against rational explanation. Scientific imagination is as much an intellectual operation as is the analysis of facts; it is an imagination that serves this analysis and prepares theories; it is an operation that undergoes the same kind of control and discipline which dominates all scientific work; it is in no sense individual. On the contrary, to the degree that it is individual, it is on a false track and can never lead to scientific results. The genius in the field of the natural sciences is not inspired by an imagination which binds together the two extremes of experience and the world, but is a genius of the intellect. Kant denied categorically that the scientist could ever be a genius, reserving this word for the poet and the artist alone. I think he is right, if we take the word in its accurate meaning.

The scientist, as contrasted with the artist, does not create an imaginative work and an imaginative world, but he observes the world methodically and compels nature to give answers to intelligent questions, under circumstances freely chosen and arranged by the observer and experimentalist. In this respect one might say that the scientist is nearer to "reality" than is the poet or the composer, the architect or the painter; "reality" in this sense means, of course, not the ultimate but the phenomenal reality of scientific objects. The scientist is a "realist" in the sense that he has to disenchant the half-poetical, half-mythical visions of nature which have their place in almost all speculative systems. Thus he might seem to be the opponent of an artistic and of a mythical world-view; but he is this opponent only if he oversteps the limits of science and encroaches upon the prerogative of the arts and of religion.

The scientist can discharge his task only if he is inclined to discipline and control his imagination and his will for the sake of his intellectual purpose; he has to subordinate the nonintellectual forces of the individual to the intellect. It is paradoxical that this very subordination cannot be carried out by the intellect alone but also requires the moral will. Without the activity of the moral self, the scientist cannot be a scientist. This relation points to the power of morality even within the contemplative sphere. The scientist can achieve his own purpose only if he exercises those virtues which point to the conquest of time by eternity: endurance, perseverance, patience, loyalty, and so on. The "pure" intellect needs these virtues in the scientist, although the result of scientific labor and toil does not preserve the individual effort and virtue; it is impersonal, objective, abstract, and rational. But it is culturally important to realize that scientific work has an educational influence upon the person in the direction of virtues indispensable not only in the field of science but in all cultural efforts as well. Thus science transcends science within the scientist.

The same can be said with respect to the collaboration of the scientists, which is demanded by scientific work. Here, too, science fosters an effort which transcends the proper aims and ends of the sciences. The scientists are legitimately conscious of this social contribution which they produce. Precisely because of the objectivity and generality of the intellect, as well as the truth which underlies scientific work, this work can unite all individuals on the earth. The *république des savants* as conceived in the seventeenth century thus paves the way to the peaceful collaboration of all races and all nations, even to a world-state. The solidarity of all scientists refuses to acknowledge any frontiers and political barriers. It is the spirit of the active spheres of cultural life which animates the community of the scientists the world over. In spite of the "world-solution" which science offers, the primacy of the "ego-solution" makes science instrumental to the end of active culture.

This same primacy is also obvious in another way. It is, after all, the ego which operates in the scientist; he can subordinate the world to the intellect and, within the world, the material and changing surface to eternal and intellectual rules only because his intellect is the same intellect as that which, according to Kant, "prescribes to nature its laws." Indeed, if the intellect of the scientist and the intellect which is the true lawgiver of the natural processes were not one and the same intellect, the work of the scientist could never succeed. Only because there is a universal primacy of the ego over the world can scientific labor achieve what it does achieve. This points to the great mystery which hides behind the polarity of ego and world, of contemplation and action, of the phenomenal and the ultimate, and which pushes cultural life forward to ever new solutions of the antinomies, and finally to faith and religion.

The Limit of Science

IN THE course of my discussion I have frequently touched upon the limit of science. Although science is one of the activities of civilization, it is by no means the only one or the most prominent or the sum total of them all. Science leaves room for other activities which supplement and limit it. The world as propounded by science is by no means the "world-in-itself" or the whole of experience; it is a limited, definite, fragmentary view of the world, correct within its scope and exact in its knowledge. Science is, therefore, not even the only branch of contemplative culture, as I have shown above. It is rivaled by art, which also offers a "world-solution" of the supreme problem, but on a higher level.

Science is limited in a twofold way; first, because it is contemplative only, aiming at a "world-solution," and, second, because it subordinates one pole to the other, while art co-ordinates the poles in their extreme opposition. Between absolute unity and absolute plurality science interpolates the intermediate stratum of generic laws, a kind of scientific realm of Platonic Ideas. They have in common with the absolute oneness the power to unite a manifold of phenomenal facts under one head, and they have in common with the multiplicity of phenomena a concrete and definite content which facilitates the subordination of the facts to the laws. The facts themselves are adapted to the laws by their subordination; they are not merely perceived but are comprehended as particular specimens of the generic laws. This intermediate stratum abstracts one aspect from the world of experience, but it does not offer a picture of the world in its all-embracing unity and its full, vast multiplicity.

The stratum of the laws also reconciles the universality and individuality of the world of experience, as indicated, in a limited and relative fashion. The consequence of this limitation is that the world is broken up by science into several classes of phenomena corresponding to the classes of laws which prevail over them. The individual multiplicity of phenomenal facts is so ordered that all of them can be subordinated to definite classes of general laws represented by definite natural sciences, like mechanics, optics, and the other branches of physics; chemistry in its various divisions; astronomy; geology; geography; biology; and so on. There is no single science of nature; neither is there one nature comprehended by science. Instead, there are several provinces of nature, but none of the sciences tells what the whole is. There is no true and absolute universality in any of the sciences, although mechanics claimed, and claims sometimes even now, to represent the basic essence of nature to which all the other phenomena should be reduced. This claim is in conformity with the mathematical priority of mechanics, but it disregards the difference between generality and universality. It ignores the truth inherent in individuality itself. This world of ours is not a mechanism, precisely because it is individual in all its manifestations. Indeed, the world itself is a kind of individual which cannot be dissolved into particulars dominated by general laws.

Some writers have suggested that the most modern phase of scientific development has opened the door to the understanding of freedom. Physics, they argue, no longer holds to the principle of strict causal necessity but provides for the reality of the accidental, which, in turn, is at the root of freedom. Even scholars of considerable training in the intricacies of epistemology and the methodology of science have supported this suggestion. Does the modern method of statistical probability really permit the introduction of freedom into the conception of the world?

This seems highly improbable from the outset, since freedom in its genuine and proper meaning belongs to the will and action of man as a self and since man's selfhood is methodically ex-

cluded from the scientific world. It is true that, by acknowl-
edging the limitation of causal necessity within the natural processes, science approaches the limit of its own world and thereby
the "supernatural" world-hemisphere of man and the self. As far
as I understand it, the step made by the modern development of
physics was brought about by the attempt to subordinate the
individuality of the world more closely to general laws than had
ever been done before. This attempt met the barrier between the
particular, which can be subordinated, and the individual, which
cannot. The nearer the scientist comes to that barrier, the more
obstacles he must encounter to his undertaking. The more closely
he approaches the full reality of observed facts, the clearer it becomes that his method cannot penetrate into the individual kernel
of reality. This kernel cannot be subjugated to a strict necessity;
it can be grasped only by statistical methods, which replace necessity by probability.

But we should not forget that probability is not a principle of
freedom or of self-determination but is itself a principle of necessity, though of a restricted kind. Statistical laws in the realm
of human acts do not support the insight into the operation of the
free will; on the contrary, they show that this operation is subject to necessity of a certain sort. If we learn that under definite
circumstances a definite number of persons commit suicide, this
does not say anything about the individual motives and the individual views of those who are the unhappy ones. Instead, it disregards all these individual factors on behalf of a general rule
which limits the freedom of the will. The contrast and contradiction between natural necessity and moral freedom is not mitigated by statistical laws; it is rather enhanced and brought into
the open. The atom particles, electrons, or whatever, for all the
indeterminateness that quantum mechanics ascribes to their motions, have no freedom at all; and this indeterminateness can in
no way reconcile freedom and necessity—it is simply a limited
necessity. Indirectly, of course, this limited necessity does point
to the limits of science and its world and in that way to the existence of something that transcends those limits.

Man can certainly be subjected to the principles and methods
of science, as biology, physiology, psychology, and sociology

show; man is definitely a part of nature, exposed to all the necessities of natural existence. Even historical life in all its cultural manifestations and ramifications is not exempt from this general rule. Natural necessity plays a part—and sometimes a very decisive part—in the historical trend of events; but how far the whole course of cultural development is determined by general laws we do not know. Whether Spengler is right in asserting that a certain rhythm recurs over and over again in that development (when we abstract from his thesis that this rhythm is bound up with the rise and fall of new cultures) it is hard to determine. It is certainly true that man, even as creator of cultural values of the highest kind, is yet a being controlled by psychological laws which he cannot evade. How deeply this necessity permeates the creativity of the mind, whether the flourishing and the decay of cultural life is partly caused by a natural rhythm that encroaches upon intellectual and spiritual impulse and vitality, I would not dare to judge. But it is certain that circumstances and conditions of a unique and individual character are involved in all historical change and that they offer the occasion on which man's free will comes to the fore.

Rhythm, i.e., the reiteration of a sequence of equal stages in a development, is a phenomenon that occurs frequently in nature and also in the arts. Organic life provides many illustrations of rhythm. Many processes in the organic body—for instance, breathing—take place in a rhythmical sequence. Birth and death, although not regulated by definite periods, are nevertheless also a kind of rhythmical reiteration. We find rhythm, however, not only in the realm of organic life but also in inorganic nature, as the change of the seasons, brought about by the rhythmical movement of the earth, shows. As the lack of determination can be regarded as the negative substitute for freedom in the world of science, thus rhythm is a kind of negative substitute for eternity.

Rhythm is the phenomenal image of the timeless validity of natural laws. It manifests this validity in a visible form. The reiteration of the same stages or phases in a movement demonstrates to sense-experience the eternal order of nature in special cases and seems to superimpose eternity upon time and the temporal processes. It is, as it were, the temporalization of eternity. Plato calls time "the moving image of eternity," referring thereby to what appeared to him to be the visible, circular movement of the sun around the earth, which determines the change of day and night and which serves as the measure of time.

Science is limited to this image of eternity. The idea of cycles is the scientific substitute for eternity. Nietzsche, whose thoughts were influenced by scientific patterns (in so far as they had any logical coherence at all), dreamed of the eternal return of all things as the highest fulfilment of his longing, since he "loved" eternity, as he says in one of his most beautiful poems. But Nietzsche was not a scientist after all, though he was (at least in some of his utterances) a representative of scientism.

Scientism

SCIENTISM transgresses the limits of science. Rarely has the scientist himself fallen victim to the temptation of this transgression, at least during the last two hundred years. In the sixteenth and seventeenth centuries, during that period of great metaphysical systems based upon the natural sciences when scientism was in its heyday, even outstanding scientists like Descartes and Leibniz indulged in the adventure of expanding scientific thought-forms to cover the universe. Today scientism is the vice of those who do not practice science itself but are intoxicated by the triumph of scientific, and even more of technological, discoveries and devices, i.e., the vice of the masses in almost all countries on the earth. Scientism has become the most dangerous pseudo-religion, pseudo-metaphysics, and pseudo-theology that has ever been devised.

The roots of scientism lie deeper than its proponents know. They extend to the very springs of culture and life. Culture tries to overcome the antinomies of experience. Science partly solves them; but a partial solution is no solution—it only generates new unsolved and scientifically insoluble problems. It thus postulates other ways of culture. But the very existence of a plurality of solutions contradicts the goal of culture; it tears anew the human consciousness which culture aims to reconcile; it generates a competition among the branches of culture, instead of bringing peace and unity. We are accustomed to the manifold of cultural activities and realms and no longer take offense at this plurality, until some tragic clash between the realms or the persons representing them reveals that there is no peace in their mere coexistence, if they are not united inwardly. But no single branch of culture seems to be entitled to unite them all or to represent their inner unity and totality. Scientism pretends that science is called upon and is enabled to carry through this high task.

The limitation of each of the cultural realms is not a mere fact, it is something that upsets the thinking mind as much as the persons who suffer from it. If the antinomies are not solved by any of the cultural activities, what good is in them? Why does mankind labor and toil for the goal of culture when the very manifoldness and diversity of activities only enhance the original split within the experiencing subject? Does not the whole undertaking of civilization thus frustrate itself? Is its meaning not endangered, if not outright destroyed, by its eventual failure to reach its goal?

These questions lie behind all attempts of any special branch of civilization to extend over the whole range of culture in order to solve definitively the common antinomies. Scientism, as we will see, is only one of the many attempts aiming at the same goal, undertaken by each of the manifold realms of culture. As science oversteps its limit and falls into the trap of scientism, so art falls into that of aestheticism, politics into that of totalitarianism (or statism), morality into moralism, philosophy into absolutism, history into historicism, and so on. Each branch has the ambition of finishing the job and giving mankind what mankind strives for in all its single efforts and works. At bottom it is a religious longing which inspires and presses man toward the final solution, the perfect unity, the absolute peace, in all these disparate aberrations.

People begin to adore science after science has deprived them of their proper object of adoration, because they need such an object and are fond of adoration. The adoration of science leads to the fallacy of scientism. Since science has achieved almost miraculous results, it has taken over the function of the miracle-

worker, and, because most people need miracles in order to believe in the existence of a power greater than man, they begin to
believe that the scientist is a kind of superman.

It is a strange paradox, however, that science—this intellectual
undertaking, this methodical and exact way of finding truth, this
most unromantic, most disenchanting procedure—should play the
role of a universal savior of mankind, a quasi-divine source of
wisdom, of the Logos (in the sense of the preamble to the Fourth
Gospel). And yet one cannot doubt that to many—perhaps to the
majority of people today—science has become the spiritual support and the inner strength to which they appeal in all the
troubles and dangers of our time. Even the Christian faith has
bowed down before this new deity in founding the denomina-
tion of a "Christian Science."

The most grotesque scientism was proclaimed by Auguste
Comte, the initiator of so-called "positivism," which is a philosophical or pseudo-philosophical fashion of scientism. He was
not satisfied to assert that the natural sciences are the only solid
basis and the entire content of philosophy, but he went on to
proclaim that this philosophy should be regarded as the only
valid religion, and he even proposed the establishment of a
"church" derived from his principles. This is the most explicit
prototype of all the following attempts at a cultural system
dominated by science.

The nineteenth century and the beginning of the twentieth
were more or less convinced that science alone could bring salvation to mankind; that in the long run it could and would cure
all human evils, not only those which originated from ill health
or natural deficiencies within man or from natural enemies without, but also all social, political, and moral shortcomings and
frailties; that psychology, sociology, and political science, if con-
ducted in the exact spirit of scientific observation and analysis,
would build up a better civilization, free from the superstition
and anxiety of former, less happy ages. Scientism was firmly in-
trenched in the heart and mind of man.

The devastating effect of this new form of superstition can
be seen everywhere. The scientific spirit invaded all the other
branches of culture and organized them according to its own

methods and ideals. This led to a general paralysis of man's spiritual imagination, which blighted the arts, enervated faith, and produced illusionary political and social ideas. The decay of poetry, painting, sculpture, and music and the rise of utopianism and ideology were the immediate consequences. Sensitive artists took refuge in an abstract symbolism or in an often artificial and sophisticated style and manner.

The most insidious and invidious influence of scientism is felt in the noncontemplative spheres of culture, which are most remote from the spirit of science. Action rests upon strong conviction, not upon experimental observation and calculation. It rests upon insight in individual and practical necessities and in the discovery of the right ways of dealing with them. Science can put means and tools into the hands of the statesman, but it certainly cannot determine the end and the goal of action. The word "ideology" arose in minds which believed that science was able to guide and to direct action. The best-known example is so-called "historical materialism," a misleading term, since the theory (or ideology) which it is supposed to designate is neither truly historical nor truly materialistic; it claims, however, to be true in a scientific sense.

Historical materialism is a pseudo-philosophy of history based upon the dogma that the physical needs of man and the economic institutions which serve the satisfaction of those needs are the backbone and primary cause of all social and political realities—and even of all the higher realms of culture. These higher realms are called a "superstructure" by the adherents of this pseudo-philosophy, which today has assumed the dimensions of a new fanaticism pretending to the authority of dogmatic truth. Economic conditions and institutions undoubtedly have a great influence upon the whole of cultural life; but, even so, they themselves are, in turn, always influenced by religious, political, and social traditions or revolutions.[4] But more important than this historical question is the hierarchical order of the cultural branches, because it is this order which should determine the action and the evaluation of good and bad in the social and political spheres.

4. Cf. Max Weber, *Gesammelte Aufsätze zur Religionssoziologie* (Tübingen: J. C. B. Mohr, 1923–34).

Only a philosophy of culture which distinguishes lower and higher spheres can decide this question. Scientism is unable to do so because, in principle, it confuses scientific and philosophic points of view, and this confusion generates ever new confusions.

If historical materialism were right, it should conclude that it is itself the product of economic facts; but then it would become false at the moment when economic conditions alter; since economic conditions have greatly altered in countries in which historical materialism was made the slogan of revolution, the theory or philosophy should have altered too. In other words, if historical materialism is right, it is an outcome of a capitalistic situation and should cease to be true when this situation disappears. This conclusion obviously contradicts its own logic. It demonstrates that it is altogether nonsense to make truth dependent upon economic conditions of whatever kind. Historical materialism is only an example of the confusion originating from the superstitious belief in the omnipotence of science and especially from the belief that any scientific theory can become a possible guide to political action. This is a fundamental error, based upon the imperialistic tendency to exalt science to the pinnacle of the supreme and absolute solution of the world-ego antinomy.

Another example of scientific imperialism's disregard for the legitimate limits of science is the attempt on the part of psychopathology and psychotherapy to claim a philosophical and religious authority and to replace philosophy and religion by scientific methods and ideas. I do not speak about the medical value of psychoanalysis; I leave the decision about this to the experts. But in the name of a philosophy of culture I must protest against the arrogant attempts to extend psychoanalysis beyond the reach of its relative merits and to presume that from its vantage point alone one is permitted to evaluate religion and to speak as the judge in any and all matters of culture, as Freud has done. Atheism based upon scientific reasons all too often forgets that it infringes the limits of a special branch of culture; it ignores the simple fact that science is incompetent to speak about matters not belonging to its territory. A philosophy of culture has to be on guard against all violations of the frontier of cultural realms and to push back invaders.

Psychoanalysis is in danger of disregarding this limitation, if the physician assumes the function of the moral educator (or of the priest). He who wishes to cure emotional perturbations is easily tempted to assume that role. Since, however, the method of psychoanalysis is devoid of ethical standards—as, indeed, all purely scientific methods necessarily are—the danger is imminent that the physician may take his healing art as a substitute for moral advice. Psychoanalysis tries to liberate the patient from inhibitions which (according to the theory) produce mental disturbances; the physician may then forget that moral life to a great extent rests upon wholesome self-control, which, seen from a psychological point of view, closely resembles inhibition.[5]

Art: (a) The Image-World

ART is another of man's efforts to solve the basic contradiction of experience which endangers his inner integrity and selfhood. Art, like science, offers its contribution in the fashion of a "world-solution." Although art does not eliminate the human ego, it takes it as only a part of the world, as determined by surroundings and involved in the universal nexus of temporal events. Art continues the work of science on a higher plane; it offers a higher truth, more comprehensive and more radical than the one presented by science.

Such a statement probably upsets and challenges most modern men. They are accustomed to think of scientific intelligence as the supreme judge in questions of truth and reality. They are proud of having defeated earlier views of the world created by an imagination allied, to a great extent, with fancy and caprice. Is it not the glory of modern science to have dismissed groundless speculations of ancient and medieval world-constructions, as Bacon demanded that it should do? Do we not know by now that only the disci-

5. Cf. William E. Hocking, *Science and the Idea of God* (Chapel Hill: University of North Carolina Press, 1944): "It is not the business of psychiatry to say what life is about nor what for any individual makes life worth living" (p. 41). C. G. Jung, *Modern Man in Search of a Soul*: "The patient does not feel himself accepted, unless the very worst of him is accepted too" (p. 270, quoted by Hocking, *op. cit.*, p. 44). See, however, the chapter on "Moralism" in David E. Roberts, *Psychotherapy and a Christian View of Man* (New York: Charles Scribner's Sons, 1950).

plined mind of science is able to find out truth in a realistic sense, while imagination may conquer the heart and generate lofty and noble ideals but cannot tell us anything about the real nature of things? Much has been said already in rejection of this whole argument.

Art does not challenge science on the ground of science. It transcends the whole scientific level. It works where science cannot work, though both have the approach of contemplation in common. What science never accomplishes—the depiction of the world in one image—is the particular and singular intention of art. The whole of the world is not subject to the principles and methods of science; it can be grasped and comprehended only by imaginative means. The world as a whole is not intelligible. It is, however, imaginable; and to this degree speculation was right, although it erroneously conferred the method of imagination upon the field of rational thought. Imagination is more powerful than the intellect, if the task be to reach the uttermost polarities of experience and to reconcile them. No intellect whatever can perform this task. It is therefore not man's finitude or the limitations of his intellect which prevents the solution achieved by art from being translated into the language of science. Rather, it is the limitation of the intellect per se which frustrates any such attempt. Even an infinite intellect, as long as it is an intellect, not endowed by and enlarged through imagination, cannot encompass the scope of the world as a whole.

Only imagination can accomplish this. Only through an image can the universe be known. The world as a whole does not exist in the way in which all the details of the world do. It belongs to another kind of reality, and it is this reality which can be grasped only by imagination. The senses are confined to single impressions and perceptions; the intellect embraces genera by means of concepts and laws; but imagination is able to adumbrate the universe. This is a wondrous capacity indeed, and the intellect will always suspect its results. The intellect is perfectly right in doing so, since the result reached by imagination completely overshadows intellectual truth and can never be made acceptable to the intellect by intellectual means. One has to have imagination, one has to know it from within, in order to measure its performance and to assess its truth.

Imagination alone can reconcile the extremes of experience—the absolutely individual and the absolutely universal, the sensuous and the spiritual. No abstract concept, no mere idea, no generic law, can ever hope to grasp the individual and concrete universe; only artistic creativity can produce the world in a mirror, a little world, a kind of microcosm in which the macrocosm is reflected. It is not the method of subordination but only the method of co-ordination which brings about this wondrous solution. The little world of art is as sensuous as it is spiritual; the opposite poles of experience are most intimately united, without any chasm. The individual features of whatever phenomena are so depicted as to obtain at the same time a universal significance. The multiplicity of detail is not subjected to an outer abstract unity but is inwardly united. The microcosmic world of the work of art does not embrace, like the macrocosm, all the details of the world but only a tiny fragment, some peculiar events, some particular persons, some individual feelings. Even so, it images the world in and through its form.

It is this form which reconciles the extremes with each other. Whereas in science the realm of laws is an intermediate stratum interpolated between the extremes of unity and plurality, of universality and individuality, the artistic form is one with the content of the artistic work, although it is possible to distinguish them *in abstracto*. The laws order real processes not contained in them; the aesthetic form orders its own content and has no relation to anything outside itself. The image-world of a work of art and the image-form of that world are actually one and the same whole. The form penetrates and permeates the content in all its detail. This wholeness generates the impression of world-totality. The image-world is absolutely independent of anything outside itself; it is, as it were, closed up, perfectly self-sufficient, balanced within itself, based upon itself, like the One of Parmenides (who was probably influenced by the experience of art, as most Greek philosophers were, especially those who think of the cosmos as the Absolute).

This form of the image-world makes the content a whole in which every part derives its existence, function, and meaning from the whole, which is the underlying, creative idea of the parts: its immanent end or *telos*. As Kant points out, the aesthetic form resembles the organic form in nature. Of course, this analogy is limited, since the image-world is a product of the human mind, while the organism is a product of nature. The organism as a living entity is related to the outside world and depends upon it; it is not absolutely ordered by the idea of the whole (the idea of organic self-preservation and self-propagation) but permits contingent elements caused by inorganic factors. Still there is an analogy between the organic and the artistic form. Recently the thesis has been defended that the development of artistic styles from a primitive to a more and more complicated and integrated form resembles the development of the organic forms in the evolution of the species. I do not dare to take sides in this discussion.

The analogy between organism and image-world has caused those systems of philosophy which assert that the world is both an organism and a work of art (as did Plato and, after him, innumerable other thinkers, outstanding among them Augustine, Giordano Bruno, Shaftesbury, and Schelling). In this way they tried to unite nature and mind by the same idea of a whole organizing itself and producing itself as the artist produces his work.

The more perfect a work of art is, the more are the whole and the parts actually one and the same unit, the whole growing out from the parts, the parts developing into the whole and determined by the whole, as the idea of the universe demands it. The contradictions within the world seem to be dissolved. Harmony is the aesthetic category expressing this solution. Indeed, as long as we live in the contemplation of the image-world, we are at rest. We feel that the tensions of the antagonistic poles are subdued, preserved but overcome. In that way the truth presented by art is not merely physical, as is the truth of science, but metaphysical. It concerns not only the existence of the phenomena of the world and their necessary connection but, at the same time, the meaning of the world, its purpose as expressed and exemplified by the phenomena. And thus not only the contradictions within the world but even the contradiction between world and ego are mastered—of course, in the manner and within the limits of the "world-solution."

"To the great poets I ascribe the power to gaze fixedly at the whole of life and bring into harmony that which is within and that which is without them."[6] Not only oneness and manifoldness, universality and individuality, but also freedom and necessity and even eternity and time are somehow reconciled to one another. This is achieved because the image-world of art depicts not only the visible universe but also the soul of man. In fact, man is even in the center of the artistic image; he is the real focus of artistic imagination. The world appears only as the reflex of man. The primacy of the ego is thus maintained in spite of the primacy of the world and in spite of the "world-solution" offered by art. Of course, man is merely a depicted man in the artistic image; it is an image-man we see in that picture, not the actual man we meet in life. This depicted man, however, is the pivot upon which the universe hinges. Therefore, drama and lyric and epic poetry, more than architecture, are the prototypes of the image-world. Music presents the inner soul, painting and sculpture present the outer appearance of man, though indirectly his soul also.

Art is more adequate than any psychology to mediate the truth about man. Who can doubt that there are infinitely more profound and more comprehensive insights into the nature, character, heart, and soul of man in the works of great poets than can be found in scientific psychology, which often denies even the existence of the soul and certainly does not undertake the study of its inner life? Homer, the Greek tragedians and lyrical poets, Dante and Shakespeare and Goethe, know more about this inner life than all the volumes of technical psychology contain. And this is not at all the fault of the psychologists; it is the necessary consequence of the limit of science as compared with the scope, the task, and the method of the arts.

The will and action of man as depicted by the poets are not deprived of their prerogative to manifest freedom. On the contrary, they appear within the image-world in the same or, more accurately, in a manner similar to their appearance in actual life, i.e., endowed with the capacity of deliberation and decision and encumbered by the judgment of conscience, which presupposes

6. Thornton Wilder, *The Ides of March* (New York: Harper & Bros., 1948), p. 33.

responsibility and freedom. But—and this is the wonder of art—at
the same time the conflict between freedom and necessity seems
to be straightened out. Although in art the person is not deprived
of the freedom which we know from experience belongs to him,
the utterances of his freedom appear, nevertheless, as necessitated
by his character and by the causal nexus of events and decisions.
Thus universal causality is brought into harmony with personal
freedom: the great riddle of metaphysics is solved. Even so
Christian a theologian as Augustine has made much of the aesthetic wholeness of the world, in order to demonstrate that individual freedom and universal causality (in the form of the will
of God) are compatible. In that way the most tragic afflictions
and sufferings can be assuaged: "The sinners," Augustine says,
"enhance the beauty of the Whole."[7]

Finally, time and eternity are also conciliated and conjoined,
as far as this is possible, by contemplative creativity. Schiller says:
"Was sich nie und nirgends hat begeben, das allein veraltet nie"
("What has never and nowhere occurred, that alone never becomes obsolete"). Art exalts all events and all actions to the level
of eternity. Time, as depicted by the poet, the composer, the
dramatist, is not the time which the scientist knows in his equations as one of the determining factors of natural processes.
Neither is it that time within which biological development proceeds (organic time), nor is it that time which we measure in
actual life (actual time). Rather, it is a time scheme peculiar to
the work of art, an especially aesthetic or artistic time. And this
peculiar time is in a profound unison with eternity; it is no longer
endless, but complete.

Whereas science is compelled to separate the timeless validity
of laws from the temporal processes, such a separation does not
take place in the image-world of art because the opposite poles
are united by co-ordination. The timeless validity of the work
of art is not dissociated from the temporal content which unfolds
in it, since form and content are only two aspects of one and the

7. Not only in his early work, De ordine, but as late as De civitate Dei (xii.
4 ff.). Cf. Nicolas Berdyaev, The Divine and the Human (London: Geoffrey
Bles, 1949), p. 86, where he speaks about the form of theodicy adopted by
Augustine and adds: "It means the prevalence of the aesthetic point of view
over the ethical" (chap. vi, "Evil").

same whole. To be sure, the ten years during which the siege of
Troy by the Greeks lasts do not actually pass in the epic of
Homer; they have a merely aesthetic existence. Nevertheless,
they have the function of actual time in the image-world depicted by the poet; they are depicted years, as the persons are
depicted persons, their acts are depicted acts, and so on. Depicted
time is time, though it passes only in the image-world and has
an imaginative character.

This imaginative time is reconciled to eternity. Indeed, it is
itself "the image of eternity" in a sense more true than is the circular movement of the sun around the earth, which Plato had in
mind, precisely because this time scheme is not circular or cyclical. It extends like actual time and yet differs from it in that it has
an absolute beginning and an absolute end and is thereby self-
sufficient, as eternity is. Actual time stretches indefinitely, end-
lessly. Its contents are not inwardly connected with one another
in a meaningful coherence but are interrupted by divergent, dis-
connected events and circumstances which chance or fate allows
to follow one another in our life. There are empty periods without meaning, lost moments and intermissions; and no meaningful
whole generates the succession of its various contents, although
we are always seeking and longing for such a continuous flow of
meaningful moments and periods in our life, in the life of other
persons, and, finally, in the history of mankind. This state marks
the finite and endless time of history.

Imaginative time is both finite and infinite, just as the whole
image-world is both a fragmentary segment of life and yet the
whole of life. Time thus takes on the nature of the whole. In
spite of its finitude, it does not point to any "before" or "after,"
any past or future which would extend outside the frame of the
work. Although the plot of a novel does not always begin on the
first page but sometimes many years before the first described
scene opens, nevertheless the time span filled by the novel has its
beginning and its end within the covers of the book; it is complete and fulfilled together with the unfolding plot. It is the time
scheme of a little world which neither needs nor can tolerate any
supplement, if the work is truly perfect. The image-time exists
by itself; it hovers above the ocean of nothingness and possesses
all its strength within itself. The beautiful "is blessed by itself"

(Moericke). The image-time is a temporal eternity, an eternal temporality.

Like the cyclical return of the stages in a natural process, the image-time of the image-world also may return at any actual time, i.e., at any moment, when we turn to it, read the epic or novel again, see the performance of a tragedy again, and so forth. But nevertheless this time scheme is not cyclical, because it happens only within its own world and in no way in our actual life. It belongs to a blessed island or oasis, and therefore it does not return but is unique. It is complete not only in that it has its beginning and its end within its own little world but also because in a masterpiece it is so rounded that the end returns to the beginning, being its necessary consequence and definitive fulfilment. This is particularly evident in music.

The image-world of art exists in its own eternity, just as its time exists within that eternity and is one with it. This is the unique glory of that reconciliation and self-realization which is achieved by artistic creation. Hegel in his *Encyclopedia* tried to imitate this self-contained, closed, and blessed character of the image-world, in order to generate the impression of a comprehension of all existence, a comprehension which would successfully rival the work of art and even surpass it because it would not be imaginative, but scientific and speculative. He did not realize that the peculiar glory and perfection of the masterpiece of art is based precisely upon the imaginative character of its performance.

The contribution of art to the activity of culture thus consummates contemplation. Art reaches the highest summit in the whole sphere of "world-solution." The antinomies of experience seem to be overcome, the human consciousness seems to be completely satisfied, totally united within itself. No wonder the poet often claims a quasi-religious significance for his work. Goethe calls true poetry a "secular gospel,"[8] and Graf Platen sings:

> Um Gottes eigene Glorie zu schweben
> Vermag die Kunst allein und darf es wagen,
> Und wessen Herz Vollendetem geschlagen,
> Dem hat der Himmel weiter nichts zu geben.[9]

8. *Dichtung und Wahrheit*, Book III.
9. *Venetianische Sonette*. "Art alone is able to attain to God's own glory and is entitled to attain to it; and he whose heart is struck by the master's work cannot expect anything which heaven could give him beyond this."

Art: (b) The Artist

ART reveals the primacy of the ego in still another way. The image-world is, even more than has yet been shown, centered around the ego. Not only is it centered in man, as poetry, music, and also, to a lesser degree, painting and sculpture illustrate, but the image-world, being the product of human imagination, is also rooted in the self of the artist; it is an image of the world, and it is also indirectly an image of the soul of its creator. Every work of art is unmistakably stamped by the individual way in which the artist sees, feels, and interprets the world. The image-world is not like the intelligible world of the sciences, an abstract, schematic, and conceptual world, the reflex of highly theoretical doctrines. Instead, it is a concrete and individual world which reflects the concrete and individual personality of its author. The artist lends, as it were, his own soul to the world which he creates, so that this individual soul assumes the function of the soul of the image-world. The animating principle in the artistic work is not the general intellect but the personality of the artist.

The image-world is therefore much more in line with the world of experience, which also centers around the experiencing self. Indeed, artistic imagination and creation spring directly from total experience; they are much nearer to experience than are the theories and laws of the sciences. The world which we experience is like the world which we confront in the work of art, and not like the world devised by physics and chemistry and the other branches of science (although biology and psychology are, of course, nearer to immediate experience than are the mathematical disciplines). For this reason it is easier to read a novel than it is to study Einstein's theory of relativity, although it is less easy to penetrate great masterpieces and to understand them fully than it might be to understand physics, if one were trained for this purpose. In principle, every man should be able to understand physics as well as mathematics because both rest upon the general intellect, while the appreciation of a work of art demands a kind of kindred soul.

Although the artistic creation is nearer to experience than is science, this very affinity between art and experience makes it more difficult to understand how art can achieve a reconciliation of the polarities and how it can solve the antinomies which arise out of experience. Is not the generality of the intellect precisely the reconciling principle in the sciences? Does not the elimination of the individual features of the self enable the scientist to arrive at a "world-solution" no longer encumbered by the contrast between the universality and the individuality of the ego? When the artist, on the contrary, does not eliminate his individuality but even makes it the very soul of the world he creates, how can such a product reconcile the opposition mentioned? And yet the fact cannot be denied that the work of the artist does perform this miracle and (what is even more startling) performs it the better, the more original the individuality of the artist is, that is to say, the more individual it is!

However, we already have the key to this riddle in our hands. If it is true that the world of experience is always the world of an individual self and not of an abstract intellect only, then it is evident that only the reconciliation of the individuality and the universality of the ego can bring about a full and true image of the world, one which concerns not only fragmentary aspects but the totality of all aspects. Therefore, we can well comprehend that a universal personality can achieve what science cannot: the reproduction of the world in an image that echoes his own soul and, at the same time, appeals to all souls which feel the harmony between the individuality and the universality of the genius reflected in his work.

The artist has to be "inspired" in order to achieve his work. He does not produce out of rational or intellectual reflections and calculations, although reflections and calculations do participate in the transposition of the inspired conception into the actuality of the work. The artist cannot generate his work by sheer will power. As a merely individual person, he cannot create. Inspiration means the fusion of the universal and the individual ego within the operation of the artist. When this fusion occurs, the precondition of creation is achieved. But it cannot be "achieved" at all, when this word implies that the effort and the aspiration of the artist alone decide. They do not decide; the artist depends not only upon himself but also upon the favor of the Muses whom he invokes.

No phrase can better describe his inner state of mind. It is not accidental that a mythological metaphor creeps in when one tries to express the peculiar method of the artist. Mythology is the poetical solution of the religious "problem." And it is the religious problem which enters when we analyze the miraculous process of imaginative creation. The artist depends upon "grace" in a pagan sense. As the fragmentary and individual character of the imaginative content of the artistic work does not hamper the universal significance of the image-world, so also the individuality of the artist does not obstruct his universal greatness. On the contrary, in both cases the fusion itself is the moving power of the reconciliation achieved.

Although the religious sphere is somehow anticipated and foreshadowed in the act of artistic creation, still the artist is not a prophet. Poet and prophet are brothers. But the poet belongs to the contemplative sphere, the prophet to that of action. The poet acts, but for the sake of, and commissioned by, contemplation; the prophet contemplates, but for the sake of, and commissioned by, action. The artist is a messenger not of the Living God but of the Muses, whose virtue and spirit are entirely contemplative. The poet, Schelling says, is born a pagan. No wonder that the great poets have some inclination toward the pagan gods, to which they frequently appeal. Even Dante chooses Vergil as his leader through hell, and his audacious idea of making the beloved woman the mediator between himself and the Blessed in heaven is certainly not Christian.

Both prophet and genius act under a kind of compulsion which does not exclude, but rather presupposes, individual freedom. The wonder of inspiration in both rests upon the fusion of freedom and necessity in their creative state of mind. Here again we see that the antinomies of experience are surmounted by and in the artist. He is certainly not coerced, as are the beasts by their instincts; and yet he is driven toward his intuition, and only when he is driven is his intuition genuinely artistic. The split between necessity and freedom as it opens in experience is closed in the blessed situation of genuine creativity.

The artist "redeems" the world in a secular sense. Depicting even man's cruelest deeds, his most tragic destinies, his most depressing frustrations, his most destructive forces, the artist exalts them to the level of eternal beauty, endows them with nobility, and spiritualizes them. His deity is Beauty. He adores her in creating his work, and thereby he produces a kind of theodicy which is more effective than any thought out by a philosopher or theologian. After all, Augustine only imitates the artist when he insists that everything truly and really existing is included in the universal order of beauty.

The instrument by which the genius accomplishes so great an effect is his imagination, which combines the opposite poles of the personality, thereby integrating man as a self. Wordsworth calls the imagination of the artist "the mind's internal heaven." Initiating the dream world of fairy tales and fables, fiction and fancy, romance and myth, and all the arts, this creative force is itself akin to its products, equally fabulous and miraculous, superrational, and to be understood only in an imaginative fashion. If it is true that man is created in the image of God, then the artist, in spite of his pagan affinity, most resembles the Creator (although the Creator in the biblical sense is more than an artist) The identity of the word "creator" in both cases is not accidental. The artist does create, as God does, "out of nothing." He is not bound by the laws of nature but is free in depicting the world as he sees fit, for the purpose of interpretation. He possesses the power to arrest the fleeting wave of time and events and to impress eternity upon the transitory moment. His hero will live as long as his work:

> So long as man can breathe, or eyes can see,
> So long lives this, and this gives life to thee

Shakespeare proudly exults. Indeed, as the image-world is a little world of its own, so the artist is a little god of his own.

The Limit of Art

IN ART the contemplative solution of the antinomies of experience culminates, but this solution itself is limited for the very reason that it is contemplative. Contemplation can never absolutely reconcile world and ego because it offers a "world-solution," which either completely disregards the existence of the human self, as science does, or treats this existence only as a part of the image-world of art. To be sure, the self of the artist impinges upon this world, but it does not figure within it. The artist as such is not known by artistic means; he, as the creator, does not appear in his work except in autobiography (which is not purely a work of art but in most cases is either historical or at least half-historical, as in Goethe's *Dichtung und Wahrheit*). A self-portrait is an artistic mirror of the artist, but this mirror makes the artist an image of his own world; it must "objectify" his self, precisely in order to be a work of art. The self as such, the living subject, can never be transformed into an image; this is the limit of art. It is the final limit of contemplation and of the contemplative solution of the antinomies.

The artist is not only the image he creates in his work, if he portrays himself, but also a living being. In fact, he is such a being in the first place and is only secondarily a creative being and the author of his works. The contradictions of experience are felt by him in an actual way, and they could be absolutely transcended only in an actual way, i.e., by means of an actual community in which the contrast of ego and ego, of world and world, is finally settled. Contemplation cannot perform this task because it does not take the other self as an acting, existing person but transforms him into an imaginative person who lives in the imaginary world of the artistic work. In other words, the limit of art springs from the fact that everything and everyone undergo a metamorphosis in the mirror of art and that this metamorphosis deprives the actual person of his actuality. This explains why the actual self-contradiction of the experiencing ego cannot be absolutely conquered by any contemplative solution, be it scientific or artistic.

This basic limitation of the whole sphere of art again generates a new tension, a new inner division of the self, and so aggravates the evil it would conquer; it generates a split between the actual and the imaginative worlds. This split is felt, and the more the artist succeeds in portraying himself in his works, the more he becomes merged in the world of his creation, and the more his actual life is regarded as merely a means for his artistic intentions. The actual world can never be completely absorbed and, as it were, replaced by its imaginative counterpart. Since this counter-

part is infinitely more harmonious and reflects the inner reconciliation of the art sphere, the insufficiency and the contradictions
of actual life are only the more deeply and the more painfully
notable; the contrast between the two spheres underlines the imperfection and the unredeemed character of the actual one. The
artist and the sensitive lover of art suffer more from the deficiencies, tensions, and tragic conflicts of human existence than do in-
sensitive and unaffected men immersed in the pursuit of active
purposes and ends.

This fundamental limit of art could not be removed, even if it
were possible to contemplate the great world in the fashion of
the little world of art, or if it were possible to comprehend the
all as the macrocosm, as Greek thinkers and even their Christian
successors, like Augustine, thought they could. In *Faust* Goethe
shows how the hero is completely dissatisfied with knowledge,
even that knowledge which enables him to look at the world as a
harmonious whole, because he feels that it does not still the infinite thirst of his mind for actual life, for a satisfaction that no
contemplation of whatever kind can possibly grant. Observing
the sign of the Macrocosm, he explains:

> Like heavenly forces rising and descending,
> Their golden urns reciprocally lending,
> With wings that winnow blessing
> From Heaven through Earth I see them pressing,
> Filling the All with harmony unceasing!
> How grand a show! but ah! a show alone.
> Thee boundless Nature, how make thee my own?

It is this infinite desire which prompts Faust to leave his study,
where he has investigated nature and enjoyed the acts, to im-
merse himself in the floods of life and the tumult of action. Led
by this desire, he is driven first from pleasure to pleasure;[10] but
finally he acquires the insight that only social work can absolutely satisfy his thirst for life and that a community in which all are
free to collaborate with one another for the sake of all could
alone redeem his heart and bring peace to the storm of his passion. Goethe in this way expresses his conviction that it is not

10. It is remarkable that among those pleasures which Faust enjoys, but only
for a short time, even artistic creation and contemplation, symbolized by his
marriage with beautiful Helen, figure.

contemplation but action alone which can calm a man's unrest, because this unrest originates from an inner conflict which no contemplation of the world, even of a perfectly harmonious cosmos, can pacify. Whether Goethe's solution is eventually satisfying is, of course, a question not to be discussed here.

Art is limited because the ego ceases to be the ego when it figures within the world as a quasi-object. The chasm between the self as an object belonging to the world and as a subject not belonging to the world cannot be filled by any "world-solution" of the basic antinomy of experience. The impossibility becomes further evident, when we consider the relation between individuality and universality in the ego of the artist. Although this contrast is reconciled in the creative genius, it is never fully so, since the universality of the genius is somewhat restricted by the fact that there are many artists and many arts and that even one and the same artist creates many works, so that art offers many "worlds," each of which claims universality. The one universal world is imaged in many forms, since there are many individual artists and even the same artist produces his works in many individual situations. This is the price which has to be paid for the prerogative of artistic creation in reaching the goal of art in many works.

To be sure, it is possible to establish a scale of the artists and to distinguish the greatest among them as the one who alone deserves the predicate "universal" in the fullest sense. One might call Homer the greatest of the epic poets, Shakespeare the greatest of the dramatists, Goethe the greatest of the lyric poets, and so on. But all such judgments might evoke some protest; besides, it might be difficult to distingish any single one of the creations of each as the epitome of greatness (e.g., the *Iliad* or the *Odyssey*). Whatever we might design to reduce the manifold of masterpieces to one only, we will always meet difficulties. In fact, such an undertaking is impossible.

In spite of the universality of the genius, artistic imagination is still the imagination of an individual man, even if he is inspired by the Muses, i.e., by universal powers imaged in a poetical fashion. The genius is the creator of his work, not the Muses. In other words, the individual man is universal inasmuch as he is a genius;

but, even so, he is human and finite and hence exposed to failures and defects, not only as a moral being, but also as an artist, as any attempt to arrange his works with respect to their greatness illuminates. It is not that the universal ego is individualized in him but that his individual peculiarity takes on the dimensions of universality in his work. The artist is not a messenger of the Living God, or even of the gods. To put it another way, art is limited because it is not religion, though it may have a religious significance.

This limitation seems to encroach upon the principle of co-ordination as compared with that of subordination. The scientist can unite scientists the world over because they are, as it were, incarnations of the Logos, that reason which "prescribes to nature its laws," while the artists have not such an inner solidarity and the art-lovers are divided by their different tastes and assessments. In this respect the scientist and science seem to be free from the restriction of art. This is true, but only in a qualified way. Scientific universality is less restricted indeed, simply because it achieves not universality, strictly speaking, but generality only, an abstract universality which sacrifices individuality and thereby wins a wider scope of acknowledgment and applicability. To conclude: both science and art are restricted, though in different ways and on different levels. If it were possible to combine the absolute generality of science with the relative universality of art, so that an absolute universality would result, this hypothetical synthesis might achieve what none of the branches of contemplation can achieve by itself. But alas, such a synthesis does not exist in the field of contemplation, precisely because it is this field.

The image-world of art is limited, also, because it images but a fragmentary detail of the world and exalts it to the height of universality. Homer might seem to embrace the whole cosmos of human feelings, situations, relations, and so on. Even so, all these contents are only a segment of the all of human possibilities, which is, in fact, inexhaustible. But each of the possibilities selected by the artist somewhat circumscribes the image of the world and thus the world itself as imaged in this peculiar way. Thus we arrive at many "worlds" again. As in the case of the artist, so in that of the world, individual items or instances are exalted as representative of the whole universe; it is not the universe itself which appears before us in an individual image, as it does when we read that God created it in six days.

Art can integrate the soul of the spectator because the work is the result of a self-integration on the part of the creator. But, as the process of creation is restricted, so is the process of its effect upon the lover of art. In both cases the redemption—if I may use this religious term—lasts only as long as the work is conceived and perceived, although the value of the work may be eternal. The reconciling power of the work cannot penetrate the whole of life (as faith can); it depends upon the presence of the work and the state of the spectator, reader, or listener, who must be engrossed in the contemplation of it in order to feel its redemptive efficacy. There is an analogy with respect to the sacrament, the sermon, and so on in the religious realm, but I will postpone discussion of this point.

Aestheticism

AESTHETICISM refuses to respect the boundaries of art and tends to expand art over the whole range of culture, making it the consummation, the absolute. Such a transgression necessarily violates all the other realms of culture, invades their legitimate territory, and distorts the meaning of their contributions. It creates the semblance of an absolute reconciliation achieved by art, whereas, in reality, this reconciliation itself is distorted by enlarging it beyond its prerogative. Aestheticism would like to make art a religion and religion an aesthetic contemplation.

In a way, all mythological religions are a result of aestheticism, inasmuch as they discharge the task of religion by artistic imagination, expressing their religious feelings by artistic production in painting and sculpture, song and poetry, music and drama, as the Greeks above all nations did in the most marvelous and convincing form. However, in ancient Greece art was not yet detached from the totality of cultural activity; it was itself religious in its origin and in its function, so that one should speak of a reciprocal influence of art upon religion and of religion upon art. The cultural realms were still inwardly united, none was autonomous. *L'art pour l'art* is the least Hellenic slogan conceivable. Even so, aesthetic contemplation was the highest goal and the guiding principle in all Greek civilization, as the German classics were right in interpreting the Greek spirit. "In God all things are beautiful, good and just," Heraclitos says, mentioning first the beautiful.[11] And even Aristotle calls the good the beautiful (*kalon*) throughout his *Ethics*.

The "ancient quarrel between philosophy and poetry" which Plato discusses in his *Republic*[12] is fundamentally a quarrel between religion and poetry, to be sure—between a religion propagated by the philosophers, who revolted against the mythological gods and their artistic representation, as Heraclitos was the first to do. "The Greeks," he says, "pray to these statues, as if a man would converse with buildings; for they do not know the true nature of gods." This invective mirrors the indignation roused by the aesthetic influence upon religious expression. It parallels the biblical prohibition of portraying God by "graven images."

Plato himself took the most active part in this quarrel by branding all the views of Homer on the gods. "The first thing," he says, "to be established in the state will be a censorship of the writers of fiction. They are telling a lie about the gods, and what is more, a bad lie. We shall be silent about all the innumerable quarrels of gods and heroes: wrangling is unholy. All the battles of the gods in Homer: these tales must not be admitted into our state."[13] Plato rejects the claim of poets to know the truth about things divine; they are too fanciful and irresponsible to be trusted. It is not poetical imagination but political philosophy alone which can be called upon to teach this truth and to establish the right religion in the state. For religion is not a matter of artistic creation, it is rather a matter of political wisdom and philosophic insight. Plato thus restricts the sphere of art, which he otherwise admires and loves.

The most dangerous and finally disastrous consequence of

11. Diels, *Die Fragmente der Vorsokratiker* (Berlin: Wertmannsche Buchhandlung, 1922), Frag. 102.

12. *The Dialogues of Plato*, trans. B. Jowett (New York: Random House, 1920, 1937), I, 865.

13. *Ibid.*, pp. 640 ff.

aestheticism is, as Plato saw, the falsification of religious truth and the enervation of moral life. If one regards art as the ultimate and absolute interpreter of the meaning of life, the peculiar conditions of the entire active sphere of culture will be distorted in a manner analogous to the distortion generated by scientism. Aestheticism and scientism have this in common: neither can do justice to actual life because they transplant it to the plane of contemplated life, on which it loses its own right and essence by appearing either as a scientifically observed, or as an artistically created, object. It undergoes a metamorphosis which deprives it of its peculiarity and destroys its actuality. Objectification kills the significance and reality of the living subject; it suppresses the responsibility and personality of the willing and acting person; it paralyzes and annihilates the very pulse of life. Contemplation is the opposite of action, and this opposition is not neutralized or placated by aestheticism but is, rather, ignored, so that life appears to be imaginative only, instead of being actual and real in the moral and religious sense.

Although, as we have seen, aesthetic imagination and contemplation can preserve the specifically human features of human life and the human personality better than scientific observation and explanation can, nevertheless they still deprive life and personality of their original and immediate presence. They deal with man not in an active, but in a contemplative, way which makes him an object and a mere part of the world without that moral freedom which characterizes man as man. The great achievement of art—its ability to reconcile freedom and necessity in the unity of the image-world which superimposes its own totality upon every event or decision that occurs within its scope—becomes perverted into the denial of freedom, because actual life lacks the totality of the image-world and does not reflect the soul of a creative artist. Art is not ultimate.

The greatest artists are inclined to extend their own artistic modes of viewing the world to actual life and thus to fall victim to aestheticism. It is well known that Goethe tried to lead his life as if it were a work of art[14] and thereby met difficulties and underwent temptations which he could overcome only because

14. Cf. the profound book on *Goethe* by Georg Simmel (Leipzig: Klinckhardt, 1913).

a great amount of moral wisdom and strength counteracted and balanced the trend of aestheticism. But his example was dangerous to those of his innumerable admirers who did not possess the same resources and yet ventured to imitate his aesthetic standards (or lack of moral standards) in their own insignificant lives. This might well be one of the many reasons why the German nation declined so surprisingly and fatefully in her moral standards and conduct during the nineteenth and twentieth centuries. Some of the Romanticists had already drawn conclusions from aestheticism with respect to moral actuality which were destructive for social morality and which weakened their own resistance when they confronted the temptation of being converted to the Roman Catholic church.[15]

In a definite way this church itself resulted partly from the blending of Christian and ancient religious tendencies and from attempting to preserve the aesthetic values and artistic inclinations of paganism[16] without giving up the moral and spiritual basis of biblical faith. This attempt certainly saved the treasures of antiquity, but it harmed the gravity and depth of the gospel and led eventually to Renaissance and Reformation.

Sometimes scientism and aestheticism covenant with each other and thereby increase the dangers involved in both tendencies. Here again Goethe is an example. The consequence of this union was that his scientific views were tinged by his aesthetic contemplation, causing him to establish a doctrine of the nature of colors which was in agreement with the sense-experience of the visible world but impaired mathematical optics and induced Goethe to assail Newton's theory. On the other hand, his scientific passion encroached upon his poetry, obscuring some passages in the second part of *Faust*.

Kierkegaard describes and analyzes profoundly, in his first great book, *Either-Or*, the sickness of aestheticism, which probably threatened his own moral and spiritual health for some time, if not throughout his life. He shows that one of the conspicuous symptoms of aestheticism is its imitation of the artistic reconciliation between time and eternity in actual life. The aesthete aban-

15. E.g., Friedrich Schlegel, whose early novel *Lucinde* indulged in libertinistic ideas, while in his old age he was converted.

16. The famous impressionist painter, Renoir, stresses this point in his letters.

dons the imperative of fidelity in his love relations because he enjoys the beauty and perfection of every new erotic impulse. He lives through the moments of his life as if each were a little world in itself like that within the work of art, closed and self-sufficient and not pointing to anything beyond itself. The happy "moment" of such a life, however, contradicts the fact that life is not a series of imaginative world-moments or momentary worlds, each possessing its own eternity, but, rather, a continuous challenge to fight merely momentary desires for the sake of moral eternity, i.e., the inner consequence and wholeness of character revealing itself in loyalty and endurance and acts of resignation.

The difference between belief in Fate and Fortune and belief in Providence and Destiny rests upon the difference between aesthetic and ethical standards and views. Fate reflects the unity and universality of aesthetic world-contemplation, while Providence reflects the unity and universality of a moral and spiritual faith in God, the creator and ruler of the world. Aestheticism sacrifices the unity and universality of the holy will of God to the same features as those realized in the work of art. It sacrifices the ideal of a perfect human community to the enjoyment of looking at the world as if it were created by a world-artist or an "Artist-God," as Nietzsche worshiped him, according to his own confession.[17]

In the twentieth century the seed sown by Nietzsche flowered. German youth succumbed to the alluring charm of his style and the fascination of his refined and learned aestheticism. In the so-called "Stefan George-Kreis," this aesthetic mode of feeling and thinking reached its zenith and enervated the hearts of the most gifted lovers of art, so that they were unable to resist when Hitler called them back into the arena of action. National socialism was itself a half-romantic, half-scientific movement in which scientism (pseudo-biological theories) and aestheticism (mythology) joined each other on the political scene, on which the barbaric fanaticism and the sadistic insanity of a new Nero used them for his own "will to power."

17. Preface to *The Birth of Tragedy* under the title "Attempt at a Self-critique" (1886).

Works and Life

CONTEMPLATIVE culture is consummated in the fine arts. The limit of art is, at the same time, the limit of the whole sphere of this culture; if there is any "beyond," it cannot be sought further on a higher level of contemplation but only in another sphere. This sphere is to be met in the realms of active life, where the antinomies of experience are solved by the attempt to unite the manifold of persons and to create a community in which the self-contradiction of each ego is removed. In this sphere we can distinguish two main areas, the political and the religious; in between them, as a mediating realm which, at the same time, is the very center of culture and civilization, we meet morality—a realm which belongs to both private and public life and which inwardly connects also the personal and the cultural spheres of human existence.

The active sphere of cultural activity is nearer to experience than the contemplative one, in so far as it is the sphere in which an "ego-solution" is sought, since the ego is the active subject of experience. While contemplation objectifies the ego and thereby estranges it from itself, action centers around the ego and is its own immediate self-expression. Active culture has the very ego as its end; it acts upon the selves, in order to reconcile them to each other and within themselves. Whereas contemplation rests upon the contents of experience, action does not rest at all but aims at a transformation of the acting ego by means of action. Contemplative activity (creativity) produces something outside the experiencing ego, a theory or a work of art; active culture organizes the experiencing selves into a living community. The contrast between works and life thus characterizes the contrast between the two cultural spheres.

The works are, as it were, surrounded by a wall that stands between the world comprehended or imaged within them and the spectator. These walls protect the treasure of knowledge and imagination, but they also draw a boundary between the image-world and the ever fluid, effervescent, boundless life which has created it. The image-world preserves this life; but, preserved, shaped, and interpreted by the artist, it is no longer the same. It is removed from its original scene. Even when the artist is able to hold fast to the original features—the fluidity, effervescence, and infinity of life—still all this is now well ordered within its frame (as, for instance, the glimmering air in the landscape paintings of French impressionists); it is cut off from the totality of experience and itself represents another totality in imaginative form. As compared with this aesthetic order and form, life is formless and without order.

To be sure, life contains the rudiments of the artistic world. Poetry and music live in the soul not only of the poets and the musicians but of every human being who is not yet dehumanized and calloused by the routine of life, by vice, or by bitter experiences. A German proverb says: "Good people harbor songs." Even the average man or woman lives through a romance, when in love, and all adventure has something novel within itself. Tragedies occur not only in the drama of the playwright but also on the scene of life. We feel that the happiest hours of life resemble a fairy tale or a legend: the chasm between art and life seems to disappear; the "wall" of the image-world seems to fall; life shines in the splendor of beauty; and beauty conquers the confusion and fragmentariness of life. And the same could be said about the relation between the plastic arts or painting and the impression made sometimes by living persons or by a natural landscape.

No doubt there is art within actual life, just as there is mathematics within the visible universe. Otherwise we could not say that science and art convey truth. The scientist and the artist only set free or separate what exists in reality, so forming it that intellect or imagination is satisfied. They continue and finish what is begun in experience.[18] But, still, life is always richer in potentialities; it is less definitive, less determinate, less total in

18. Conrad Fiedler in his *Philosophie der Kunst* derives painting from the inner impulse ever present in immediate perception to bring the process of forming, which is inherent in the act of seeing, to completion. In a similar way, Benedetto Croce holds that the work of art is the truth immanent in the object of sense apprehension. The same is suggested by Bergson when he says: "Si nous pouvions entrer en communication immédiate avec les choses et avec nous-mêmes, je crois bien que l'art serait inutile, ou plutôt que nous serions tous artistes, car notre âme vibrerait alors continuellement à l'unisson de la nature" (*Le Rire* [82d ed.; Paris: Presses universitaires de France, 1947], chap. iii, p. 115).

itself than is the work. There are art and science in reality, but reality is not only what art and science know and tell about it; it is never to be known entirely by art and science: the antinomies of experience cannot be absolutely resolved on the plane of the work, precisely because actual life would then be meaningless or its meaning would be distorted and estranged, as we have seen.

Although the work has its value and significance within itself; although the image-world is rounded and complete as it is; although the frame or the theater curtain closes it off from the actual world and from actual life, yet the works have their vital function within life. They not only grant an image and through it the truth about life; they also mold life; they educate and civilize man; they exalt his mind and soul; they mediate moral wisdom and prudence hardly to be learned otherwise. They have a place, not only within contemplative, but also within active, culture. As the scientist and the artist themselves are not only scientist and artist but also citizens, moral beings, and religious believers (of some kind) and as the work they produce has a function and meaning within their nonscientific and nonartistic humanity,[19] so also it has a function and meaning within the active and actual life of the student and the spectator, who themselves are more than merely students and spectators. The works, as it were, participate in life in spite of their contemplative isolation and blessed perfection.

This shows that life is more comprehensive than the work, that the active sphere of culture embraces within itself the contemplative. The works, then, do not lose their connection with their own source. As they arise out of the constantly creative impulses of life, so they remain in continuous contact with life, sharing its inexhaustible fulness and its changing destinies. Indeed, the work itself changes together with this change, since it takes on ever new faces and voices, echoing new life, new tasks, new visions, and new experiences. Great books are always new books. They constantly reveal new wisdom and insight corresponding to the ever changing circumstances and conditions of life. Shakespeare

19. Goethe called his works "fragments of a great confession": they were written to smooth the raging waves of his passionate soul, and they fulfilled that end.

as we love him is no longer the poet of the sixteenth and seventeenth centuries; he has grown, together with the growing soul of mankind; he may shrink, together with the shrinking soul of darker centuries. And the same is true with respect to the meaning of architecture, music, painting, and sculpture. Only thus do the works retain their own vividness and vivacity.

All culture strives to reconcile the polarities of experience. All culture therefore, whether contemplative or active, serves life and is alive. But active culture is directly bound up with life itself; it is the culture of life in a definite sense. Active life does not produce works which stand over against life, but it forms life directly, its stuff is life, and its result is life. There are no separating walls between the results of active culture and the activity which brings them forth. On the contrary, result and activity are in steady inner exchange, mutually stimulating each other, correcting each other, and enlarging their common horizons. Active culture never results in a product besides its own activity; instead, the result of its activity is further activity. Active culture, therefore, never arrives at its end, not even in the relative sense in which science attains conclusions of a definite sort. The result of active activity is itself immersed in the fluidity and effervescence of the ever changing scene of actual life.

Actuality and activity are akin to each other not only linguistically but also in their meanings. Actuality means that the reality of the self, of its experience and its life, depends upon its activity. The self is not real in the same sense in which everything else, even the works, is real, because its reality is not objective or the result of self-objectification but rather of its activity. The self is real only in so far as man is active in realizing himself; this activity is the indispensable presupposition of man's existence as a self. He is real only to the degree to which he makes himself what he is: a free subject that decides and determines himself in willing and acting. Kant and Fichte have emphasized this truth again and again, and the modern existentialists are only the successors of the great idealists in this doctrine; unfortunately, they have distorted it by conceiving man's freedom without taking into account that this freedom is inseparable from the obedience to the moral law.

Man's active activity aims at himself as a moral ideal. Only in the active sphere of life is this goal directly sighted and pursued, while contemplative productivity in science and art only indirectly aims at man's self-realization. To be sure, artistic and scientific activities are activities because the self also realizes itself through them, though merely indirectly, by the detour of the works. The work-world of science and art is not actually, but only theoretically or imaginatively, real, i.e., in a secondary fashion. It borrows its life from the life of the self that actualizes itself by means of its activities, be they those of science and art or those of the political and moral spheres.

Man gains his reality as man from his own activity; only in being active is he real or does he make himself actually real. What we call "life" in the human sense is this activity without which man becomes only the object of contemplation or falls victim to the aims and ends of other persons who utilize his physical or intellectual gifts. What we commonly mean by "reality" is derived from man's activity and actuality. The "real" world in this sense is the world in which we work and realize ourselves. In a word, it is the moral world. Things are real in so far as they are related to my obligations and duties, and I myself am real in so far as I fulfil those obligations and duties or fail to fulfil them. It is from this point of view that Fichte rightly says, "The world is only the material of my duty," or things are in themselves what we ought to make out of them.

One may say that in the active sphere man makes himself the work of his cultural activity. There is no other work in this sphere except man himself, the community of persons who realize themselves. Therefore, the result of active life is personal and actual, as much as is the activity which brings about that result. Active culture is a sphere not of works but of life. Its goal is not to comprehend and to construct the world (i.e., contemplative reality) but to comprehend and to construct man (i.e., active reality) and the world only for the sake of man. In the active sphere man becomes the architect of himself, of society, and of the state. While contemplation demands that man disengage himself from life, that he should not be involved in the objects he investigates and comprehends, and that he look at them in a disinterested mood, action demands that man engage in life, that he be interested in the human world of intentions and actions, and that he feel himself responsible not only with respect to the truth of his comprehension but with respect to the ends which he pursues in actual life.

In a way, active culture, like contemplative culture, results in self-objectification of a special sort, but not in works. Institutions arise out of actions. They are organizations of people. They regulate life and its ends. They "form" the relations between men and their obligations and duties. They are relatively stable and self-contained. The most conspicuous among them is the state.

The State

THE state does not exist like an object or even like the work in the sphere of contemplative culture. Neither does the work exist like an object of the natural sciences, for it is a work only in so far as it harbors a meaningful world, a theory, or an image, and neither theories nor images are objects in that sense. Rather, they convey the truth about objects or about reality. They cannot be known except by a response to the truth or the meaning which they convey. In so far as works are objects, they do not belong to the world of the senses but to the world of meaning. The state does not even exist in that way. It has no body, as a theory has which is expressed either in words or in symbols, like a poem printed or recited, a drama performed, a painting on a canvas, and so on. Works exist in a quasi-objective fashion in the form of a meaningful body. Institutions do not exist as meaningful bodies. In vain would we seek for such a body representing the state (although one speaks of the "body politic," but in a metaphorical sense only). To be sure, there are buildings and monuments, documents and implements, and other physical realities which are expressive of the existence of the state; but none of them represents the state as does the canvas a painting, the book a novel, and so on. An institution exists mainly and truly in the consciousness of persons and as an arrangement of their interrelations, their actions, and their offices.

Whereas works (scientific, technical, or artistic) offer a

"world-solution" of the ultimate problem, institutions offer an "ego-solution." Whereas works unify persons only indirectly by unifying their worlds, institutions unify persons directly, and only indirectly their worlds. And, whereas the unification of worlds is brought about through the medium of the work by a theory or an image-world, the unification of persons (or their selves) is brought about by an organization which creates one single quasi-organism in which each person has a more or less distinct function and office (or "station," as Bradley calls it). This quasi-organism is represented by a head—be it a king, a dictator, a leader, a president, or whatever. Each manifold of persons organized may be called a "community"—be it a family, a social group, a party, or a municipal body, a political or a religious community. The state is the most tightly and most deliberately organized community on earth, although not the most intimate or the most inwardly united.

There are communities joined by common bonds like language or by common remembrances, habits, legends, and so forth. Some of these communities, like peoples or nations, are politically organized and formed by the state. One of the most important common bonds is that of common cultural trends. The state not only is thus itself the product of cultural activity but also contains cultural activities within itself. This distinguishes the state markedly from science, technology, or art; so much so that sometimes the term "culture" is used in contradistinction to politics and is reserved for the sphere of work-creation.

The state exists only in the form of an ever new activity or ever new actions performed by the head and the officials (including all citizens in a democratic state); it exists only in a way of life. Political life aims at constantly new attempts to organize and to unify the community so that the contradiction between the manifoldness and the oneness may be resolved by the creation of one ego comprising all the ego-subjects belonging to the community. This one ego represents the universality and the ego-subjects represent the individuality of the ego, so that this contrast no longer leads to conflicts and struggles either between persons or within each person. The task of the state as a cultural realm springs from the antinomies of experience and consists in their pacification: it is not a merely biological task like that of the anthill, the beehive, or any other statelike union in the kingdom of brute animals, nor is it a merely economic task, as some politicians suppose, although, of course, economic needs and ends do play an enormous part in political action and reaction. The supreme task of the state is, instead, metaphysical; it concerns the contradictions of experience, especially of self-experience in individual and collective life.

Since the reconciliation of the universality and the individuality of the ego is the supreme task of the state, it is obviously wrong to contrast these two polarities by overstressing either the interest of the individuals to be reconciled within themselves or the interest of the state in reconciling all the individuals within itself. Both extremes should be avoided in a true theory of the state. Neither does the state exist for the sake of the individuals only, nor do the individuals exist for the sake of the state only. These one-sided aspects forget the basic task of the state, which is precisely this: to unite the poles of "either-or" and to bring about their inner synthesis. The state may be called the "universal ego," since it exists in every self, made real and powerful as a special self-existing ego, or it may be called the "common ego" of all the individuals united politically.

Clearly, the state does not exist merely on behalf of the happiness of the individuals, as democratic philosophy sometimes interprets its ideal. If this were true, it would be impossible to understand that the state is entitled to demand the supreme self-sacrifice from the citizen in war. This demand can be justified only if it is recognized that the state is a kind of superior ego, a supreme end of the life of each individual. Only if the state represents such a metaphysical end can the total sacrifice of life and happiness be vindicated.

But, further, the state does not exist for its own sake, so that individuals are nothing but objects of whom the state can dispose at will as mere means for its own ends, as totalitarian doctrines of all shades assert. If this were true, the individual would be of no greater value than a beast, a tool, or a physical energy. Indeed, the citizen would rank no higher than the individual bee in a hive or the individual ant in a hill. But then the state itself would lose all value, as the hive or the hill has no more value than the bees or the ants. In which case the state would not be a state at all. The state has its grandeur and majesty only because there is grandeur and majesty in the individual, namely: the universality of the self which makes each self the self of the world in which the individual lives, and the self of the community of which the individual is a member and without which he would not even be an individual in the human sense.

The state is this universal ego of each member of the organized community, set apart as their universal ego and therefore far superior to each member. The state is thus a separate ego, a kind of independent person representative of all the members. This is most obvious when the state communicates with other states and declares its will to them. "The United States takes the position . . . ," or "the United States does not agree . . . ," or "the United States is willing to support China . . ."—in all these examples the state functions as a will in its own right. This will is neither the will of the majority nor the will of some high-ranking officials nor the will of the President, although it is true that decisions originate from all these sources. But in the end it is the will of the state itself which is expressed and which has an authority higher than any of the citizens. The will of a madman like Hitler would never have moved the world, if this will had not become the will of the German Reich, representing more than a hundred million individuals organized in one single state.

The will of the state is more than a will *in abstracto;* it has the power to carry through its decisions, the power to act. Action is the life-element of the state. The state is a living ego, to be distinguished from the life of the individuals, even the most powerful and most authoritative among them. This is a mysterious reality, if compared with the reality of the individuals who have bodies and physical energy and are real in the sense of natural entities. The state is not a natural entity, although its own power and action would be impossible without the employment of individuals and the physical energies used by them. The reality of the state can never be understood by those who deny that there is a reality besides that of nature and natural entities. They will always mistake the state for individuals or for one individual in the state, as the king of France did when he said, "L'état, c'est moi!"

The state is will and power and the agent of its actions, as much in its relation to the community, which is organized by the state, as in its relations to other states. As the supreme will of that community, as its universal self, the state is the supreme legislator, executive, and judge. The individual legislators, executives, and judges in the state are only commissioned by the state; they are state officials of various types and powers, and even the president in a democracy is not exempted from that rule. In a democracy of the Western style the people are the source of the sovereignty of the state; but, even so, they are not themselves the state any more than the French king is. "The people," however, is by no means a simple term, as many think it is. What does it mean?

Certainly, individuals are not "the people," at least not in so far as they are not yet organized by the state. As unorganized individuals they have no power or even the possibility of expressing their will, and none of them could pretend to represent "the people." Only as organized in a state do "the people" represent the source of sovereignty. "The people," then, are the community itself, politically united. The emphasis laid upon the sovereignty of "the people" is derived from the pretense of kings or other dynasts to represent not only the will of the state but the supreme source of this will, so that all other individuals are excluded from any possibility of shaping or influencing decisions and actions, at least legally and metaphysically. The democratic philosophy, instead, recognizes the profound truth that every individual in the state is endowed with the same universality as any other individual or that, metaphysically, all individuals are equal in this respect. But this profound truth does not or should not impair the other truth that the state has a will of its own and that its supreme source is the universal will living in each member of the community. The question arises, then, as to what degree the individuality and universality of the ego are united in the will of the state; but this question will be discussed later.

One thing, however, is immediately evident: that a despotism is no true state in the metaphysical sense because in it the will of the state does not represent the will of all individuals but only of one individual made universal, so that the antinomies of experience are not solved but are only strengthened and deepened by such a pseudo-solution. The individuals are deprived of their royal property—the universality of their selves—and the despot himself therefore does not really represent the will of the individuals or the community organized in the state; rather, he wills and acts as an individual only. No solution of the ultimate contradiction is achieved thereby. The contradiction is only hardened by the contrast between the individual will of the dynast and the will of the individuals and by the contrast between the pretense of the despot to represent the universal will and the fact that he does not do so. He is a real head of the state and this state itself is a real state only to the degree to which the extremes of universality and individuality do coincide in the monarch—a happy accident that sometimes occurs in history.

Only to the degree to which the individuals are really united would the contradiction between their manifoldness and their oneness be dissolved. And the same can be said with respect to the other categories. Freedom and necessity, time and eternity, are also reconciled to each other in a true state, but only inasmuch as the state fulfils its task, which ultimately surpasses the entire political realm. In a sense those polarities, too, are harmonized. The state compels the citizens to act or not to act, according to its laws; but these laws are given by the citizens' own universal will, so that they are free in obeying them. The state not only satisfies the temporary needs of the community but represents their cultural aspirations, which aim at eternity. However, in both directions definite limitations exist which manifest the limit of the state altogether.

The Limit of the State

A CERTAIN analogy between the state and God is evident. Both represent the universal will, superior to the will of any and all individuals. Some thinkers, therefore, have been inclined to exalt the majesty and sovereignty of the state to such a degree as to deify it, as the Roman emperors and oriental despots deified themselves—they identified their own will and power with the

divine. Commonly, Hegel is decried because he has allegedly deified the state. Although it is true that he expressed in some places
a view which can easily be misinterpreted in that direction, he
was never so foolish as to ignore the deep chasm between the authority and sovereignty of the state and those of God. The state,
according to his political philosophy, is the summit of the "objective spirit," but this spirit is the antithesis of the "subjective
spirit" of the individual; there is a synthesis called the "absolute
spirit" above this disjunction, and it is here that his system
reaches out to the concept of God as revealed in religion. Furthermore, Hegel was aware of the analogy between the state and
God and called the state the "earthly god," indicating that there
is a vast difference between the two, in spite of their similarity.

The analogy is instructive. As we shall see, the realm of religion is actually more akin to the political one than it is to that
of science or art. Both the state and God are, first of all, willing
and acting beings like the human self, though on a level on which
the opposite poles of humanity no longer contradict each other
but are reconciled to, and united with, each other. Both state and
God own "power, kingdom, and glory," although the state owns
them only in a limited, God in a limitless, way. The analogy and
yet dissimilarity of state and God sometimes generate awe mixed
with horror when the state is estimated—so when it is called "Le-
viathan" by Hobbes or "the coldest of all cold monsters" by
Nietzsche. The state is a monster precisely because it is not divine but in some respects resembles the divine. It disposes of the
individuals in an irresistible way; its power over them is un-
equaled "on earth"; and yet not only does the state have a limited
power, but its power is used for limited, and often abused for
devilish, ends.

The political realm of culture is limited because it corresponds
on the level of action and life with science and not with art. The
state is the product and the manifestation of an activity that has
its parallel in the subordination of the particular under the general, that is to say, in a method which transforms the extreme
polarities of the universal and the individual into intermediary
opposites which no longer possess the same contrariety but can
be brought together by rational means. The universal converted

into the general is less pretentious, less concrete, and less real; it is real, like a principle, an axiom, or a theory but not like the self that experiences itself. The particular, in its turn, is also less real, less immediate, and less total than is the individual; it can be logically subordinated to the general and thus reconciled to its opposite in a methodical way. In science and in politics we meet the same method of subordination, of rationality, and of a mediating synthesis.

The state, of course, is limited most obviously, as long as it is confined to a definite community and lacks the dimension of an all-embracing world-state. But, even if political wisdom succeeded in bringing about such an absolutely universal state, the principal limitation of the political realm would not be abolished even then. This limitation rests not so much upon the limited number of individuals united by the state or even upon the fact that most states as we know them are limited by the specific language and culture of the people organized in the state (the exceptions only confirm the rule) as upon the method in or through which the people are organized and united, the method of subordination. Even in those states in which neither a despot nor an absolute monarch reigns but "the people," the will of the state never represents the will of all individuals but that of a majority. The minority accommodates itself to the will of the majority, which is recognized as the will of "the people."

This principle of democratic constitutions cannot be improved; it inheres in the very limitation of the state itself, and it is therefore recognized as binding by all individuals, whether they belong to the majority or to the minority. It points to the inner boundary of political decision and action. The political will does not concern the full totality and concrete actuality of life but only aims and ends of a specific sort, namely, those which can be attained by the subordination of the individuals as particular citizens to the general will of the state. The will of the democratic state is not, as Rousseau was the first to see, the will of all (*volonté de tous*) but a general will (*volonté générale*), a somewhat abstract, formal, rational will creating a somewhat abstract, formal, and rational unification of all individuals. General principles, like the fundamental laws of the constitution, the

codes of jurisdiction, and the laws, decrees, and decisions resolved by the legislative body, determine the conduct of the
state. By these means certain regulations are laid down to be observed and carried out by the judiciary and the executive.

These principles, laws, and regulations are akin to those which
science investigates and discovers in nature, i.e., they are equally
general, abstract, and rational, so that they dominate wherever
they are applied, but without determining the concrete and individual in its full reality. As the facts of science are subject to the
laws and species only in so far as they are particular instances or
specimens, so the citizen likewise is subject to the laws and regulations only in so far as he is a citizen, i.e., as he represents the
type or the genus of a citizen in a particular fashion. Accordingly, it is not the individuals in the fulness of their reality who
are united with one another in the state, but they are united as
citizens only, in the way that facts are united by science as patterns only and not in their individual uniqueness. The political
community is, though not a mere administrative union, nevertheless not an inner relationship among the individuals; it does not
unify the souls and hearts but merely the intellect and the will
(I deliberately use the singular because it is the general intellect
and the general will living in the citizens which are implied). This
makes the state as "cold" as it appears to be. Of course, there are
occasions when the body politic seems to expand upon the totality of the citizens as concrete souls: during national festivals
or in the danger of war. Since the citizen as such does not exist
but is merely an abstract constituent of the full personality, this
concrete personality may in rare moments be aroused in the totality of his existence. Since it is active life and not contemplative
creativity only which is concerned in the sphere of politics, the
boundaries among the realms of this sphere are not so sharply
drawn as they are among the realms of the contemplative sphere.

In a similar way the political realm is separated from the moral
and religious one in a specific sense. As science establishes an
intermediate, intellectual department between the absolute, polar
oppositions, in order to subordinate the phenomena of nature
to the intellect, so also the state interpolates the department of
governing persons and governmental institutions between "the

people" as the manifoldness of individual persons and their absolute oneness, in order to subordinate the citizens to the intellectual will of the state. As science fails to penetrate the very substance of the natural entities and their individual relations, so also the state fails to penetrate the inwardness of the individual citizens and their relations. The state cannot command the will in its inner intentions and motivations, it can only direct the outer conduct and actions. As science is necessarily "legalistic," so is political power. Therefore, the judiciary is the most powerful weapon of the state in its relation to the citizens and even with respect to its own prerogative. Law and right are inseparably connected.

The state cannot hope to make its citizens morally good but only to make their conduct legally correct, i.e., to subordinate their actions to the law and to protect them against violence and outer injustice. Plato, in sketching his ideal state, did transgress the boundaries of the political sphere. He was prompted to do so because in antiquity the boundaries between the political or legal, the moral, and the religious domains were not yet distinct. The state combined all activities aiming at a community. The state was the only existing "ego-solution" of the contradictions of experience. Consequently, in his scheme the state took over what we would call the "duties and prerogatives" of the church. Indeed, his state was a church, as far as the idea of a church could be conceived by a pagan thinker. It is well known that Plato's idea, in turn, influenced the establishment of the Roman church through the mediating instrumentality of Augustine.

The state itself, as much as the citizen, is an abstract person and unreal, in so far as it is abstract. The state lacks the fulness of individuality; it certainly has no soul and no heart. It is a rational will and will power only. It is a general will, just as the intellect of the scientist is general. Of course, the difference between "world-solution" and "ego-solution" causes differences between science and state. Science is not a person like the state, not even in the abstract and rational sense in which the personality of the state exists. The state is an ego, precisely because the "ego-solution" demands that the product of cultural activity should be itself an ego—the common ego of those who are active—and that this common ego should be active in generating and regenerating itself through the activity of the individuals.

The state does not correspond to the scientist, but to nature as understood by the scientist, while the scientist himself corresponds to the statesman who devises the means by which the state is to be constructed and maintained. As the scientist is confined to the operation of the intellect supported by scientific experience, so the statesman is confined to the operation of the rational will supported by political experience. His personal, individual feelings and inclinations are as much to be eliminated as are those of the scientist. He has to subordinate his whole self to the general interests of the state, so that his private life often suffers from this sacrifice.[20]

As there is a scientific imagination, so there is also a legitimate political imagination; only the routine diplomat or the bureaucratic functionary of the state would dispense with it altogether. But, as scientific imagination has to be disciplined and, as it were, rationalized, so the imagination of the statesman has also to be trained and subjected to rational ideas which are feasible and advisable. Only an irresponsible leader of a state, like Hitler, indulges in merely individual and arbitrary fancy, thereby ruining the state and himself. It is the privilege of the artist to combine both his most individual imagination and the universal demands of his work and work-world. In the area of cultural action, only the prophet resembles the genius, but the prophet transcends, as we will see, the whole range of culture.

The state is limited, also, because it is closely connected with the lower realm of economics, as science is closely connected with that of technical purposes. Both science and politics serve the

20. In his novel *Anna Karenina*, Tolstoy depicts Anna's husband as a politician so completely devoted to his political task that his whole personality is absorbed by impersonal considerations and intentions. When Anna falls in love with Vronsky, he is alarmed: "For the first time he pictured vividly to himself her personal life, her ideas, her desires, and the idea that she could and should have a separate life of her own seemed to him so alarming that he made haste to dispel it. It was the chasm which he was afraid to peep into." Then he resorts to his conscience as an official of the state and deals with the affair and conduct of his wife as he is wont to deal with the affairs of the state and the duties of his office. The effect is, of course, tragic, and the gulf between himself as the statesman and the husband is at the bottom of the entire tragedy, which ends in disaster.

needs and wants of men, although this service does not constitute the real task and mission of their cultural activity. The state, even more than science, is bound up with the lower level because in the sphere of life the different realms are not so cut off from one another as they are in the sphere of contemplation. Although the real task of the state is the unification of individuals and not the satisfaction of their needs and wants, still the two aims can be separated only *in abstracto* but not in life. The state is the political organization of the community, i.e., not only of the persons but also of all the interests common to them. Among these interests the most vital ones are the economic.

The community is a living unit composed of beings who are not only spiritual selves but also organic bodies. The state has to protect and promote their physical welfare; this is the precondition of protecting and promoting their higher cultural needs and aspirations. Science can abstract from the lower interests and seek for pure truth on behalf of truth because science is, in principle, impersonal and objective. Politics, on the contrary, is, in principle, personal and subjective, serving the individuals by approaching the "ego-solution" of the antinomies of experience. Therefore, politics cannot be disentangled from economic necessities. Rudolf Stammler, a renowned German jurist and political scientist, has defended the thesis that law is related to economics as form is to matter.[21] I will not discuss here this interesting theory, but it seems to me that the whole task of the state (including legislation and jurisdiction and also the executive) is related to economic affairs as form to matter. The state cannot help considering incessantly the possibilities and necessities of economic life, if the higher goal of justice in the commonwealth is to be reached.

On the other hand, cultural activity hampers the extension of a political community, since it separates nation from nation, and this separation makes the political unification of all nations difficult. Since the highest realm of contemplative culture—the realm of art—depends upon the individual language and spirit, differences between different races and nations generate different cultures and cultural habits in life, and these differences produce many grave

---

21. *Wirtschaft und Recht nach der materialistischen Geschichtsauffassung: Eine sozialphilosophische Untersuchung* (Berlin: De Gruyter, 1896).

obstacles to a world-state. As long as such a state is not yet created, those differences, combined with economic needs and rivalries, lead necessarily to competition and eventually to hostility and war. War, of course, reveals in the most visible and the most terrible way the limitation of the state. The second form in which this limitation is revealed in political life is the counterpart of war within the state itself, revolution. Like war, revolution is the outcome of a tension between individuality and universality which has not been placated and pacified by the state.

Statism

WAR and revolution indicate not only the limit of the state but also the political way in which this limit is transgressed in order to reconcile the polarities of experience which are unreconciled in the existing political form. War tries to settle the competition and hostility between nations; since the mode of settlement is political, the remedy cannot be of lasting success. Revolution tries to eliminate existing injustice or conditions felt as unjust by a stratum of the people, majority or minority; since the result is a new political arrangement, this arrangement might again produce malcontents who might wish to overthrow it in order to generate a more satisfying one; but no war and no revolution can change the fundamental limitations of the whole political region, simply because they are themselves political measures.

War might aim at a state which would ultimately comprise all nations—the whole world. All so-called "imperialistic" wars, indeed, are intended to solve the problem of competition in that way. The Roman Empire was the most impressive result of such an attempt; it united the whole civilized world around the Mediterranean and the Atlantic and settled for many centuries the problem of a world-state. The British Commonwealth is another great attempt in a widened geographical scope. A British Commonwealth combined with the United States might be the solution of tomorrow. But none of all these attempts can ever hope to remedy the evil absolutely because it is rooted in the very nature of the political form of reconciliation, which is limited in principle.

Revolutions in modern times have been partly motivated by

ideologies geared for the overthrow not only of a particular state-constitution but of the state-form altogether. So-called "anarchism" is an outcome of the limit of the state; the anarchists believe in a stateless state—a contradiction in terms. They believe that people can live together peacefully without being coerced by law and police. This belief is of either a religious or a utopian character. If it is religious, its political expression and action are inadequate and doomed to fail; if it is utopian, it transgresses the limits of the possible and, accordingly, must have devastating consequences, since politics is the field of the possible. Utopianism best illuminates the limit of the political reconciliation. It points to the necessity of a higher realm in which the politically irreconciled polarities of experience would be reconciled on a new level, but it commits the error of arguing that the state should be abolished because of its limitations and that the higher level of a religious reconciliation should be anticipated in a political and also super-political fashion. Utopianism is the expression of a confusion originating from the disrespect for the specific form and limit of the political realm. And this confusion, in turn, is the consequence of a lack of religious faith, which alone is the adequate response to the inadequacy of the state. For religious faith is the one legitimate form of utopianism because it is faith in an ultimate reconciliation which cannot be obtained by political or, indeed, by any cultural (i.e., human) activity or aspiration.

Anarchism is a kind of utopianism, and utopianism is a kind of anarchism; both have the same source and seek for the same kind of solution. Both are right as to the motivation of their creed and action; both are wrong as to the means and ends by which they try to reach their goal.

While anarchism and utopianism accept the possibility of the politically impossible, statism tends to enlarge the prerogatives and activities of the state, so that it swallows up and replaces all initiative of the individuals. This represents another attempt to disregard the limit of the state, resembling scientism and aestheticism in their respective regions. Statism presumes to extend the limit of the state so that all civilization would turn political, and the political solution would include all other solutions of the basic contradictions and would consummate them all. The term "totalitarianism" is therefore completely correct. The totalitarian state pretends to be the real source of scientific truth, of artistic perfection, of technical and economic devices and planning, and, finally, of moral and religious education and guidance. All these different branches of human activity and faith are unified and completed in the enormous scope of the totalitarian state, according to those who believe in that state. One can understand the fanaticism and ambition of those believers, since they have staked everything on the state, for better or for worse. The totalitarian state resembles, in this respect, the Roman church and those ancient despotisms in which the monarch was supposed to be the deity and in which all civilization was concentrated in his hands. It was characteristic that Stalin on his seventieth birthday was celebrated as the greatest scientist, engineer, artist, economist, and militarist as well as being almost divine.

There is one important difference among the kinds of "imperialism" in the different realms of culture: the contemplative realms, according to their limits, cannot even pretend to embrace all the realms of culture. They pretend only to solve their respective tasks to such a degree as to satisfy the human heart and intellect completely by settling absolutely the contradictions of experience. The "world-solution" offered for this purpose cannot, however, replace the "ego-solution"; man can never be coerced into accepting scientism or aestheticism as religions; such a coercion would contradict the very principles on which science and art are built. The "ego-solution," on the other hand, definitely embraces the "world-solution," because it is the ego that works in the contemplative sphere and seeks self-reconciliation or because all culture finally aims at a solution which would pacify the human heart, torn by the tensions and splits originating from experience. And the state can coerce people to believe in its totalitarian power, or—more correctly—the totalitarian state can and does apply coercive devices in order to evoke belief in its power from the soul of every citizen.

In a way, every state embraces all the activities and aspirations of its citizens, since the state is not a work but an institution uniting individuals. The state—every state—does promote the sciences and the arts, religion and morality (with more or less success, according to the spirit in which the state itself is governed or governs itself). Science does not include the other branches of culture, nor does art include them; but the state, as the organized community of its members, does include their entire cultural activity as part and parcel of its own activity. However, the state which respects the natural and logical limit of its power does not presume to be itself the author of science and art or to be able to produce scientific truth and artistic perfection. Unfortunately, the wisdom of political self-restraint is as rare as is humility, and the temptation to expand the range of the state is greater, the lower the level of religious insight and devotion. Only after having lost her ancient faith could Germany be conquered by totalitarianism.

German naziism was a curious mixture of aestheticism, scientism, and statism, made efficient by modern technology. It was the opponent, but also the heir, of historical materialism, and it was also the heir of German romanticism—the two most powerful, but antagonistic, currents of nineteenth-century thought or feeling. It was, like Nietzsche's pseudo-philosophy, a materialistic romanticism or a romantic materialism—a perverse monster. Therefore, every utterance and every action of the Nazis was necessarily ambiguous and led to deceit, but it was difficult to say who was more deceived, the deceiver or those who accepted the deception.

Russian communism stood godfather at the birth of this monster. This form of statism is not so perverse as naziism; a certain trend of utopianism gives it an idealistic tinge, and the lack of romanticism gives it a political seriousness and efficacy. Nevertheless, the arrogance and the megalomania of statism are also immanent in communism, and therefore the same or even greater dangers arise out of it for the culture of Russia and for the security of the world beyond Russia. The Communists are convinced that their ideology is scientifically grounded and sound; but they understand by "science" the pseudo-science of historical materialism. This creed makes the confusion of economics and social politics a principle because its adherents believe at bottom in one cultural realm only: economic power. This statism is therefore based upon an all-embracing economicism, which is the real tyrant not only of those Russians who are enslaved under its regime but even of the enslavers themselves, who are the victims of their own dogmatic creed.

CHAPTER V

Morality

State and Morality

POLITICAL life and moral life are intimately connected with each other, although it is not easy to say exactly in what way. As the Nazi state illustrates, politics can be extremely wicked and destitute of moral conscience. The law and the judiciary can be used by a profligate state leader for his vicious purposes; diplomacy is notoriously the art of concealing one's thoughts and of expressing canny and polite lies. "Might is right" is a melancholy reminder of political history. Even though Machiavelli was a cynic, still there is much truth in what he recommends; and many a statesman denied this truth, only to practice it the more recklessly, as, for instance, Frederick the Great. It is sometimes difficult indeed to distinguish rigorously and effectively between a state and a well-organized and disciplined gang of robbers. On the other hand, the greatest philosophers—men like Plato, Aristotle, Kant, and Hegel—have insisted that the state is a moral institution, and Hegel even believed that the state is the culmination of the moral sphere. To be sure, all these thinkers distinguished the existing states from the ideal state, and they expressed their view or vision of the state not as it is in history but as it ought to be, or as it is according to its true idea.

In fact, all existing states are both immoral and moral, admixtures of ideal communities, pursuing moral ends and organized according to moral rules, and robber societies, founded by selfish men who submit to a common rule and a common ruler only in order to save their property and pursue their "happiness," a vague word which may or may not have a moral connotation, according to individual opinions and desires. But even in a robber society certain virtues are afforded, a certain code of rules is to be observed, so that at least the appearance of moral conduct is not absent. Of course, the ultimate end of the robber company prevents each member from having a good conscience, even if he adheres to the rules and acts in agreement with them, supposing that he knows and understands that end. Morality is not an outer form of action but an inner motivation; it concerns the spirit and the mind of the will or, we may say, the heart of a man, rather than his behavior isolated from his heart. In so far as the state cannot reach this inner center of man but merely directs his outer actions, the political and juridical dominion is not in itself of moral character.

However, this statement must not be exaggerated; Kant and Fichte, especially the latter, were inclined to separate the legal and the moral principles too rigorously. Fichte went so far as to assert that the state should be so ordered that it would function even if its citizens were devils. Indeed, the state of Satan in Milton's poem does operate well, and so did the Nazi state, if the outer order and efficacy, in a military sense, are made the criteria of order. This overemphasis upon legal and military order prompted Hegel to fall into the other extreme and to conceive of the state as the highest manifestation of morality, the synthesis of the outer —legal—and the inner—ethical—order. What is the truth?

I think it lies between those extremes. As we are not permitted to learn from scientific errors and illusions what science is or what the goal of scientific knowledge is, so also in the case of politics we must turn to the best state, in order to ascertain what the state and its goal are. Astrology and alchemy are sciences only as to their outer form and appearance but not as to their substance and truth; they can be compared with the satanic empire in Milton's poem or with Hitler's caricature of a state. Culture on all its levels and in all its spheres is always threatened by demonic misuse of its forms and methods, but this fact does not deprive it of its real meaning and significance. The state at its best is not severed from morality but rather is based upon it and has an ethical character in all its manifestations. On the other hand, this character is not, as Hegel teaches, absolute. On the contrary, it suffers from the innate and essential limit of the state as discussed in a previous chapter.

Since morality is the very center of man, it is necessary to, and, indeed, operative in, all cultural activity. The scientist, as much as the engineer or the artist, is not only an intellectual or spiritual worker and creator but also a moral being; he is a moral being first, and only secondarily a scientist. To be a scientist requires an "intellectual conscience," as Nietzsche puts it; to be an artist requires an aesthetic conscience. Without the operation of the conscientious will, no work, no creation of any worth, is possible. This relation shows again the primacy of the ego and of man's active life in all realms of civilization. Morality is nowhere absent from human existence; on the contrary, it is the very heart of this existence. Reality is of moral essence. Morality is the substance and the basis of culture throughout.

As science and art presuppose conscientious workers, so, and even more so, does the state. Since the state is not a work but a living institution, it is even more deeply rooted in the conscience of man. The antinomies of experience cannot be solved if the individual does not dedicate himself to this task. To dedicate one's self to a task is the very nerve of morality. Morality, therefore, is rooted in experience. It is rooted in selfhood. To be a self is to be a moral self because a self is a self only inasmuch as it makes itself a self, and this task is the supreme moral end. To be a self presupposes at least a minimum of loyalty, of permanence in striving and willing, of endurance and steadfastness, of consistency in acting and doing. All these virtues are therefore metaphysical as well as moral; indeed, the root of morality is metaphysical, just because it is to be found in original experience and in the self as self.

In the realms of contemplative activity the self dedicates itself completely to the creation of the work; to fulfil this task is the sole virtue of the worker and creator, in so far as he is this and nothing else. But he is always more than this. He is always also a fellow-man (even as a worker he is a fellow-worker), and as such he is morally obliged to dedicate himself not only to the task of his profession but also to that of building up a good and just community, of which he is a member, whether he likes it or not. For this reason, morality unfolds in the sphere of action and only there gains its true and full meaning and significance. The scientist or the artist may be great in his own field but poor and miserable in life. He may know how to compose, how to sing, how to paint or to write poetry, and yet he may not know how to live, how to be a friend or a neighbor, a son or a husband, a citizen or a diplomat.

The state cannot be a good state if its citizens and its statesmen, its judges and its administrators, are not conscientious. Morality is thus the most solid pillar of the state. If morality is low or declining, the state is in imminent danger and may collapse at any time, as the German state collapsed in 1933.[1] Although it is true that the state cannot control the heart, nonetheless the heart controls the state; and the soundness and vigor of the state depend upon the degree of honesty and fairness alive in those who are at the helm and in all citizens alike.

What Is Morality?

THE discussion in the last chapter circled around the problem of morality without directly attacking it. Of course, this sketch of a system cannot deal with the ethical problem as ethics must do. I must confine myself to the basic problem of the nature of morality seen from the perspective of the philosophy of culture and faith. Is morality itself a cultural activity? Is its realm to be regarded as belonging to the political field in its wider range? This was the position of Hegel. The preceding discussion has already rejected this claim. Although the state needs morality on the part of its officers and citizens and although the end of political striving is in line with the moral end of building up a good community in which the manifoldness of the individuals is united in the one ego, the particular form of this unification in the state is not morally satisfying. Morality points, obviously, to an end which transcends the limit of the state because it concerns the inner motivation, the character, and the heart of man.

Not only does morality transcend the boundaries of the state, but it transcends the boundaries of culture altogether, if we un-

1. Former Reichskanzler Brüning told me, when I came to the United States, that he had found himself unable to govern because he could no longer trust the character, honesty, and integrity of those who surrounded him, before the Nazis came to power.

derstand by "culture" an activity that produces special works or special institutions. We may say that culture in this sense is historically real, while morality has its domain in the secrecy of private life, in an inner realm which does not appear in the outer world and does not manifest itself in a visible way. To be sure, the institution also is not so visible as is the work of art or the result of scientific investigation, but nevertheless the state has an outer reality; its regulations are published; its officers, its judges, and its administrators appear in public as representatives of the state; and its documents, its symbols, and its weapons are visible signs of its powerful reality.

Morality has no such reality; it cannot be directly seen; it has no insignia or symbols, no documentary witness, no weapon that could defend the moral person in this world; it has no cultural realm of its own. It is indispensable in all realms; it is the real strength of man in all the directions of his creative activity and action; but, even so (or perhaps just on account of this?), it has no special place within the system of civilization. It does not belong to the public and historical scene of life, although it might be felt by the public and recognized publicly. There is no cultural branch called "morality," although there is no culture at all without this secret and private exertion of the innermost will. All cultural aspiration is also moral aspiration, all cultural achievement is also moral achievement. But, in spite of this most intimate and indispensable function of morality within civilization, morality itself does not result in any special cultural effect. In so far as there is any cultural effect of moral exertion and operation, it is itself hidden, and, according to biblical wisdom, God alone sees into the heart. Even the doer himself can never be sure to what degree his motives are or are not pure in the moral sense.

Cultural activity in creating works and institutions produces, as it were, a world within the world, a second world, a world of culture, which differs from the first or natural world in that it is meaningful because it is the effect of man's purpose and mind. This meaningful world is nevertheless a world like the natural universe, in that it has an existence of its own, apart from the inner will of man, though dependent upon that will and, in the sphere of action and institutional life, even partly overlapping the private

exertion and action of individuals. Man lives not only within the
visible universe but also within this meaningful world of culture,
which is the object of historical investigation and description.
Over against that world, man is an ego, a private person, a secret
self, an invisible soul, a striving will; and in this inner sanctuary
his morality operates.

To summarize: a new contrast between ego and world ensues
from the contrast between culture and morality. Man expresses
himself more deeply in morality than he expresses himself in culture because in morality he does not objectify himself but works
upon himself alone; he is concerned with himself, he is the target
of his exertion and action, and he remains an ego, or rather he becomes an ego in a deeper sense, after having exerted himself, than
he was before. The "inner" function and significance of morality
means exactly this: that the self does not objectify itself, that it
does not construct a "world" out of itself as it does in culture, but
remains within itself, "civilizing" only itself. A German poet
(Storm) has written:

> Der eine fragt: was kommt danach?
> Der andre: ist es recht?
> Und also unterscheidet sich
> Der Freie von dem Knecht.[2]

The "free" man does not depend upon the world, the fettered
man does.

Morality is this inner exertion and operation of the self upon
the self, whereby the self is integrated and developed. But, then,
is not morality a very egotistic and selfish thing? This would be
the case only if that inner exertion were without relation to the
supreme goal of civilization—if the moral person were not concerned with the end of the good community. But the truth is that
the moral person is just as much concerned with that supreme end
as he is with himself; that he acts upon himself only in order to
promote the good society; that in working upon himself he tries to
make himself an instrument for this highest goal of civilization.
Civilization is not its own end after all; its end transcends all
its works and all its institutions—indeed, all its results. But the ego

2. "One man asks: 'What will result from my action?' The other man asks:
'Is it right what I am doing?' This difference reveals who is free and who is
a slave."

is included in that end, since it is the self-contradiction of the ego which motivates all cultural action and which is to be overcome by this action.

In and through morality man strives to reconcile the individual and the universal ego within himself, within his own ego. It would be most foolish to call such an enterprise and exertion "selfish." Yes, it is selfish in a sense, namely, in that sublime, ethical sense in which each of us has to be selfish so that his self may be the center of his existence and of his world—the center of his character, the representative of his moral worth. Without the self, man is indistinguishable from the beast; he is no subject in contrast to objects; he is not man. Therefore, it is his duty to build up this self, to care for it and defend it against attack from without and from within. In that sense man has to be "selfish" indeed. This self is identical with his moral substance and core.

This moral self, this innermost and most secret self, is the seat of moral freedom and moral eternity. Man cannot be free without pursuing the task of reconciling what is individual and what is universal in him; he cannot attain eternity without subordinating the temporal in himself and in the world to the eternal center of himself. Only moral strength enables man to free himself from the pressure of temptations, be the tempter outside the self or inside; only moral courage and endurance can free man from that fear and anxiety originating from his inner conflict and self-contradiction, which is intrinsic to his self as he experiences it.

In this wider sense, morality does belong to civilization and is ever its core. It also belongs to civilization in so far as it is man himself who has to civilize himself in the moral direction or in so far as morality is a secular exertion and springs from secular experience. It is true that morality is incomplete and insufficient as long as it relies upon itself alone; but, even so, it is morality precisely in so far as man does rely upon himself and does work upon himself out of his own resources.

Conscience, Law, and Guilt

THE state coerces its citizens to comply with the law; police and military power are essential in the political sphere. Morality does not coerce man to comply with its own law, except by one very powerful inner weapon—a bad conscience. The word "conscience" indicates the inwardness of its power; man is together with himself, and he is conscious of himself and of his own motives if he is plagued by remorse. Indeed, the tribunal and the penalty of morality live within the human consciousness itself. Man is split before this tribunal into the judge and the perpetrator; the judge represents his universal, the perpetrator his individual, ego. The split between them indicates that man has failed in his exertion to unify himself and to resolve the self-contradiction arising out of his self-experience.

The wondrous power of conscience (not articulated in pagan language because the inwardness of the Christian consciousness was still absent) confronts the self with itself; where the public, the outer, the cutural, world ends, there the private, the inner, the moral, ego begins and unfolds its silent, but extremely loud and intensive, voice. Conscience is the place where the two selves, which are at bottom one and the same self, meet and act upon each other. A struggle arises from this encounter, for it is the very existence of the self which is at stake. The first philosopher who saw the tremendous power and the momentous significance of this struggle and its outcome was Socrates. It was a Greek form of biblical wisdom which appeared in him among the wise men of his nation. Plato, who was still under the immediate influence of his great teacher when he wrote his first dialogues, renders this discovery in the following way: "When the soul descries herself in herself, she passes there into the realm of the pure and the eternal and the immortal and the unchangeable, and since she is akin to this, she ceases to err. . . . Is this not the state of the soul which we call wisdom?"[3]

Plato, far more than Aristotle, was aware that morality rests upon the inner conversation of the soul with the soul and that

3. *Phaedo* 79.

philosophy is the continuation of this conversation. Plato was therefore much nearer to biblical faith than was Aristotle—a fact well known and appreciated by the first Christian theologians and philosophers and forgotten or ignored only by the Aristotelian Christian thinkers of the thirteenth century.

Conscience is the inner voice of morality; it pleads for the universal ego in its struggle with the merely individual ego that would like to revolt against it; it pleads thus for the reconciliation of the two ego-aspects by means of a subordination of the individual to the universal one. Since the two aspects or perspectives are not united from the outset but, on the contrary, are separated and therefore sometimes in controversy with each other, morality strives after the unification of the self with itself and with the community of all selves. Since this community does not exist as a moral society but only as a society of individuals each of whom has in his conscience the norm and goal of the ideal community,[4] morality announces itself in the form of an inner legislation, commonly called the "moral law." Conscience is simply the reflex of that law.

Some moral philosophers hold that Kant's doctrine of the Categorical Imperative exaggerates the rigorism and formality of the moral law. There is some truth in such a view, I believe. But more important than the debate concerning this character of Kant's ethical philosophy is his discovery that morality consists in the consciousness of a law which is neither identical with any conventional or habitual attitude nor motivated by any consideration of expediency or profit (not even of "the greatest happiness of the greatest number of people"), but which commands unconditionally.[5] This great insight was a philosophical transposition of biblical ethics based upon the commandment of God. Its merit rests upon the demonstration that the character of an inner command is inseparably connected with the moral consciousness. Indeed, he who denies this interconnection does not understand himself and his moral consciousness and conscience. Responsibility, moral approval or disapproval, striving and exertion, conflict and deci-

4. Cf. Reinhold Niebuhr, *Moral Man and Immoral Society*.
5. Cf. H. J. Paton, *The Categorical Imperative* (Chicago: University of Chicago Press, 1948), pp. 58 ff.

sion—all these instances of moral life point to the same conclusion: that this life consists in finding out what I ought to do and in obeying or disobeying my conscience or the inner voice of the moral law.

The Greeks had great difficulty in expounding the nature of guilt because they did not see or admit the commanding character of the moral law and the freedom of obedience or disobedience in facing this command. They interpreted disobedience as an error of the intellect in determining what is good for the doer; they did not recognize (at least in their philosophical reflections) the revolt against the law on the part of the individual will. This revolt makes it perfectly clear that the ego is split within itself and that the original self-contradiction of the two-sided ego is only aggravated and, indeed, repeated by the repudiation of the moral command. Only an absolutely unified ego, not split into individual and universal aspects of the will—only an ego that is no longer human but divine—can live a moral life without the consciousness of a law that commands what one ought to do in contrast to what one would like to do if one were nothing but an individual will. Whether such an absolutely unified ego can still be called "moral" may be questionable and will be discussed later.

The momentous gravity of the moral law which prompted Kant to speak of it as being "holy," thus inadvertently admitting that he touched upon the religious realm in describing the unconditional character of the law (without, however, admitting it consciously and in principle, as Socrates had done), originates from its metaphysical significance. What the moral law commands is not derived from any "empirical" wish or need or opportunity, not even the welfare of mankind (since it is better that mankind perish than that the law be disregarded). Rather it aims at the solution of the fundamental contradiction inherent in experience. Morality offers (or commands) an "ego-solution" more satisfying and substantial than the political (and juridical) one because it aims at a community which is more inwardly united and at peace than the body politic can ever be. While civil law regulates the outer region of action, the moral law regulates the inner region of decision, thus operating nearer to the source of friction and strife

between the individuals or (what is the same thing) between the
two opposite aspects of the individual self.

The term "integrity," which expresses the moral goodness of
the person, points to the aim of morality—the self-integration of
the divided person. To the degree to which the person attains integration, to that degree he attains integrity, i.e., "wholeness" of
his ego, completion of the moral exertion. But this completion can
never be absolutely accomplished by any human being. Man is always on the way; he never reaches the goal by his own exertion
and action. The most obvious illustration of this deficiency is
guilt. No man is free from guilt of some kind and weight. As man,
he cannot avoid guilt because guilt is the outer manifestation of
the inner split and self-contradiction belonging to the very nature
of self-experience. Although morality is a more inward and therefore more intensive and more effective form of an "ego-solution,"
still it is defective because guilt is unavoidable.

Personal and private guilt is like error in the field of science;
like imperfection in that of artistic creation; like shortcomings in
legislation, jurisdiction, and administration; like crime against the
cvil law, but infinitely more momentous and grievous than all
these failures and frailties of human activity. Here the innermost
substance of the self is violated or, rather, violates itself. Here the
same ego that feels the antinomies of experience as the source of all
sorrows and conflicts of human life contributes voluntarily to
this very source and aggravates its darkness. Here the same ego
which commands itself to subordinate the merely individual and
antiuniversal tendencies of the impulses and the will to the universal law subordinates, in strict opposition to the law, its own
universality to its individual arbitrariness and lawlessness. Here
the same ego which strives with all its strength after its integration
wilfully disintegrates itself.

This astounding and alarming phenomenon clearly shows that
human effort to fight the antinomies of existence is limited. As
long as guilt strains man, he cannot hope to release and redeem
himself. But guilt is not an abnormal deviation from the path that
man treads. It belongs to the normal way of life, it characterizes
man as man and is part and parcel of his moral destiny, as all the

dramas and epics of all nations in all epochs of history disclose.
Man is man and not divine, because he incurs guilt:

> Ihr stosst ins Leben uns hinein,
> Ihr lasst den Armen schuldig werden
> Dann überlasst Ihr ihn der Pein,
> Denn alle Schuld racht sich auf Erden.[6]

So sings Goethe, not in a Christian, but in a pagan, mood.

The phenomenon of guilt demonstrates that morality does not succeed in reconciling ego and world by means of an "ego-solution." By succumbing to temptations, by yielding to merely individual incentives and impulses, man allows himself to be defeated by the world, be it the world of outer, physical elements which threaten or induce him; be it the world of inner, emotional motives; or be it the world of cultural works or institutions which persuade him to violate his conscience. In all cases he sacrifices the freedom of his decision, his very selfhood, to the compulsion or constraint of energies outside his own center. He also fails to reconcile his temporality with his eternity, for guilt always involves some form of abandoning the virtues which profess the victory of eternity over time; he permits transitory and fleeting motives to prevail over loyalty, endurance, consistency, and constancy.

The Limit of Morality

THE phenomenon of guilt and moral frailty lays bare the full limitation of the moral reach. Although morality is a more satisfying way of reconciling the opposites of the ego within the ego, and thus the opposites of ego and world, than is the reconciliation brought about by the state in its legislative, administrative, and judicial performance, it still belongs to the way of subordination. Although the law of conscience does not command from outside the human self but rather is its own indigenous command, still it presupposes and establishes two sides within the ego—one legislative, administrative, and judicial; the other subject to the

6. "You [gods] thrust us into life, you let the helpless become guilty, then you leave him to misery, for all guilt is punished on earth."

authority and sovereignty of the former, as the citizen is subject to the authority and sovereignty of the state. Morality still operates like the state on the lower level of active civilization, as does science in the sphere of contemplation. Morality, in spite of its high rank and central position within the system of culture, still does not correspond with art; its method is not that of co-ordination and fusion but that of subordination, so that the polarities of experience are not unified in their polar opposition except by intermediary stages. The very term "law," equally characteristic of science, politics, and morality, betrays the similarity of the methods of dealing with the antinomies in all these regions.

As in science and the state, so also in morality the ego is never at the end of its striving and doing. It never reaches its goal, as the masterpiece does. It never truly reconciles the opposites. Guilt is only the most obvious manifestation of this deeper deficiency. There are other manifestations. Morality by no means accomplishes what is missing in institutional action; it does not finish what is begun in the state, as art finishes (in a way) what is begun in science. Legality and morality supplement each other; both are one-sided, since what characterizes the one is missing in the other (this is the reason why Hegel thought it necessary and possible to unite them in one highest ethical realm which he conceived as "state" in the ideal sense; it is his greatest blunder, however, since the state is never "ideal" but always, and by its very nature, confined to an ever imperfect, ever growing or decaying, status—a fact that he recognized in his philosophy of history but did not sufficiently consider in his concept of the ideal state).

The state is the region of outer legislation and action; morality is the region of inner legislation and action. The two supplement each other without producing one great whole which would fully reconcile them. In part they do produce a whole, but in part they separate and may even contradict each other, as the phenomenon of the "conscientious" objector shows and as all revolutions and wars illustrate. In a totalitarian state it may be morally meritorious to defy the laws, as it may be morally blameworthy or outright wicked to obey them. On the other hand, although the glory and triumph of morality consist just in its inwardness and invisibility (in its "weakness" as seen from the point of view of physical and political strength and power), this confinement to the inner realm of the person is also a real weakness, since it points to the unfinished and deficient status of human society.

As it would be an achievement to create a state in which shortcomings and crimes would no longer occur, so that no police and no courts would have to exist to apply means of coercion; as it would be an achievement, indeed, to create such a world society that wars would no longer be waged, armies no longer be necessary; and as it would be the most desirable and the most moral status if in this way politics became completely moral, so also it would be desirable to make morality efficient in an outer form— to blend it with the state. Utopian ideals of all sorts, anarchistic or socialistic or technical, as well as the oft repeated constructions of ideal states (by Plato, Augustine, Hegel), disclose that such a fusion of the political and the moral would make both perfect and would settle their disputes and remove their one-sidedness.

The "ego-solution" would be complete and absolute only if it were neither one-sidedly an outer arrangement, belonging to the cultural and historical world, nor one-sidedly an inner self-regulation of the individual ego, but a combination of the two. For man is both soul and body and he acts by an inner and an outer manifestation of his will. The manifoldness of persons is preconditioned by their spatial and temporal separation or by their living in a world of space and time. The division of the self into a worldly and an ego-aspect cannot be overcome until both are harmoniously united and reconciled to each other; only thus can world and ego be brought into harmony and all the tensions which cultural and moral activity try to solve be perfectly eliminated. Morality alone cannot accomplish this task.

Morality does not co-ordinate the extremes of experience. The commanding ego is not an all-embracing universal will which would include all the individual selves within itself; rather, it is a relatively abstract, general, and rational will, like that of the state, though inward in nature. Such a will sets forth principles, rules, and maxims of conduct and manifests itself in the form of an inner code; such a will commands and demands obedience and submission on the part of the individual will. Morality, after all, does not truly and fully outshine legality; on the contrary, it is a kind of inner legality. It interpolates between the uttermost poles of universality and individuality the contrast of moral reason and natural desire, impulse and passion; and it subordinates the vast individual and ever changing plurality of the "inclinations" (Kant) to the identical, permanent, and inflexible order of reason. Such a subordination is possible only at the expense of the individual for the benefit of the general, whereby the individual is transformed into the particular and regarded as an example of the general principle.

In this way the moral law falls short of a full recognition of individual motives. The situation is never rational and can never be completely analyzed in such a way that the moral law would be applicable. The law always mishandles the person somehow because it always mishandles the situation somehow. (This is the truth of psychoanalytical theory.) A judge who could see into the heart would discover the distance between the general rules and the ever individual motivations and would therefore no longer subject the latter, as particular instances, to the rules. On the contrary, he would understand the absolute and unique individuality of the person and of the situation; he would feel the incongruity between temptation and resistance power in the individual; and he would therefore be moved by mercy. He would consequently warn the jury not to "judge," but to be merciful; not to condemn, but to forgive. (He alone, however, and not the psychoanalyst, is allowed to warn in that way.)

The inner conflict is another symptom of the insufficiency of the moral solution. In many cases antagonistic commands or sets of maxims meet one another in the heart, and the will is hard pressed by both. A right decision is certainly not always possible, because reason cannot weigh the exact difference of urgency or of importance between them. Thus conscience cannot evade a choice which leads to self-accusation and self-condemnation. There is a moral ambiguity in the soul.[7]

7. This has been forcefully expressed by Simone de Beauvoir in her book *L'Éthique d'ambiguïté;* however, the author mistakes the ambiguity of moral decisions when she asserts that this ambiguity can be made a moral principle itself, instead of admitting that it indicates the limitation of morality altogether. Although moral decisions may always be ambiguous, even so, ambiguity cannot be made the principle of ethics and so be regarded as the supreme moral principle.

Morality is limited also with respect to the criterion and the validity (or sanctity) of its principles and commands. The form is general and does not allow of exceptions; but the content varies from epoch to epoch, from nation to nation, from culture to culture; and the individual conscience is by no means infallible. Precisely because of the disparity between the individual situation and the general law, uncertainty and confusion may easily arise, so that the will may find itself without any guiding light.[8] Then the appeal to a hidden legislator who is more than a legislator because he embraces the full totality of the actual situation can alone free the moral person from his anxiety and perplexity. But morality does not provide for such an appeal. This again is its limit.

Moralism

"MORAL action is that great and only experiment in which all riddles of the most manifold appearances explain themselves," says the poet Wordsworth.[9] The temptation to regard morality as the one and only source from which we can learn ultimate truth is greater than the temptation of scientism, aestheticism, and statism, since morality is the innermost center of the human consciousness and since experience in the secular sense does not grant any vista beyond the horizon of morality. The most profound thinkers have had recourse to the moral consciousness as the ultimate position that man can reach. If I abstract from the founders of the world-religions those who were also rooted in moral experience but interpreted it in the context of religious experience, the most outstanding names are Socrates and Kant,

8. In Tolstoy's *Anna Karenina* a passage lucidly narrates such an impasse in the life of Vronsky, Anna's lover. I cannot refrain from quoting it in full: "Vronsky's life was particularly happy in that he had a code of principles which defined with unfailing certitude what he ought and what he ought not to do. This code of principles covered only a very small circle of contingencies, but then the principles were never doubtful and Vronsky, as he never went outside that circle, had never had a moment's hesitation about doing what he ought to do. . . . Only quite lately in regard to his relations with Anna, Vronsky had begun to feel that his code of principles did not fully cover all possible contingencies, and to foresee in the future difficulties and perplexities for which he could find no guiding clue. . . . Of late new inner relations had arisen between him and her which frightened Vronsky by their indefiniteness."

9. Quoted by W. R. Inge in *The Platonic Tradition in English Religious Thought* (1936), p. 71.

both of whom believed in moral reason as the supreme light of the supreme knowledge, as the only guide in the darkness of human existence. Both were convinced that moral reason alone can show the direction not only of the path that man has to choose in life but also of the road that leads to philosophic truth. Both believed in the "primacy of pure practical reason," although this phrase is Kant's.

Indeed, morality is best entitled to give us the clue to the understanding of man's self and of his cultural aspirations, since morality is, as it were, omnipresent in human life and productivity; since it is the ultimate root and the ultimate goal of all human activities, the purpose of all man's purposes, the end of all his ends, and the path to his own self-integration. Culture culminates in this aspiration; it reaches its zenith in the moral achievement which embraces and unites them all. If there is any land beyond the border of morality, it can no longer be conquered by man's own activity and self-civilization. It would presuppose morality as the highest level that man can reach by his own effort, but it would finish what is unfinished in that realm. Religion claims to perform this task. Of all religions, that of the Bible especially makes this claim; but even the most primitive religions are concerned with conduct, oblige man to do or to omit certain acts, and try to unite the believers in the most intimate, most ultimate, and most obligatory way.

Moralism claims that morality itself is sufficient; that it opens all the doors to religious truth or even grants this truth itself; that nothing is needed beyond moral reason and insight. Moralism, in other words, disregards the limitation of morality in pretty much the same way as that in which scientism disregards that of science, aestheticism that of art, and statism that of the state. Of course, there is a vast difference between the kinds and degrees of this disregard. Even the most outspoken and resolute moralist would not deny that there is something outside the moral ken which transcends human knowledge. Socrates, as well as Kant, emphasized this barrier of human knowledge and insisted only that within the scope of humanity the moral consciousness is ultimate and that religion can be true only in so far and inasmuch as it agrees with the principles of moral reason and insight. Kant, however, in his last writings was convinced that the moral law

and moral knowledge alone really matter in man's life and that
even his faith should be reduced to the conditions of his morality;
that the only true religion is the "religion within the boundaries
of reason alone," wherein he understands, by "reason," moral
reason.

Apart from political reasons, which certainly were very strong,
the execution of Socrates can be interpreted as a result of his
failure to recognize the limit of morality and reason. He certainly did not want to "introduce new gods," as the indictment
runs, but he did believe that the moral guide within his breast
was the highest judge of his deeds and that man by reason can
find out the will of the gods. The judges probably scented this
trend of moralism in their greatest compatriot and feared it
would spread; they feared that the established religion might
be harmed by this trend or that the initial disintegration of this
religion might be promoted and not cured, as Socrates himself
believed. The vast difference between the moralistic attitude of
Socrates and the philosophic interpretation and dissolution of the
Christian faith by Kant is, of course, this: that Greek religion
needed the moral uplift and transformation which the philosopher instilled into it, while the Christian faith is the very root of
Kant's moral philosophy.

The most conspicuous and fateful example of moralism is the
attitude and faith of the Pharisees—the immediate negative condition of the "protest" of Jesus and of the rise of the new faith
based upon him. Pharisaism believes in the necessity of ritual and
ceremonial observances as the indispensable and sufficient precondition of man's salvation. There is a religious meaning and
content in this faith, but there is also a typically moralistic taint
in it: the conviction that certain acts which man can, and ought,
to perform are able to bring about that absolute self-integration
and justification which is at the root of the idea of salvation; that
by sheer moral strength the basic deficiency of man's moral capacity can be eliminated; and that man in this way can redeem
himself—can finish the task of his self-civilization. Paul makes no
distinction between the ceremonial and the moral law in this respect; and this distinction, momentous though it is, nevertheless
is of no importance when the moralistic trend within Pharisaism

is considered. The only issue for Paul was the question as to whether or not man is able to perform what morality, according to his conviction, cannot perform.

In his *Phenomenology of Mind* Hegel has subjected Kant's moral Weltanschauung to the severe test of his dialectical logic. The gist of his penetrating criticism concerns Kant's moral formalism, which is a consequence of his moralism. Since Kant made the moral law absolute and unconditional, he had to make it "the mere form of a law." But he did not realize that this form alone does not command anything and that it is therefore no law at all. Hegel ironically fashions his attack on Kant by demonstrating that Kant's moral law is rather an immoral law, just because it pretends to command man without doing it in fact. This is the crucial point in moralism which does not recognize the limit of morality, a limit that manifests itself in the chasm between the unconditional majesty of the moral law and the fact that it is always conditioned when it really functions in life.[10] Hegel thus reveals the limit of morality and of a moral Weltanschauung, i.e., a philosophic view which is circumscribed by morality as its ultimate principle.

Unfortunately, Hegel himself thought man's reason could transcend the horizon of morality by its own effort and insight and arrive at an "absolute knowledge" which outshines moral reason but does not altogether outshine reason. Hegel believed in the possibility of reconciling the self with the self, and thus solving the supreme task of culture, by speculative insight and dialectical method. He believed that culture can finish its undertaking by its own resources and that philosophy is the instrument by which this is done. He thus proclaimed that human thought (identical with divine thought) overcomes the antinomies of experience and achieves man's salvation. Philosophy exalted in that way rivals religion, or even surpasses religion, since the solution offered by the dialectical method is assumed to be more adequate and effective than that of the Christian faith.

In our own time we have seen a grotesque form of moralism rise in the existentialism of Heidegger and his French disciple Sartre, a moralism without a moral law and without any standard

10. Cf. above, pp. 170 ff.

at all. Heidegger is a kind of perverted Fichte, perverted by his denial of an ego that would be more than the individual self; it is rather this individual self alone, deprived of its universality, which demands an absolute recognition and value. But, although Heidegger cancels the universality of the ego which makes it an ego in the true sense and which alone raises it above the level of the world, he claims for this degraded ego the same authority and metaphysical dignity which Kant and Fichte attributed to the moral self. The individual self is its own master and goal, it authenticates its own end, not in so far as it is the author of a universal law and participates thereby in a universal community but rather in so far as it is isolated and grounded in itself alone, free from any compulsion and any relation to other selves.

The principle of autonomy is enhanced in this supermoral system in such a way as to thwart its moral meaning. It is the haughty self that defies all moral obligations and rests upon its own uniqueness and "existentiality"; it is the self-reliant and self-sufficient individual which asserts that he is authentic, inasmuch as he faces death as his ultimate "end." The anticipating experience of "my" death, Heidegger argues, makes me absolutely independent not only of any community or law but also of nature outside and inside myself; it exalts me over all merely causal or legal conditions up to the unconditional. In facing death, I face the Absolute, and thus I myself am absolute, if I live according to the vision of my death. Sartre has drawn the conclusion that the free human being is free not only from all compulsion of nature and society but also from God; for, if God existed, man would not be absolutely free, he would not be able to decide upon his own action out of himself alone, and thus he would not be man in the "moral" sense of the term.

The existentialism of death reveals one important truth, namely, that man, even as a moral being, is involved in a destiny which transcends his moral capacity and autonomy. He cannot conquer death, and thus he can never become absolutely free; indeed, he can never become absolutely a self or an absolute self. Death reminds me of this limitation which the moralist is likely to forget or to deny. As a mortal being, I am in the hands of something or someone higher than my own strength, be it physical or moral.

I cannot surmount that wall which involves me in the causal nexus of nature and history and which thus confines my inner freedom and my moral autonomy.

But it is the error of this kind of existentialism to conclude that the anticipation or the consciousness of my death can bring about what is lacking in my moral selfhood. I do not gain an absolute "courage" or any other moral value, as Heidegger asserts, merely by facing the inescapability of my death. I rather learn from this knowledge that I can never become absolute; that my self, in spite of its freedom, is also limited; and that in this respect it belongs to the world and shares the destiny of all living creatures. The tendency to exalt my freedom beyond the limits set for me does not reach its goal but degrades and diminishes the real dignity which I possess as a moral being; it deprives me of the greatest virtue—the virtue of humility in facing my finitude and the infinity which is beyond my secular experience. This virtue, like all virtues, is rooted in the moral consciousness, which itself depends upon the universality of my ego.[11]

The Limit of Culture

THE limit of morality is the final limit of culture. Man cannot transcend his moral consciousness, he cannot achieve what is essentially beyond his moral capacity, either in action or in thought. The philosophy of culture reaches its own end, therefore, when it analyzes and comprehends morality and its limit. Therein it limits itself. Kant was right in this respect, I hold. Morality is the beginning and the end of all human activity because the human self is itself only in so far as it is a moral self, i.e., finds itself as standing under the moral law or laws and strives to reconcile the universality of the law with the individuality of its situation, or its own universality with its own individuality. Culture is only the totality of all possibilities which the moral self encounters in realizing itself, be it as scientist or engineer or artist, as statesman or citizen, as official or private person. Man himself is the center of culture, and morality is his own

11. Cf. Marjorie Grene, *Dreadful Freedom* (Chicago: University of Chicago Press, 1948).

center. To realize himself by uniting the polarities of his nature, thereby uniting the contrasting sides of experience—world and ego—this is the inner motive and the ultimate end of all his toil.

But all the splendor and all the riches of culture cannot or should not deceive us that the end is never reached, or is even within the reach of man. Morality itself sets a goal that is beyond all possible aspirations and achievements. Morality transcends itself according to its own terms and postulates. It points to some end which is no longer within its own horizon. In other words, the antinomies of experience do not find their final and definite solution within the compass of morality; they are, on the contrary, only stressed and strengthened. Morality itself demands a transition which morality can never attain. This is the self-contradictory character of a "moral Weltanschauung," as Hegel has rightly seen. There are antinomies within morality with which morality is unable to cope. There is a light beyond the moral radius which nevertheless seems to kindle the very light of morality itself.

This is a paradoxical situation indeed. But it is simply the human situation, as we find it in our experience. We are torn by divergent claims, we try hard to assuage this tension and to generate a complete harmony. But, in spite of wonderful works and victories, the tension remains, and new tensions arise; the harder we press, the further we go, the richer the harvest is, just as new heads grow upon the hydra when the old ones are cut off. Culture is a tragic undertaking if it is not supplemented by a faith which assures us that it is not destitute of meaning, although it cannot be finished and although it does not bring the ultimate satisfaction for which we long. And what is true with respect to culture is true with respect to the whole of our life, since our life is ours only inasmuch as it is devoted to the goal of self-civilization, for we are selves only in so far as we realize ourselves, i.e., in so far as we make ourselves real selves.

The question of whether there is any faith that could transcend our moral capacities and the whole realm of moral exertion, is weighty; it concerns the other question of whether or not culture and life have a meaning which surpasses that studied so far, which is immanent in culture and life. Since this immanent meaning is endangered by the impossibility of an ultimate solution of the basic antinomy, be it in the sphere of contemplation or in that of action, the question of whether a meaning transcending this immanent meaning exists or not is of the utmost importance. It is a question of life or death in the ultimate sense of these words; it is the question as to whether or not tragedy is the inevitable and definitive end of life or whether there is anything "beyond tragedy." As long as we dwelt within the system of culture, the limit of each realm was not of such fateful consequence, since the possibility seemed to exist that another realm would supplement the deficiency of the one analyzed and that, at the end, perhaps all the realms taken together might provide a sufficient guaranty for the existence of an ultimate meaning of all the realms and activities of culture. Thus it seemed that the arts supplemented, deepened, and widened the truth of the sciences and, again, that the whole sphere of contemplative creation and works might be supplemented by that of active life, so that the sum total of all these realms would assure us of an immanent solution of life's problem.

Now, however, we face the final limitation of culture in all its spheres and realms, the final doom of all cultural effort and productivity, the final frustration of all exertion, since the spheres and realms do not supplement one another or grant a final solution, if regarded as a whole. Now we confront the possibility that, on the contrary, all cultural activity might only generate forever new inner contradictions, forever new barriers which inclose us in the circle of our finitude without ever opening up access to the absolute goal. Now the basic contradiction, which urged us to go ahead and work out all the cultural possibilities, seems to stifle us, so that all the satisfactions and achievements grow pale.

This is the experience of our own times. After centuries of cultural optimism we have arrived at a point where this optimism appears as a frivolous and shallow attitude, which feels secure and happy within the limits of finitude without realizing that such security and happiness are ultimately devoid of meaning if they are not supported by a faith that sustains their meaning, since they cannot sustain it themselves. Nietzsche's "nihilism,"

Dostoevski's message illuminating the questionable and desperate character of human life as long as it is not lived by faith, Van Gogh's paintings, which seem to express the same truth, and many other interpretations lead to this conclusion. This also is perhaps the positive implication of Heidegger's philosophy of death.

It is not only moral reason but the cultural consciousness and conscience as a whole which postulate a faith that would save the meaning of life. But neither moral reason nor the cultural consciousness as a whole can fulfil the postulate. It was Kant's greatest error, generated by the optimism of practical reason in which his whole epoch indulged (as the simultaneous French Revolution proves), to believe that the postulate of moral reason can be fulfilled by moral reason or that a rational faith could fulfil it. A rational faith must always be confined to a faith in reason, but it is this very faith which the postulate aims to surpass. In postulating faith, moral reason transcends itself or, more accurately, postulates something that entirely transcends its own capacity and domain.

Two considerations may conclude this chapter of the philosophy of culture. First, as I have already pointed out, the logical scheme of the system of culture demands a realm within the sphere of action which would correspond with the realm of art within that of contemplation, a realm which would deepen and widen the realms of politics and morality in a way analogous to the function of art as compared with that of science. It demands a higher level on which action would bring about a completion and perfection not attainable on the lower level. On that higher level co-ordination, instead of subordination, should create a community in which laws, be they outer laws like those governing the state or be they inner laws like those governing the will of every individual, would no longer mediate the opposites but in which, instead, universality and individuality in their absolute polarity would be fused as they are fused in the work of art and in the image-world. We have to inquire whether such a realm can be discovered and how it would look.

Second, we should not forget that the whole system of culture as developed in this philosophical treatise abstracts deliberately and methodically from any experience that might be called religious. But such an abstraction is artificial. Life is nowhere destitute of such an experience, nor is culture in any of its realms. On the contrary, as history shows, there is no civilization that is not tinged by some kind of religion, be it ever so primitive or "atheistic," i.e., without a worship of gods or godlike beings. Some emotional or intellectual or volitional relation to reality as such, or to existence as such, characterizes man as man, even if he is not aware of such a relation in any distinct or elaborate fashion. Man cannot live without having some views or visions about his place in the universe, without feeling dependent upon some power greater than he (this is the substance of Schleiermacher's definition) and without regulating his life according to those views and feelings. Even less can he build up a culture without such a religious relation to the ground of all that is, of all that he experiences. Religion in this vaguest and widest sense may be defined as the inner relation to the totality of experience, i.e., to that totality in which the differentiation between world and self has not yet taken place or has not yet assumed the character of a distinct consciousness. Of course, religion is not merely this inner relation, but it is always, at the same time, an articulation of this relation, however dim this expression may be.

III. Faith

CHAPTER VI
Preliminary Considerations

Religious and Mystical Experience

THE inner relation to the totality of things and the whole of experience may be called "mystical" if it has not yet been articulated or interpreted by religious expression. In that sense there is a mystical experience at the foundation of all religions or of faith in its generic sense. Since the experiencing consciousness can never express this mystical ground culturally because culture never arrives at its goal, when it would be able to grasp the unity of world and ego in fulness to its own satisfaction, mystical experience needs another kind of articulation, which it finds in religious faith. The original split of world and ego could never be experienced if the original unity of this opposition were not also experienced. But this experience of an original unity of all the contents of experience beyond the division into world and self is mute as compared with the language of science and art, of politics and morality. It cannot express itself in a cultural form, because all cultural forms are based upon the original split within experience, and try in vain to return to the original unity. Mystical experience rests upon the ground of this original, ineffable unity of those opposites which language and thought, work and action, distinguish and never completely reunite.

Mystical experience, as the Greek word indicates, implies silence, although the mystics are often very eloquent in pronouncing the incomprehensibility and inexpressibility of the contents of their mystical experience; but they always borrow from religious faith or dogma and point to something that lies behind or beyond the contents of faith and dogma and that cannot be expressed, except in a negative form (negative theology). The *via negationis* is the highway of mystical "philosophy," because at bottom this philosophy negates its own means and because it is this very negation which gives it a positive content. Although this "method" seems to contradict itself, it is, nevertheless, the right way to enunciate the truth of mystical experience, the way of the *docta ignorantia*, as Nicolas of Cusa has called his mystical philosophy.

Life is surrounded by the mystery of ultimate reality, that reality which secular experience and secular culture can never reach, since both breathe and create in the atmosphere of the original split and contradiction characteristic of man's consciousness. But this atmosphere is felt to be less than ultimate; otherwise man would not strive to improve his situation by achieving self-reconciliation and self-realization through his cultural exertion. Behind the secular and cultural atmosphere another one is longed for which would not be determined by the disunity of world and ego, of ego and ego, and of the antagonistic poles within each ego, but which would enable man to live in complete harmony and peace. As our earthly atmosphere is circumscribed by the firmament, so our cultural atmosphere borders a higher one which we cannot grasp and in which we cannot breathe as long as we are divided within ourselves, i.e., as long as we are cultural workers and citizens of cultural institutions.

Mystical reality may be compared with the ocean as the ancients conceived it, the limit of the solid earth which it encircles. We know now that there is no such circular ocean around the stable land but that the oceans surround many continents, which can be regarded as big islands in one ocean, since all the oceans are connected with one another. So also the cultural realms may be compared with the continents, while the one ocean out of which they emerge symbolizes the mystical reality which encompasses them with its waves. Or, to use the metaphor of the atmosphere, we now know that the earth moves around the sun, that it moves continually through the firmament, as the cultural sphere moves through the mystical medium, but protected against it by its own atmosphere, so that the uncanny and superhuman environment does not penetrate into our daily affairs, except on those occasions when we are aware of our own finitude and of the infinity that surrounds us. In former centuries these and similar metaphors (the Bible is full of them) could be used in a more powerful and more naïve way, because science had not yet interfered with them. But even now they have some symbolical function, when we remember that science neither solves nor eliminates the ultimate mystery of existence.

Religious faith is always an articulation of that ultimate mystery which surrounds us and which we "experience" in a strange fashion, namely (as the mystics rightly say), in such a way that we feel it exists, without feeling what it is; we recognize its power, but we are unable to perceive or comprehend it. As soon as we attempt to describe or conceive it, we fall victim to contradictions, or we have to be content to speak in negations, secretly knowing that we cannot describe or conceive it precisely because it is what it is: the "ocean" or the "firmament" beyond the land on which we stand and the atmosphere which we breathe. The moment that we try to express what it is, we distort or destroy it. Hegel thought that, by a methodical destruction of the distinct and definite meanings of logical terms, he could grasp it; but he did not grasp it any more than "negative theology" has been able to do.

Religious faith loses its original and true meaning when it is deprived of the mystical experience out of which it arises and which it interprets or articulates. If taken at face value, literally or, as Origen calls it, "somatically" (i.e., in the way in which the visible world is taken), religious language degenerates into superstition or idolatry. Only the mystical undertone of this language makes us guess that it points to the inexpressible and incomprehensible. Only mystical experience enables us to "understand" in the legitimate way what is not understandable in any other way. Only mystical experience guards against that dull and spiritually lethal literal understanding of religious language which contributes so much to antireligious feelings. Those who rightly revolt against the blight of such a misunderstanding flee into science, art, politics, or morality, if they identify the nonspiritual and nonmystical (both are the same) literalism with the essence of religion.

An English divine[1] interprets faith as "a delighted acquiescence in mystery." He admits that this definition is not complete, but he claims that it hits a constitutive element within faith. I am sure it does. Faith without this delight is no longer religious faith. Faith, from the outset, is in a paradoxical situation. It concerns that very element which cannot be grasped or known with the tools of science or thought—indeed, by any means at all—and which nevertheless is supposed to be grasped and known by faith. The true believer delights in this paradox because he is aware that it is inseparably connected with the peculiar "object" of his faith and because that faith would not be worth while without this paradox. There is always a secret silence in all religious utterances; they speak when they articulate that silence, as God speaks in the biblical record with a low, whispering voice and not in the thunderstorm.

Secular experience is secular only to the extent that it takes place against the foil of mystical experience, which always surrounds and lures it to penetrate deeper and deeper into its impenetrable darkness. Cultural consciousness and life can be compared with daylight, while mystical consciousness and joy can be compared with the wonder of night, as the romanticists often did. But if night swallows up the "common sense" of the daylight worker, if he loses himself in the delight of the beatific vision, culture and life are rightly alarmed and protest against this perversion; for man must perform his daylight task and pursue his goal of self-reconciliation, even if faith assures him of a harmony and peace which he can never reach by his own labor and aspiration. Mystical experience remains mystical throughout man's existence and by no means allows him to dispense with his own efforts. This also is a paradox in need of illumination.

Mystical experience, paradoxically, concerns what cannot be experienced; it is the experience of the nonexperiential, the comprehension of the incomprehensible. We experience the certainty that there is something behind or beyond all experience, because we experience the antinomies of all experience and the impossibility of getting rid of them by cultural productivity. Science

1. T. H. Brabant in *Time and Eternity in Christian Thought.*

PRELIMINARY CONSIDERATIONS

and art, politics and morality, bring us only to the edge of the abyss; they never fill it. Art, more than science and politics and even more than morality, seems to express successfully the inexpressible, to reveal the veiled, to make manifest the wonder of night in the language of day. Not only a poet like Dante, who speaks the language of religion, but even a "secular" poet like Shakespeare seems to possess the key to the ultimate mystery of life and reality. Again, Rembrandt seems to reveal it by painting the darkness within the light or the light within the darkness. Indeed, art is the most mystical among the cultural branches.

But art gives us only a contemplative account, confined to the image of the world and to an image-world; it can never touch upon the deepest truth because this truth concerns the original unity of world and ego and not solely the world, even if interpreted by the ego of the artist and imbued with his inner self. The artist may be a mystic himself—and all great artists certainly have a mystical element within their creations—but the artistic expression remains, nevertheless, a daylight expression, in that the means are taken from nonmystical experience or from adopted religious symbols and images.

Mystical experience refers to the original unity which makes us feel that the disunity implies a contradiction. In that negative sense, mystical experience is the presupposition of secular experience and secular culture. But the original unity is never "given," it is always veiled as long as experience remains mystical, and it remains mystical even when revealed. Original unity seems to be lost, since we find ourselves in a situation of tension and conflict and cannot assuage it by any cultural achievement. The Bible expresses this experience by the story of paradise and the Fall. "Originally" we were in perfect harmony with ourselves, with our fellow-men, and with the mysterious background of all secular experience (called "God"); we lost paradise through our own fault, and now we labor hard to regain it by our own resources. This wonderful story reveals the mystical truth through a veil. It applies the moral consciousness in explaining the chasm between the original unity and the disunity which permeates all our secular experience and culture.

Even our cultural effort could not be enacted if we lacked the inner certainty that, through labor, we could return; this conviction presupposes, of course, that there is a unity and harmony behind and beyond all the conflicts and perplexities which we commonly experience.

Morality and Faith

RELIGIOUS faith is inseparable from mystical experience. However, it does not arise without an articulation of that experience and therefore also contains cultural elements. Yet, being mystical, faith does not belong to cultural activity but transcends it, despite the cultural elements inherent in the articulation of mystical experience. Besides the cultural elements in the narrower sense of the word (meaning science, technology, art, economics, and politics, including jurisprudence), faith also has a moral element which unfolds its significance, especially in biblical faith, although it is not altogether absent from any other religion. It is so prevalent in biblical faith that one might almost say that biblical faith is a moral articulation of mystical experience. Of course, morality is developed and thereby transformed on the level of faith, so that it is no longer morality, any more than art is science. In faith the rational and legal characteristics of morality are surpassed, as the rational and legal characteristics of scientific truth are surpassed in and by art. Faith no longer subordinates the individual to the universal but co-ordinates both, fusing them so that their antagonism disappears and a full reconciliation of these poles is brought about.

This reconciliation of the opposites is not the result of a moral effort. Morality cannot reach this goal, it cannot completely reconcile the individual and the universal ego within the ego or within the community of moral persons. If morality could perform this task, religious faith would be unnecessary—indeed, meaningless—as the moralist thinks it is. Faith attains its dominating and imperious position in life by the way in which it surpasses morality and finishes what is unfinished, although "postulated" by morality. Faith brings morality to completion and solves its task, which remains insoluble within its own limits. The following discussion will defend and carry through this fundamental insight, first pronounced by Kant, although the Kantian form of the postulate and his idea of rational faith have to be rejected. Faith cannot be rational in the Kantian sense, that moral or practical reason not only postulates the completion of morality but even fulfils the postulate by means of its collaboration with theoretical (or scientific) reason, in which practical reason has the primacy. Kant did not recognize the part that mystical experience plays within faith; he refused outright to accept or to acknowledge such an experience (although he admits in his book on "religion within the boundaries of reason alone" that there are "mysteries" in the Christian religion which reason cannot comprehend).

Faith is faith precisely because it is not rational only but contains an element which might be called "supra-rational" or "extra-rational," an element that does not necessarily negate reason but fulfils a mission which reason, be it theoretical or practical or a synthesis of both, cannot fulfil by itself alone. Even faith in reason itself is not simply a rational attitude but shows that man is more than a rational being even when reason works in him or through him. The presence of faith within life indicates that man is unable to know absolute and total truth about reality, life, and himself by means of reason alone. Since we can never know the future, faith is necessary and present, even if it is of no genuinely religious origin. What is faith in this most general sense?

It is, first of all, a kind of confidence or trust (*fides*) which is based on no secular knowledge of any kind. If the validity of trust can be proved in a scientific or logical way, trust is no longer trust but knowledge. Kant is right when he says that faith is akin to the practical attitude, but he is wrong in identifying this attitude with practical reason. Trust is not rational certainty, though it is of practical import and relevancy and though one might call it "reasonable," which term, however, does not propose that reason can demonstrate or generate the authenticity of trust. Trust in reason means that we trust reason to conquer wherever it is in operation. Such a trust is by no means guaranteed by reason; it may even be fallacious. It surely is fallacious when it is extended to ultimate truth.

Faith unfolds its power only because life is surrounded by riddles insoluble in a scientific or logical (rational) way. All men "live by faith," although their faith is not in every case religious but is often nonreligious or outright irreligious—for example, faith in reason or man or in one's own capacity, luck, or talents, or faith in culture, history, or any other secular source (one's country, friends, class, money, and so on). Man cannot live without faith, simply because he does not know enough to live by knowledge or science. Faith in science is probably the most common and widespread faith on earth today, although the atomic bomb has vehemently shaken its value and illuminated its illusory character.

Faith is possible and necessary because man does not now and never will reach the goal of his aspirations, cultural as well as moral. Or, in other words, faith is possible and necessary because life is threatened by the frustration of all human endeavors and exertions in every field of activity, be it contemplative or active. Faith derives its strength from the experience that there is something behind or beyond the horizon of the secular which, in contrast to it, is properly called "mystical." Even secular faith of the kind just mentioned could not exist without the existence of this mystical element in life and consciousness; the momentous question is, therefore, not whether or not faith is or should be permitted to unfold its role but rather: What kind of faith can most effectively and most truly perform the function that faith should fulfil in life?

It is "reasonable" to say that "a moral faith" alone can perform this function. I do not mean a faith in morality or even a faith derived from morality but a faith which moves in the direction of morality and follows its direction to the very end, thereby transcending its limits. This can be done only by a faith which articulates mystical experience, thus breaking through the insurmountable barrier of all merely human, that is, cultural and moral, energies and revealing the ground out of which human uncertainty, frailty, and self-contradiction rise. This ground opens up, not to secular, but only to mystical, experience; for it contains the original unity which is lost the moment that secular experience and activity set in. Since morality is the central and ultimate energy that man can mobilize, it is evident that true faith should supplement and finish what is initiated, but cannot be finished, by morality. Therefore, it is reasonable to say that faith should "reasonably" be moral and mystical at the same time.

Moral reason has to join mystical experience (not theoretical reason, as Kant proclaims), in order to arrive at religious faith. However, religious faith cannot be constructed upon, or anticipated by, the synthesis of morality and mystical experience; it requires an articulation of a special kind in order to be religious. Kant probably was aware of this requirement when he proposed that theoretical reason should be united with moral reason for the sake of rational faith; but the articulation which takes shape in religion is not properly theoretical. Rather, it supplements theoretical knowledge as well as moral action by a peculiar power, namely, spiritual imagination, about which more will be said subsequently.

Kierkegaard is right: seen from the secular aspect, only a leap can lead to faith. To be sure, there are leaps even within the secular area. There is a leap from contemplation to action, and there is a leap from science to art or from science to technology. There is even a leap from mechanics to other branches of physics, from physics to chemistry, from chemistry to biology, and so forth, although modern science tries hard to unify all its branches and may succeed in finding some most general equation valid for all laws of nature. However, all these leaps within the cultural system are negligible as compared with that from culture to religious faith; for this leap has to abandon the "solid" ground of secular experience altogether and soar to the lofty heights not of speculation but of an articulate mystical experience, no longer controlled by reason or measured by artistic standards. It is obvious that, because of the mystical element indispensable in faith, religion is less protected against counterfeit, illusion, superstition, and idolatry than science is protected against similar aberrations. Even within the "truest" religion, some traits or expressions may be erroneous or misleading; not all Christian churches can possess equally the Christian truth, even if one takes into account that the cultural element inherent in all religious articulation changes from land to land, from epoch to epoch, from language to language, and therefore demands changes within articulate faith too.

But religious truth should not be compared with, or opposed to, scientific or speculative truth at all, since religious faith belongs to the sphere of action, not to that of contemplation. Faith is true, in so far as it promotes the "ego-solution" of cultural activity, though not by cultural means. Faith is true to the degree to which it promotes the generation of a community in which the contrast between ego and ego, between community and individual, and between universality and individuality is abated and the conflicts arising out of that contrast are eliminated. Faith is true, in other words, to the extent that it is morally good and just and generates moral goodness and justice.

The Religious Articulation of Mystical Experience

MYSTICAL experience cannot be expressed except by a special kind of imaginative language which all religions exhibit, even those which, like some Asiatic forms, are either predominantly moralistic or speculative. All religions deal with a reality which cannot be experienced in the secular sense but which underlies this experience, interprets its meaning, and demands a certain attitude from man. This reality has a mystical character; only mystical experience can come into contact with it, and all religions serve the purpose of advising man how to come into contact with it. From the point of view taken in this philosophy of experience and culture, mystical experience concerns the original unity of world and ego which are disunited in secular experience and so remain, despite all cultural attempts to reunite them. Only a transsecular experience can reach that original unity and thereby overcome the split in man's consciousness which is the source of all his conflicts and all his struggles, as it is also the source of all his cultural aspirations and exertions. For this reason there is an absolute chasm between secular and mystical experience and also between all cultural spheres and that of religious faith, in spite of various mutual relations between the two opposite spheres. The imaginative language which articulates mystical experience must therefore be of a peculiar kind and function; it must allow the preservation of the mystical character of the experience out of which it arises, i.e., it must be mystical itself, in its structure as well as in its meaning.

Any interpretation of this language which disregards its origin and its intention necessarily fails to understand its meaning and is therefore a misinterpretation. The full meaning can be understood only by those who share the faith expressed in it, by those who are acquainted with its meaning from within the faith. In this respect, however, religious language does not essentially differ from any other; scientific or artistic, political or juridical, language can also be fully understood only by those who know it from within their own experience, by the student of science or art, of politics or jurisprudence. The difference is only this: that religious language presupposes mystical experience which articulates itself in it, while the cultural languages do not presuppose such an experience. Only he who is aware of the insurmountable barrier which prevents secularity from ever reaching the mystical ground of reality, only he who consequently longs for an expression of mystical experience, can understand the "grammar" of religious articulation and of faith.

Faith is, in the first place, a certain trust in that ultimate reality which is "revealed" by the articulation of mystical experience. Only in the second place is it an "assent" to propositions, as faith was defined by Clement of Alexandria. Unfortunately, this definition has been taken as the essence of faith by the Roman church since the time of Clement up to the present, as the "grammar of assent" by Cardinal Newman shows. If the element of "assent" is overemphasized, an intellectualism encroaches upon the innermost soul and life of faith, which has the consequence that the believer believes first in those "propositions," the dogma, second in the church which formulated the dogma, and only third in that ultimate reality itself which is the real and true addressee of religious trust and loyalty.

It is not the dogma but that peculiar articulation of mystical experience which is the first mediator between the ground of existence and the consciousness of the believer. The believer needs such a mediator because mystical experience as such is mute and uncommunicative. It is communicative and creates community only if it is articulated intelligibly, although still mystically, i.e., in an imaginative language. While trust and loyalty may be called the practical elements within faith which indicate that faith belongs not to the contemplative but to the active sphere of human life; that faith represents not a "world-" but an "ego-solution" of the supreme task; that faith is not a solution resembling that of science and art but rather one resembling that of politics and morality; the imaginative elements may be called "quasi-theoretical." They represent the quasi-objective elements which constitute the content or the object of faith. But, since faith is not a kind of science, the "object" is by no means to be taken in the sense of the object of scientific knowledge and investigation but rather, like the term "objective" used in practical life, as the point toward which one moves, as the goal of a direction pursued by action.

Faith offers an "ego-solution," although not in the cultural sense. It is not a solution which human creativity or action could possibly produce, since such a solution could never articulate mystical experience; it transcends the whole condition of human culture and the whole situation in which man finds himself. The solution of faith overcomes the barrier of this situation and presents to the human consciousness that original unity and harmony which are disturbed in secularity. Secularity can be simply defined as the state in which the original order is disorganized. Man can never return to this order as long as he lives in the spirit of secularity; and, in so far as culture is the consequence of that spirit, man is barred from reaching the point where self-contradiction completely disappears. Faith is the mystical victory of the original harmony over secular disharmony and advancing disintegration.

Religious imagination portrays an absolute ego which is in the state of undisturbed inner harmony and which enables the believer by means of trust and loyalty to participate in that blessed state. Not all religions discharge this task equally well; some do not sufficiently recognize the character of the "ego-solution" but try to release man from his plight by half-philosophical means, as Hinduism does; or they depict the state of peace and salvation in an impersonal way, as Buddhism does; or they are predominantly moralistic, as is Confucianism (Nietzsche calls Kant "the Chinese of Koenigsberg"). Other religions, the so-called "pagan" ones, do not sufficiently recognize the oneness of the absolute ego but indulge in a half-artistic imagination of many gods. Against this pagan polytheism Greek philosophers as well as biblical prophets revolted, emphasizing the oneness of God, his moral purity, and his eternal rule. But the philosophers were unable to supplant the polytheistic religion of their country, for the very reason that they were philosophers, who therefore thought it possible to produce by means of speculation the right concept of deity and disregarded the mystical character of the task and the impossibility of scaling the cultural barrier by human effort alone, disregarding, in other words, the distinction between culture and faith.

Greek philosophy was seduced into attempting a speculative solution because the Greek mind was predominantly determined by artistic imagination, as the great cultural works of Greece testify. Naturally, Greek religion was determined by this creative spirit of the nation, and only the great moral strength and courage of Socrates counteracted the aesthetic trend of Greek culture. Plato was stimulated by the commanding personality of his teacher to undertake the most vigorous attack against the gods of Homer, but he also finally tried to replace them by speculation; thus he became the founder of "natural" or rational or philosophic theology. Artistic imagination and philosophic speculation have in common their reliance upon contemplation as the supreme capacity of man in reaching the supreme solution of his problem. In fact, it was a kind of half-poetical, speculative imagination which prompted Plato to build up his theological knowledge. But he was still aware of the inadequacy of such an attempt, as the reservation with which he utters his theological suggestions clearly demonstrates. He felt dimly that the supreme task cannot be solved by means of speculation, that God—the true God—is hidden from any human thought and inquiry. Only Aristotle was bold enough to teach his metaphysical theology as if speculation were capable of disclosing the ultimate mystery in a satisfying fashion. It is well known what a fateful step this was and how deeply it influenced the entire subsequent history of Christian thought and even of dogma and dogmatics.

Pagan or mythological religions, because they are dominated by poetical imagination, offer an articulation of mystical experience which is neither merely contemplative nor truly active. The Olympian gods were not only figures in Homeric epic, nor were they merely beautiful statues; rather, they had a religious existence: they were sincerely worshiped and adored; generation after generation of devout Greeks bowed down before them, felt protected or else punished by them; and even Plato, in spite of his speculative renovations, continued to adhere to the sacred tradition of Greek ritual (there was a place for the service of the gods in the Academy). But, even so, the contemplative and artistic character of Greek religion and, indeed, of all pagan religions is evident. The gods are a plurality because the religious articulation of mystical experience is still dependent upon a religious "world-solution." Behind the gods looms the Cosmos as the real Absolute. The gods are only inhabitants of the world, being but partially distinguishable from men by their greater physical strength and a kind of immortality.

To be sure, certain characteristics of the gods, even in Homer, point to a dim inkling of the fact that they represent a state of sublime superiority of mind and will. They enjoy an inner peace and calm which men never enjoy; they are without serious sorrows, without sickness and fear; they hover between a superhuman knowledge and a certain ignorance of their own destiny; they are, and yet are not, absolute, or, measured by the biblical God, they are, and yet are not, divine. This ambiguity, which finally brought about their downfall, corresponds with an articulation of mystical experience which stands between a "world-" and an "ego-solution." Inasmuch as the gods belong to the world, they resemble finite moral man: they quarrel and fight with one another and are even threatened by a Titan, like Prometheus. Plato is especially polemical against all these far too human features in the gods—their strife, unrest, vice, and folly—and his own picture certainly approaches the living God.

The term "articulation" itself is somewhat ambiguous. It seems to suggest that man by means of his imagination depicts the unknown and unknowable ground of all existence, while actually the foregoing discussion was to show that man is not able and not

entitled to grasp this ground by any power of his own mind, because man's mind is at all times confined to the state of self-contradiction which is the state of his finitude and life on earth. Can this
ambiguity be expurgated?

Imagination and Revelation

THE articulation of mystical experience must imply a certain
kind of instruction, otherwise it would be entirely unworthy
of communicating truth about ultimate reality, i.e., religious truth.
Although this truth is neither scientific nor artistic and in no way
serves contemplation, as does contemplative culture, it could not
represent any "solution" of the supreme task, it could not rightly
reconcile man within himself and with his fellow-man—in short, it
could not have any value at all (let alone a value higher than that
which all cultural works and achievements possess) if the articulation of mystical experience offered by religious faith were not in
a peculiar sense "true." It has to be true, not in the sense of any
knowledge which the sciences or the arts grant, but in the sense in
which a political idea or action can be right or in which a moral
ideal can be a true ideal. It should be true, in other words, in the
sense that it truly fulfils what it intends and proclaims to fulfil.
Reality in the mystical sense (which nevertheless is a "realistic"
sense, since ultimate reality is "really" beyond the limits of all
nonmystical knowledge) can be known only in a mystical fashion, that is to say, in an imaginative way which truly conveys
its meaning.

The service of imagination in conveying this meaning, however, seems very doubtful. The diversity of religions, if nothing
else, indicates how dubious imagination is as the vehicle of religious articulation of mystical truth. Besides, imagination is suspect
anyway. It is not a trustworthy instrument of expressing truth, as
so many fanciful theories (promoted and adhered to in prescientific times from the oldest periods until the dawn of modern,
mathematical and exact science) disclose. How can we assume
that the most difficult, the most hidden, of all problems should be
solved by an intellectual power of so suspect and so frail a nature?
How can we agree that the most fundamental, vital, inclusive,

and profound truth should be left to the tribunal of a judge so easily deceived—to a tribunal which lacks all logical rules and, indeed, all criteria distinguishing truth and falsity? How can we earnestly believe that imagination can better be trusted than speculative metaphysics, which labored in vain to discover ultimate truth? Imagination, of all human powers, seems least fitted to impart so important a knowledge.

These objections, however, are not so conclusive as they may sound in the ears of rationalistic thinkers. We have seen already that imagination has a part even in scientific discoveries and hypotheses. Poetry, furthermore, does attain to a truth to which science has no access, especially to the truth about man himself. This consideration is the more decisive, since, although religions do not speak of man, they speak about the reality of the absolute ego. The diversity of religions merely shows that religious imagination is by no means infallible but is subject to illusions which can, however, be discovered by religious feeling itself, even without prophetic gifts, as Greek criticism of Greek mythological religion proves. How else would Heraclitus and Xenophanes, Socrates and Plato, have been able to reject the Homeric gods and to conceive of deity in a worthier fashion, in a fashion approaching biblical revelation?

But the main question concerns the ambiguity of the term "articulation," i.e., the relation between the human aspect of imagination and its mystical truth, which transcends all human possibilities. This ambiguity can never be fully eradicated. If we tentatively adopt the biblical conception of revelation, even in its crudest form of verbal inspiration, the question occurs as to how man can understand the language of God. Does God speak in a human language? Is man able to interpret this divine-human language in the way in which God himself meant it? If we consider that it is difficult even to understand another man's mind, when ultimate ideas and visions are concerned; that the genius cannot be fully comprehended by the ordinary man; that the distance between man and God, according to the Bible itself, is infinite, in spite of man's resemblance to God; that the Bible expressly says that God's thoughts are not our thoughts and his ways not our ways; if we remember that Jesus himself tells us again and again that man can never know the full truth and that even he himself did not teach it but left it to the spirit to reveal all truth; if, finally, we learn from Paul that now we know in part and that only "if that which is perfect is come, then that which is in part shall be done away,"[2] then we cannot doubt that biblical revelation is tinged by human understanding.

Of course, the term "articulation" does not imply that man "produces" by his imagination the biblical image of God. He does not even produce the mythical images of pagan gods in the same way in which he produces science and art or the institutions in the active realm of culture. We can distinguish reproductive, productive, and responsive imagination. Memory illustrates the first, artistic creation the second, and political planning (including juridical and administrative legislation) the third. Religious imagination is responsive not to the call of finite tasks but rather to that of the ultimate and absolute task "solved" by faith. Imagination on all levels and in all realms is human; but on the level of faith it also transcends humanity, and only thereby does it articulate mystical experience.

The correct and adequate expression of this superhuman significance and function of religious imagination is revelation. By this we mean that the ultimate ground of reality articulates itself in our human imagination and that our minds and wills are responsive to this self-articulation. This, indeed, is a statement of faith. It cannot be proved by any logical means that the living God who reveals himself and what I have called "the ultimate ground of reality" are one and the same. This is impossible, if for no other reason than that revelation would not be necessary should logic or metaphysics succeed in proving this identity, since then human thought could prdouce the revealed knowledge by means of its own resources. Revelation would become in that case a merely imperfect and inadequate or, as it were, popular metaphysics, like Aristotle's conception of mythological religion and Hegel's of religion in general. But this is false, even with respect to paganism. However insufficient pagan religions may be, they are at least religions and not metaphysical systems or popular versions of such systems. They are religions because they fulfil a function no metaphysical

2. I Cor. 13:10.

knowledge could ever fulfil. No human mind can contrive gods, although the particular stories of the gods, their description by poets, their representation by sculptors, and the like are human creations. But they are gods, precisely in so far as they are not merely artistic figures invented by man, but rather personifications of "the ultimate ground of reality," experienced in mystical fashion and articulated by religious imagination.

But if this is so, why does the biblical religion alone claim revelation as its source, while pagan religions do not raise that claim? Pagan religions do not pretend to be revealed because they have not arrived at religious truth of that height and purity which characterize biblical revelation. Even the Greeks felt that the human portion in the picture of the gods was too prominent to be contributed to the gods themselves. They felt that the gods as described and comprehended in their myths did not reveal, but only dimly represented, the hidden reality which they nevertheless interpreted to the devout pagan believer. In a sense, one may therefore rightly say that man contrives gods; but such a statement is not true without a subtle qualification which adds that it is not the divinity of the gods but only their specific traits, number, and qualities which are contrived (although, as we have seen, even those particularities suggest that some features are genuinely divine when measured by biblical standards).

Mythological religions are much too human and cultural to be revealed. They do not truly reveal the divine, or the divine does not truly reveal itself in them. Biblical religion insists upon revelation, because in it the truly religious substance comes to the fore and manifests itself in purity and perfection. One may even go so far as to state that only biblical religion is truly a religion, while all other religions are too strongly shaped by human imagination or speculation to be so. Paganism means exactly this: that its gods are "false" because the religious quality has not yet imposed itself sufficiently upon human creativity and productivity. Biblical religion is true because it has reduced to the indispensable minimum the human part in the articulation of mystical experience. Consequently, biblical religion alone is permitted and even urged by its own standard of truth to insist that its truth is revealed or that the living God himself is its founder and its interpreter.

If we assume (this can be done even without faith) that biblical religion is true in the religious sense, then we must conclude that its truth could not have been expressed in any other way; that revelation alone is the right and only adequate form in which the specific content of biblical imagination could have been transmitted. Only revelation can convey the true content of mystical experience; only the true content of this experience can be conveyed by revelation. In other words, in revelation religious imagination attains its mature, "classical" form; only in revelation does it assume its fully and purely religious manifestation. The true God cannot be articulated by human imagination. He can be known only in so far as he articulates or reveals himself. This is a philosophical, not a religious, statement.

Religious imagination in its pure and genuine manifestation is no longer mythological but revelatory. It no longer originates from man's own creativity in the contemplative realm of cultural activity, but it serves active faith which is based not only upon mystical experience but also on moral conditions. Revealed religion and biblical faith are thoroughly moral. Revelation permits religion to be pure and perfect, not only in so far as the living God, in contrast to the pagan gods, is adequate to mystical experience but also in so far as he embodies perfectly the solution of the moral task. Of course, both the mystical and the moral truth are intrinsically connected with each other. God can be truly moral only if he is also truly mystical. He can accomplish morally what man cannot accomplish, only because he is not contrived and created by man's imagination but reveals himself as the true and only God, the Lord.[3] To be sure, revelation can be received by man solely through the medium of imagination, but this imagination is no longer of a secular kind; it is no longer contemplative but serves man's moral activity and brings it to completion. Faith is, first of all, trust and loyalty; it is only secondarily a kind of imaginative knowledge derived from the active attitude which needs this knowledge for its moral function.

God's revelation, in other words, turns first to man's will and heart, and imagination is but the instrument through which God's

3. The fundamental error of Feuerbach and all the Feuerbachians (like Santayana today and Unamuno before him) is that they disregard this most important point.

word is received; the real recipient is not imagination but will and heart. Pagan religions are pagan because this true order of rank is not rightly respected or because a luxuriant imagination overgrows the inner spiritual voice of the mystical "ground of reality." The term "myth" should, in accordance with its historical meaning, be reserved for mythological religions; it should not be applied to revealed religion, because its imaginative language is nowhere imaginative for its own sake but always for the sake of delivering its moral and mystical message.[4]

Philosophy of Faith and Christian Theology

THE moment when I speak of God as the Lord of biblical revelation, I no longer speak as a philosopher but as a theologian in the religious sense, i.e., as a man of faith who is committed, or commits himself, to submit his will and heart to the God who revealed himself to Moses and the prophets and who sent his Son to redeem mankind. Philosophy, defined as man's self-understanding, ends where man, his experience, his activity, and his cultural achievements end and God's creativity, God's commandments, God's acts, and deeds begin. However, faith itself mediates between man and God and is therefore to be understood in a twofold way, by philosophy and also by theology. It was this twofoldness which generated the ambiguity of the term "articulation." Faith is a human attitude toward God. In so far as it is human, it can be grasped by human, i.e., philosophical, means, at least in part. In so far as it is an attitude toward God, it is subject to a religious and theological definition.

Many philosophers speak about God as if the meaning of this term were self-evident, completely forgetting that they cannot adopt the biblical name without also adopting biblical revelation. When the ancient philosophers spoke about "the god" in contradistinction to the gods and to the divine, they declared, or at least tried to declare, what they meant thereby. Modern thinkers naïve-

---

4. Against this rule I failed myself when I wrote my little book on *The Religious Function of Imagination* (New Haven: Yale University Press, 1941).

ly take the holy name from the Bible but then more or less reject biblical revelation and disregard the warning that man should not abuse the name of the Lord and that he cannot be known except by his own word. It is a great merit on the part of Karl Barth and his disciples to have emphasized so powerfully and convincingly that philosophy has no legitimate right to talk about God in the sense of the Lord and that it cannot talk about him in any other way, if the philosopher pretends to be a Christian. Of course, Barth stands on the shoulders of Kierkegaard. But this makes his merit no less great and his truth no less true.

Although I cannot understand faith save from within faith, I can nevertheless philosophize about the nature of faith and even of biblical faith in its contrast to pagan religions, as I have done in the previous considerations. I hold that it is possible to recognize the excellence and uniqueness of the Christian faith even from the point of view of philosophy, i.e., without any definite commitment in an "existential" fashion, according to which the philosopher is himself a believer and a Christian theologian. The "transition" from philosophy to Christian theology, from a secular self-understanding of experience and culture to Christian theology, is a delicate problem indeed. It leads to the final question as to whether philosophy itself is not always influenced by the religious or nonreligious disposition of the philosopher, and in what sense and to what degree such an influence must be accounted for. However, I will postpone this and similar questions for the moment and concentrate on the relation between the philosophy of faith, as here developed, and Christian theology.

The mediating link between the two antagonistic positions is "mystical experience." It is true that this experience is not accessible to everyone in the same way as secular experience is; from the religious point of view, it is grace which enables man to experience the original unity represented by the living God. But, as long as the content of mystical experience is not interpreted in the fashion of biblical revelation, it is accessible to every human being, at least as the contrast to the divided and self-contradictory consciousness of secularity and thus as a goal of longing or of hope. The very despair which is the necessary consequence of disbelief indicates that every man is able to recognize the significance of mystical experience, if not with a positive, then with a negative, attitude. Despair is the negative acknowledgment of the existence of God.

Of course, the philosopher cannot speak in a strict and logically satisfying manner about the "object" of mystical experience, precisely because this object is mystical and needs religious articulation to be expressed. The philosopher can only indirectly hint at it, as I have tried to do. Phrases like "ultimate reality," "mystical reality," "ultimate mystery," "the original unity," or "the ground of reality" are neither ontological nor epistemological definitions. They are only indicative of the incomprehensible and inexpressible content of mystical experience. Later on I shall recur to this intricate and subtle problem. All these phrases point to the final and absolute solution of an inescapable, but insoluble, problem.

Faith has a double face. It looks back into secular experience and supplements it, and it looks forward to an experience inaccessible to man, even to the believer, be he ever so ecstatic a visionary. Philosophy may speak about faith as trust in the content of mystical experience articulated by revelation as the living God. But such a definition is utterly insufficient and, from the point of view of faith and of a theology based upon faith, almost blasphemous because faith itself and theology, too, do not allow of any understanding that transcends the boundaries of faith and theology. Thus a certain antagonism between a philosophy of faith and Christian theology is as inevitable as is the ambiguity of articulation. Christian theology is not permitted to speak of any mystical experience not yet articulated by biblical revelation, and therefore of no mystical experience at all. This is a philosophic concept which might illuminate the nature of faith from the point of view of secularity, but which disappears into nothingness from the point of view of faith itself and of sacred theology. A philosophy of faith can be a link between secular thought and sacred theology, but only from the perspective of philosophy. Theology itself does not need such a link; it does not even tolerate it, according to its own logic.

On the other hand, biblical revelation and Christian theology are not fitted to supplement philosophy in a philosophical fashion. Faith does not deliver "concepts" which could fill the gap of igno-

rance that limits human knowledge and thought and makes speculation about ultimate reality vain and arbitrary. There is no "theological metaphysics," as there is no "metaphysical theology."
Systems like that of Thomas Aquinas or, in our own time, of William Temple are not satisfactory because they disregard the limit
of philosophy as well as the leap of faith. There is no "concept" of
God in the Bible but rather a "holy image," as Origen calls it. This
image cannot or should not be transformed into a concept, since
it is its very excellence and essence that it is not a concept but an
image through which the living personality who commands our
life is experienced. As the political state in which I live and work,
which protects me but also requires that I obey its laws and serve
its purposes, is not a concept but a living being like (though also
unlike) myself, so God is a living God in whom "we live, and
move and have our being."

Philosophy may dare to conceive of faith and the God of faith
as it also conceives of politics and the state as the self of the political community; but, even so, it must be aware that there is a fundamental difference between the political and the religious realms,
since it is man who builds the state and administers it, while it is
God who founds the community of faith. The state is a province
of the cultural world, but God does not belong to this world, as
he does not belong to the world in any sense at all. The duality of
ego and world is definitively surpassed in him. This is the exact
meaning and function of his mystical being, in whom the antinomies of experience and culture are finally and absolutely resolved.
There is an impassable abyss between the cultural and the religious
spheres, between the philosophy of faith and the word of God
himself. "The wisdom of this world is foolishness with God"[5] and
"the foolishness of God is wiser than men."[6]

God is "foolish" precisely because his wisdom is not of this
world or because it flatly contradicts secularity and all human
"solutions" of the ultimate problem. This contradiction rests upon
the contrast between God and man as expressed in the language of
Christian theology; it rests upon the contrast of original unity and
experiential disunity, as expressed in the language of philosophy.

5. I Cor. 1:25.
6. I Cor. 3:19.

There is a gap between the two languages which is filled by revelation, never by philosophy. Philosophy of faith can only point to revelation from outside; Christian theology stands inside and pronounces in a logical form what God has pronounced in the form of prophetic and inspired messages in and through which he speaks. Philosophy of faith turns thus to the "Gentiles"; it is necessary and helpful in teaching those who have lost their faith, the Gentiles among the Christian nations of today. This service of philosophy seems to be not without profit, even though it can never generate faith in those who stand outside. It may, however, be able to remove some intellectual and cultural obstacles which hinder man's reception of and belief in the message of God. The following attempt to make the content of biblical faith philosophically suggestive will, I hope, serve this end.

Secular experience and thought cannot prove the existence of the living God, although it can find some traces of him which point to his existence. The philosophy of faith can show that, and in what way, the content of Christian faith does "solve" the ultimate task of culture which culture can never solve.

CHAPTER VII
Culture Consummated by Faith

Faith, Truly Totalitarian

RELIGIOUS faith, whatever its content may be, is not a particular realm within culture but transcends culture altogether and thus is able to integrate it, to embrace and permeate
all its realms. One can characterize faith and religion as the inner
and the outer side of one and the same entity.[1] It is even gram-
matically impossible to build a plural of faith, but it is possible to
speak about religions, and we do speak about them—we compare
them, we treat them as historical facts, as factors in politics and
culture and so on. Religion can be regarded as a particular sphere
in cultural life which is related to all other spheres but is also distinguishable from them, manifesting itself in particular institutions, habits and customs, norms and manners, dogma and doctrine, buildings and costumes, and the like. Faith, though dependent upon religion, often deviates from its public manifestations.
While organized religion is a public institution and has therefore
a quasi-cultural appearance, faith is transcultural and private.
Religion exists, like science and art or even more like the state and
the civil code, as a self-dependent, relatively separated, entity;
faith, on the contrary, exists only within the believer in his most
secret and ineffable inwardness. However, this distinction, true
though it is, is somewhat artificial, since both faith and religion
are bound together as the upper and the lower surface of one and
the same thing.

Since faith is the ultimate and all-embracing power in the human soul, nothing whatever can remain untouched by it. The

---

1. Cf. the kindred distinction between *fiedes qua* and *fides quae creditur.*

whole personality is, as it were, informed by one's faith. Indeed, the self is as much integrated by faith as is culture. Faith, by completing culture, first completes morality; the seat of faith is the seat of morality, too: the heart of man. To be sure, only faith in the biblical sense fully corresponds with this description, for only in biblical faith is this inward and intimate, this moral, substance of religion developed and brought to perfection. In this sense, the biblical religion alone knows what faith is; only the biblical God demands and grants faith in this genuine, moral as well as mystical, meaning. The philosophy of faith speaking about the relation between faith and culture is therefore Christian, even if it remains philosophy and does not become theology.

Either faith is true, or secular philosophy is entitled to speak about God in an authoritative way; the two cannot be combined. Atheism is a spurious philosophy if it is true that faith alone can speak with respect to the existence of God. If God exists, as faith contends that he does, only faith knows that and how he exists; consequently, no philosophy whatsoever has a legitimate right to dispute his existence. Man cannot contact him except by the mode of faith; therefore, faith and God are inseparably united as far as human knowledge of God is concerned. We do not know of any god except God, and we know God through faith alone. This is exactly the credo of the Christian faith, and one stands outside its circle if one pretends to know God in any other way.

On the other hand, faith completes and integrates culture altogether, including science, art, politics, and morality, by articulating mystical experience, which is all-pervasive. The philosophical justification of the religious claim lies in the insight that faith of the biblical kind is the competent and trustworthy (i.e., religious) interpreter of mystical experience. Even the very meaning of the term "existence" cannot be understood except from within faith, since God does not exist in a secular sense. In this respect, curiously enough, the atheist is even more right than the theist.

Faith can complete and integrate culture for the very reason that it does not itself belong to culture. Mystical experience assures us that culture is not self-completing, as, in turn, the incompletion of culture assures us of the validity of mystical experience and authenticates it. Inasmuch as mystical experience concerns the transcultural, the ultimate, solution of the antinomies of experience, its expositor, religious faith, interprets this ultimate solution in an articulated manner. To be an adherent of faith means to believe in the validity and authority of this interpretation. This belief implies trust in God as the supreme and only "Interpreter" (to use Royce's term[2]). And, since mystical experience both hides and reveals the ultimate solution of the antinomies of experience, its interpretation is not only a self-interpretation of God but, at the same time, an interpretation of secularity—indeed, of the totality of man's life, his aspirations, his sufferings, and his conscience.

Faith is the truly "totalitarian" power on earth, the only one which is permitted and commissioned to raise that absolute and all-embracing claim. Bolshevism and naziism produced only counterfeits. God alone, since he comprises the totality of existence, is entitled to demand absolute obedience and discipleship. He alone controls not only the conduct and outer actions of man, as the state and the civil law do, but also the inner intentions and motivations of man's decisions, his will, and his heart. Thereby God controls the whole domain of culture. Faith is either truly and legitimately totalitarian, or else it is "vain imagination," an arrogant illusion and an extravagant deception, as rationalism thought when it spoke about the "three impostors"; there is, indeed, no middle ground on which faith could stand. It is either all or nothing; Brandt[3] is right in this respect, although he errs in confusing the claims of God and his own claims—a confusion all too often committed by men both within and without the church.

Faith completes and integrates culture and experience. Only in faith does culture receive its ultimate verification and sanction. Science without faith in God might be nothing more than a game with conventional rules, as some positivists think it is. Art without faith in God (or the gods) is not much more than an entertaining and joyful pastime and a pleasant deception. Homer is as great as he is because he believed in the gods of his religion and Aeschylus is much greater than Euripides because he still respected and worshiped them. The architects of the medieval ca-

2. In Josiah Royce, *The Problem of Christianity* (1913), II, 219; cf. John E. Smith, *Royce's Social Infinite* (1950), p. 7 and *passim*.
3. In the drama of the same name by Ibsen.

thedrals, Dante and Petrarch, the painters and sculptors of the
Renaissance—all of them were able to perform what they did
perform because they had faith, although this faith often devi-
ated widely from the ecclesiastical dogma. The same is true with
respect to modern poets, musicians, and artists, although many
of them like to express their faith not in the language of the Bible
but in that of pagan imagination or of a mystical experience
which they express in an individual style.

Science and art do not easily agree with biblical faith because
this faith has grown not out of contemplative culture but out of
moral experience and therefore completes this experience first
of all; only through the medium of moral experience does it complete the other realms of man's cultural activity. Science can
never answer the question of who is the "Giver" of the contents
of immediate experience and who gave the laws to nature, without appealing to the Creator. The artist cannot close the gap
between the image-world of his work and actual life without
appealing to God as the model and the greatest of all artists.
However certain the scientist and the artist may be in discover-
ing truth and in creating beauty, the last confirmation of the
value of their findings and doings is given only by a faith which
assures them that truth and beauty are rooted in the very essence
of all things; that, despite the enduring incompletion of all their
works and of the whole sphere of contemplative culture, these
works and this sphere participate in the absolute and final goodness of him who enables the scientist to investigate and to control nature and the artist to build his image-world.[4] No speculative metaphysics can furnish man with this faith; on the contrary, speculative metaphysicians rely and draw upon the source
of some faith in some gods or in God; out of merely intellectual
insight or reasoning they could never have arrived at their views.
Even the modern system-builders like Spinoza, Descartes, Leibniz, Fichte, Schelling, and Hegel are still nourished by the spiritual food of religion. When religion decays, culture follows suit,
as ancient history shows and as the European development in
modern times can also prove.

4. The simplest and, at the same time, the surest way of avoiding scientism,
as well as aestheticism, and statism, as well as moralism, is faith in God.

Since culture nowhere comes to its own end; since even morality ends in unsolved tasks, in perplexity and conflict, in guilt and remorse, religious faith alone can save man from despair and can sustain his confidence in culture and in himself. Otherwise frustration and self-contradiction would destroy his creativity and even his aspirations. Only a superficial and fleeting satisfaction can deceive man into the belief that he can live by himself and by his own achievements. Cultures, and even culture itself, may pass away and die; God alone never dies.

Biblical Faith "Solves" the Antinomies

THE antinomies of experience, based upon the contrast of ego and world, are "solved" by biblical faith. This solution, however, is not a speculative deduction of the antagonism of ego and world from a supreme principle, as metaphysical systems have offered, especially Neo-Platonism in all its manifold ramifications from Plotinus through Hegel; it is not a logical but, according to the essential character of faith, a mystical and moral solution, a solution which grows out of the active sphere of culture and consummates it on a transcultural plane. It is an "ego-solution," but the ego which brings it about is not the human, the finite, the self-contradictory, ego of man, who, by a supreme effort and by an extraordinary vision or action, would liberate himself from the frailty and insufficiency of his status and crown the works and institutions of civilization by a towering superstructure. Such a supreme exertion and such an extraordinary achievement, even if the Nietzschean superman were its author, could never transcend the basic limits of cultural activity and could never absolutely conquer the basic antinomy of world and ego. Plotinus appealed to a state of ecstasy; but this ecstasy is only a substitute for religious faith, a mystical rapture not articulated, and thus it is not any expressible solution of the supreme task. This task surpasses man's capacity; it can be discharged by no inspiration whatever, except the one presented by that religious articulation which reaches its zenith in biblical revelation.

This revelation begins with the story of Creation, which at once, in a great vision, "derives" the duality of ego and world by depicting God, the absolute ego, as the only and sufficient ground and author of the world and of man, thus "solving" with one mighty stroke all the torturing problems which speculative systems try vainly to solve. Of course, the Bible does not "explain"; the Bible "reveals." God the Creator is no principle, nor can he be derived from any principle. He is, he speaks, and he acts before the inner eyes of spiritual imagination. But we feel that this is the supreme solution; the absolute ego is neither a metaphysical principle nor deducible from any principle. What has been called an "existential" solution of the supreme problem is here given in the most powerful and most convincing form because it is the Supreme Being which "begs the question" by his existence and activity.

Indeed, if there is any solution at all of the ultimate problem, if there is any articulation at all of the original unity, the absolute one, the ground of all existence, it is this simple but majestic, this immediate and absolute, affirmation that the beginning is the Beginner acting out of his own unfathomable and incomprehensible will. If there is any solution of the antinomies, it is such a solution which presents the sovereignty and autonomy of the ego as we experience it within ourselves, but exalted over human frailty and self-contradiction. The absolute idealists were right, after all, in what they intended to say; they were wrong only when they dared to say it in terms of logical speculation. It can be said only in the dramatic or epic language of revelation. It can be said only in an "existential," i.e., in a nonphilosophical, fashion.[5]

God the Creator may be conceived as an artist who portrays the world but not only in an image, for his picture is rather the actual world which we experience. But such a conception does not exhaust, in fact, it does not even touch upon, the real substance of the figure which Genesis exhibits. This Creator who creates by way of decree should better be compared with the founder of a state. The world as created by the Logos is not so much an artistic work as it is an institution or organization

5. It is a great irony of history that precisely the concept which Kierkegaard proposed in order to emphasize the impossibility of any philosophical solution of the speculative problem—the concept of the existential thinker—has been misused in order to build a new philosophical solution of that problem.

in which man has to work and live. The visible universe, created on the first five days, is only the frame or the scene, the background and the foreground, of the human drama. God creates the world for man; man is not only the temporal, but also the volitional, end; he is the proper and ultimate purpose of the whole creation. The universe is, as it were, the house in which man is supposed to live and to be master over all other creatures. The subhuman world is merely the campus, as it were, of this vast, universal institution, and God is the sovereign, the supreme lawgiver, the ruler, the Lord of the human community. The universal ego of the state and of the moral community is enhanced and brought to consummation in the divine Creator.

Only this conception "solves" definitively the contradiction of world and ego. The world as God's creation is no longer opposed to his self; he does not confront it as his counterpart. The polarity of world and ego is surpassed by the absolute ego, which is the author of the world and of man, so that the world is absolutely dependent upon his will and purpose—is nothing but the instrument of this will. In God the world is one, as he himself is one. Only the absolute transcendence of the Supreme Being as portrayed in the Bible offers that "ego-solution" of the antinomy which is no longer limited, as all the cultural solutions have been. Only the Creator God is absolutely exempt from all the restrictions which the pagan gods suffer. He is not only, as the Greek theologians had demanded, the sole god. He is also unrestricted by the world, by conditions and circumstances. He is truly universal; he is as vast and superior to man as the universe is; and yet he is himself a self, an ego, a will. He is an individual like man. He is the absolute synthesis of universality and individuality, as he is the absolute synthesis of unity and manifoldness.

This figure, more than the demiurge in Plato's *Timaeus*, fulfils the requirement of being "beyond the substance" which Plato states with respect to the Idea of the Good. Karl Barth says in his dogmatics that this Idea, compared with the living God, is only an idol. But the truth is that the stammering words Plato uses when he tries to describe the glory of this supreme Idea are intended to express something which has come to light here in Genesis. The Creator God unites in his figure the Idea of the

Good with the personality of the world-architect. He is as absolute, universal, and ideal as the Idea but as personal, individual, and active as the demiurge. But he is neither so intellectually nor so mythologically conceived as Plato's concepts are; rather, he articulates what mystical experience and moral postulate prescribe in combination. He is the ground of all things, but not in a speculative fashion so that human logic could conceive of him as ground and derive from him logically, ontologically, or cosmologically world and ego, mind and soul, and all things, as Plotinus and Hegel thought possible; it is not such a logical process but a commanding and acting will which calls the world into being and cuts off all questions which the human understanding is prone to ask. Thus the transrational character of ultimate truth is assured from the outset, and man's relation to ultimate reality is based upon his relation to a supreme will rather than upon his theoretical insight.

Only such a "solution" can be satisfying, just because it does not satisfy the searching and brooding intellect. The supreme task cannot be discharged by the intellect; it cannot be discharged at all by man's own endeavor. It can be discharged only by faith, and faith, in the last analysis, is obedience and loyalty. Since the antinomies are, at bottom, expressions of an inner disunity of the ego or of man's self-contradiction, they can be healed by one remedy alone, an attitude which cures the inner split and conflict, and this attitude can be only an inner one, a personal and devotional attitude toward the very heart of all things; it can be only an attitude that involves man's will and heart. Faith is this attitude. It cures because it obliges man to be cheerful and high-minded in confronting the supreme author of himself and of the plane on which he lives and acts.

The "solution" of the antinomies by faith is therefore a "practical," and not a theoretical, solution. It is a solution which agrees with the centrality of will and heart in man's consciousness and with the essentially moral substance of man's life and action. It is a solution adapted to the whole personality instead of being a privilege of the understanding alone; it is a solution not of contemplation but of action. And, above all, it is a solution not of the subordinating reason but of the co-ordinating imagination, which serves to fuse and to reconcile the extreme poles of reality as man experiences them within himself. Only spiritual or religious imagination can perform this service. This imagination is more "realistic" than the bare intellect or speculative reason can possibly be, because the reality concerned is not an abstract, contemplative sphere of Ideas; rather, it is like man's own reality, primarily a moral one which extends throughout the world in which man has to exert himself, in which he suffers from conflicts and afflictions, in which he meets his "neighbor," and in which his character develops. This world is predominantly moral and spiritual, as all dramas and epics reveal.

Of course, there is no rational or logical proof that this solution is true. If such a proof could be given, it would prove only that the solution is not the right one; for a rational god does not actually live; a rational proof could never cure the heart threatened by self-contradiction and despair. And yet there is a certain logic in this translogical solution, as the foregoing considerations were an attempt to show. The heart has its own reasons, of which reason is unaware, as Pascal insists. The philosophy of faith must disclose these reasons of the heart, since the heart is that center of man's consciousness which alone can bring about the complete integration of the whole man. Such a philosophy fulfils the original motive of philosophy, the "love of wisdom," since faith, far from being scientific, is rather what the ancients called "wisdom."

A rational solution would be no solution at all; it would finally prove to be irrational and absurd, while the transrational solution alone is consonant with its task and is, in this respect, the only reasonable one. The rationalists should respect this rational dialectic, which alone does full justice to the intricate problem of ultimate reality.

Faith can consummate life and culture because it does not belong to culture and therefore offers not a rational, i.e., a cultural, solution but one which is rooted in the fact that man's life and reality as such are of a mystical nature. God is not to be experienced as the sun and the moon, gravitation and electricity, hydrogen and helium, plants and beasts, or even as science and art, state and morality, but as belonging to a stratum of experience deeper than all these contents. On the other hand, all these contents are included in mystical reality and are therefore integrated and interpreted by faith, which alone encompasses them all in the brilliance of one great light.

Faith finally solves the antinomies of freedom and eternity. God the Creator is absolutely free, since all restrictions of freedom originate from the fact that the will is engulfed in the world. He is absolutely eternal, since time is only the reflex of the inner disunity of man's consciousness and his finite will. And yet, by creating the world and the finite ego, God is the author of both necessity and time. Faith solves the antinomies because God is known as their supreme source. However, this entangles faith and thought in difficulties. If God is the supreme source of the solution of the antinomies, how can he be their supreme cause too? Why does he create world and man, if both are subject to the destiny of disunity? Why does he, who is the perfect and absolute unity, create something imperfect and relative—our world and ourselves? One may answer that this question should not be asked if man is wise, if he has faith. This is certainly a wise answer. But it has implications which will be developed further along in the discussion.

Sin

THE philosophy of faith may be called "pistology," while theology in the Christian sense is a "logic of God"—of that God who is seen through the "eyes of faith," to use the poignant term of Paul Minear.[6] Pistology deals with faith in a philosophical manner, while theology uses the language, grammar, and logic of heart and imagination in order to systematize and rationalize, as far as possible, the content of biblical revelation. Sin can be interpreted in a theological way, but it can also be discussed in a pistological way. Pistology, through acknowledgment of the peculiar right and rank of theology, can relinquish God and his relation to man as its proper subject and take, instead, faith as the consummation of culture based on mystical experience and articulated by biblical revelation. Although the two ways partly

6. Cf. his book of the same title (Philadelphia: Westminster Press, 1946).

cover the same field, the point of view is somewhat different, since pistology ascends from experience and culture to faith, while theology begins with the doctrine of God and descends to world and man. But both have this in common, that they deal with the specific logic suitable to the specific content of Christian faith.

Pistology, therefore, has to discuss the problem of sin not by starting from the Fall but by comparing the nature of secular guilt with that of sin in the religious sense. There is doubtless a certain kinship between the two concepts, but there is also a gap between them comparable to the more inclusive gap between the secular or cultural and the religious or spiritual spheres. One might say that sin is a kind of guilt, but guilt is not a kind of sin; for guilt belongs to the idea of man, whether he is conceived in a religious way or not; but guilt, regarded from the perspective of man's relation to God, takes on the specific meaning of sin. His-torically, the moral and the religious are always closely inter-woven in all cultures and at all times. All nations ascribe to guilt a certain religious connotation, i.e., they consider it to be not only a moral failure, a violation of the moral law or of moral rules, but at the same time a violation of an order represented by divinity of whatever kind. Prometheus, in the tragedy of Aeschylus, has transgressed the *logoi* of Zeus; Orestes, in aveng-ing the murder of his father, not only commits a moral (and ju-ridical) crime but also provokes the punishment of the gods, who pursue him in the figures of the Eumenides; in the same way, the heroes in the plays of Sophocles and even of Euripides transgress laws which are both moral and divine, but Euripides begins to separate the two orders and to regard moral guilt as something apart from sin against the gods.

The meaning of the term "sin," however, takes on a new seri-ousness in the Bible because the whole conception of the relation between man and God is immensely deepened and any estrange-ment of man from God infinitely aggravated in its context. As the term "sacred" in paganism is far less opposed to "secular" than is the biblical term "holy," so also sin in the pagan sense is less spiritual and less mystical than it is in the biblical sense. Since paganism as a whole fails to distinguish rigorously between motive and action but regards guilt in the first place as a crime against a quasi-juridical code, so pagan sin also is an overt act which trespasses against a divine code. Sin in the Christian sense, on the contrary, is an inner alienation from God, although this alienation must bear bad fruit in the realm of action. For even thoughts which have not appeared, and perhaps never will appear, in the outer world are as sinful as if they had already appeared. God "sees in secret." This inwardness of sin is, of course, most emphasized in the New Testament.

Sin, as compared with guilt, is not merely a moral category, it is rather, and in the first place, a religious category. It concerns the relation between moral evil, in all its forms and manifestations, to the ground of all being, as experienced mystically and articulated by religious imagination. It concerns, therefore, not only a breach of the moral law, as dictated by a moral code or by moral reason, but also and primarily a breach of the bond between man and deity. Conscience is then no longer a conversation between two selves within the self, one representing the individual, the other the universal, aspect, but between the human self and the voice of God. As, in the case of the civil law, the state represents the universal pole of the self and is endowed with the power of pursuing and punishing the transgressor, so, in the case of religious life, God takes the place of the state. But now the power and the authority of the universal self is infinitely strengthened and enhanced because this authority is both external and internal, a power not only over my body but also over my conscience and over my whole destiny; therefore, God neither uses nor needs a police force and an army: his arm is stronger than any state or any human community can be.

In paganism the gods do possess an army that pursues the criminal: the Erinyes, who only in the *Oresteia* of Aeschylus finally settle down in Athens, where the city-state takes over their office so that politics and religion mingle. Biblical religion, on the contrary, stresses the infinite superiority of God over the state. In the Old Testament, God is the head of the state of Israel, but this does not mean what it means in Athens, where Athena is the head; Israel is exalted over an earthly and political community by the covenant God makes with her. The state is no longer a state in the political sense, it is a holy community, and the people are supposed to be holy priests—a priestly nation that serves not their own interests but God's alone. "For thou art an holy people unto the Lord thy God; the Lord, thy God hath chosen thee to be a special people unto himself."[7]

Paganism does not know holiness in the biblical sense, and therefore it is unacquainted with sin and sinfulness as the opposite of holiness. Man is sinful because he is in opposition to the Holy God. This aggravates secular guilt by extending it to cosmic or ontological dimensions. Not only is man as a sinner in conflict with himself, his fellow-man, and the community of moral beings like himself, but he is immersed in a conflict which has an absolute and ultimate significance involving the destiny of the whole world as well as the destiny of all mankind, since it means an offense against the creator of both the world and man. Sin in this sense is sin against the Holy God, i.e., the moral is interpreted as the mystical and the mystical as the moral. Thereby both are extended; the moral is no longer limited, as it is in the secular sense, and the mystical is no longer mute and inarticulate. Sin implies lack of trust and loyalty. Man, yielding to sin, deserts the eternal God, his highest judge, and turns to "foreign" gods. Sin is thus both moral guilt and religious idolatry.[8]

Does this identification of moral and spiritual transgression not endanger the purity of the moral law? Does it not eventually lead to a superstitious conception of the law, confusing what is essential and what is merely occasional, what is "categorical" and what is a ceremonial custom or a ritual observance? This danger cannot be denied, and Kant emphasized it so much as to reduce religion to morality in order to avoid, once and for all, the pitfall of superstition. However, Kant neither saw nor respected the limit of morality as discussed above, and therefore he did not recognize the part that religious sanction of moral laws plays. The

7. Deut. 7:6.

8. "The Bible might aptly be described as the drama of man's effort to flee from God. . . . All such roads of escape lead to idolatry, for one of the basic urges of idolatry is man's desire to initiate his own relationship to God" (Minear, *op. cit.*, pp. 16 f.). What Minear calls man's "own relationship to God" could pistologically be called "man's cultural or culturally determined relation to the mystical ground of his existence."

danger of superstition is counteracted by the danger of moral nihilism or pharisaism (moralism); both of them represent a sort of
superstition, so that Kant evades one danger only to be caught in
another. There are dangers all about. Man cannot escape them absolutely. But Protestant Christianity at least knows the danger of
ecclesiastical superstition; by stressing the significance of the individual conscience and the immediate relationship between the
soul and God, Protestant faith mitigates as much as possible eccle-
siasticism and legalism.

But how can the fact of man's sinfulness in its Christian interpretation contribute to the ultimate "solution" of the antinomies?
Does this interpretation not, on the contrary, immensely aggra-
vate their destructive power, as it also aggravates the meaning of
secular guilt and secular punishment? Is it not infinitely worse to
confront the wrath and the punishment of the eternal God whose
domain has no limits and who is invested with an authority beyond
which there is no appeal? Biblical imagination enhances the formidable consequences of sin by the conception of hell and of eternal suffering which the sinner has to undergo in the future life.
No wonder that the Roman church was able to profit from such
a pressure exercised upon the conscience of its believers. Here
again the Protestant church has mitigated the fateful effect of the
Christian faith by the doctrine of grace, which permits man to appeal to God directly instead of being compelled to implore the
leniency of church officials. But the basic question is not answered
thereby. Sin actually worsens the inner split of man's conscience,
instead of healing it. The split seems to become incurable, since it
is no longer a split within man's conscience alone but a split between man and the very ground of being. Sin makes this split eternal and definitive, as the picture of hell, even if deprived of the
vicious ecclesiastical misuse, graphically illustrates. This interpretation is by no means arbitrary, after all. It is intrinsically necessary according to the logic of the heart, since the moral is ultimately immersed in the mystical ground of existence which faith
articulates.

Law and Love

FAITH consummates politics in pronouncing God as the King of Kings; it consummates morality in pronouncing the Kingdom of God as that moral state in which the antitheses of universality and individuality, of unity and manifoldness, of freedom and necessity, and of time and eternity are definitively surpassed. This is done by love, taking this word in the sense in which man is commanded to love his neighbor as himself and to love God with all his heart and with all his soul and with all his might,[9] i.e., without any restriction whatever. Jesus confirms this basic commandment and demonstrates it by his own life and death. Faith in fulfilling this supreme law is love in action. It is a mystical love, since its roots are religious. Love of neighbor is neither sentimental nor ecstatic, nor yet erotic in the Greek sense; it is the "fulfilment of the law."[10] It establishes that community in which every member is willing and able to identify himself with every other member, because each considers everyone to be, like himself, a child of God and therefore united in God, the Father of us all.

This sublime and, at the same time, simple conception "solves" all moral problems, conflicts, contrasts, and contradictions. It is like a magic wand which metamorphoses this tragic world of ours with one stroke into paradise. It is like an enchanted fountain in which the sick soul of man can recover by bathing. But, although love is this simple prescription which consummates all moral prescriptions, it is not easily performed; in fact, it is more difficult to live in accordance with this prescription than it is to live in accordance with any other, any minor duty or obligation. In a very profound sense it is no "law," no prescription—indeed, no obligation at all—but it transcends the contrast between desire and duty, between inclination and obligation, and between a general law and individual impulses or interests. It leaves behind the whole sphere in which these moral oppositions prevail, and it opens up an entirely new level of life on which the moral categories are replaced by a transmoral, because transrational, co-ordination of the polarities within the ego and between self and self. In and

9. Deut. 6:5.   10. Rom. 13:10.

through love the supreme "ego-solution" is made real and manifest, for in and through this mystical, and yet so simple, "commandment" man is made a co-worker with God and a fellow-sufferer in the struggle of life—a struggle which is eternally victorious because it is not only man's but God's cause in which man is involved and for which man fights.

Inasmuch as the Kingdom of God is established, God's government is made efficient. In this mystical kingdom there is no place for hate, envy, greed, lust, arrogance, impatience, or vanity; the entire host of vices and moral deficiencies is banished. Man is integrated within himself and reconciled to every other man. The absolute community is the community of love because in this community alone the principle of subordination which governs the moral realm, its norms and its judgments, is completely transcended by the principle of co-ordination. In the realm of action, love corresponds to beauty in the realm of contemplation; it is beauty active in the heart and soul. Only through love does faith become the summit of all other levels and realms of human life and activity. Only through love does faith overshadow all cultural achievements, real and potential. "God is love" is the most sublime, the most exalted, "definition" ever given. In this revelation all revelation is brought to an absolute and final end.

Paul in his great song in praise of love explicitly exalts love over knowledge, prophecy, and even faith. Love is more than all of them because it directly conjoins man with man and man with God. It is the mystical bond, the *unio mystica*, between the finite and the infinite ego. We know in part, we prophesy in part, but love makes us perfect. Hope and faith leave uncertainty, but love gives absolute certainty. Love is mysterious because it unites what is separated; it unites the opposites so completely that they become one and the same life, one and the same self. As secular love unites two persons more deeply than any other bond can do, how much more does spiritual love melt away all differences and all oppositions!

Faith culminates in the love of God, which is both man's love for God and God's love for man.[11] Spinoza insists that man cannot

11. Cf. Paul Ramsey, *Basic Christian Ethics* (New York: Charles Scribner's Sons, 1950), pp. 116 ff.

wish that God love him, if he understands the essence of God. But he goes on to say that God loves himself with an infinite love and that man's love for God is a part of that infinite love with which God loves himself. Does this not annul his former statement? If my love for God is a part of God's own love for himself, do I not then participate in this love in such a way that God embraces my love to him within his infinite love? If God loves himself and if I am a part of God, does not God then love me too as his own part? What more can I desire?[12]

In so far as man reaches this summit of faith, his self-contradiction, his anxiety, his uneasiness, and his ever lurking despair are conquered. With this love in our hearts, we are truly "more than conquerors," as Paul says; "for I am persuaded that neither death, nor life, nor angels, nor principalities, nor powers, nor things present, nor things to come, nor height, nor depth, nor any other creature, shall be able to separate us from the love of God, which is in Christ Jesus our Lord."[13]

But the greatest and the most mysterious of all the wonders of divine love is the forgiveness of sin. By stooping down to the repentant sinner and by accepting him again into his fellowship, God has shattered the ultimate barrier to the "solution" of the antinomies; the gates of hell are pulled down, and Satan is defeated. This is the greatest victory of love over all the contradictions of existence, since guilt and sin represent the severest and most offensive of all. Forgiving love finally closes the gap between man and God, and thereby all the gaps which divide the human self. By graciously receiving the sinner, God "reconciles the world unto himself" and thus reconciles world and ego by his love. Repentance implies the return of the creature to the Creator. The sinner has turned away from God, thereby widening the original split within himself to the utmost, so that a reunification seems impossible; now, by returning, he opens the way for the definitive reunification. The action of man (repentance) and the action of God (forgiveness) condition and supplement each other. Thus in

---

12. Spinoza, of course, secularizes and rationalizes mystical love. In replacing religious faith by philosophic speculation, he wants to extend culture beyond its legitimate limits. But religion has taken "vengeance": his "geometry of God" issues in an ecstatic exultation.
13. Rom. 8:37 ff.

the love of Christ the love of God reveals its fulness and faith attains its fulfilment.

The transformation of guilt into sin facilitates and provides for the final "solution" of the antinomies of experience, which persist and even harden in the cultural spheres and which culminate in guilt. By this transformation the way is paved for the decisive and definitive reconciliation which alone can do what no cultural effort and exertion, no moral goodness, and no speculative boldness can achieve. To be sure, it is a religious and therefore a mystical and imaginative solution; but this alone is adequate to the task. Man could not even wish that such a task should be discharged in any lesser form, by any less wondrous "method." In the long history of philosophy, including even Christian philosophy, only very few have recognized and respected this divine "method" in its entire scope and significance. Only Christian theology saw and expressed the truth, but the theologians were unable to convince the philosophers.

What is the secret of this divine "method"? From the human point of view or from the perspective of pistology, faith accomplishes its hardest task because it liberates man from the isolation and loneliness which is his part as long as he relies upon moral freedom and conscience alone. The modern existentialists have brought out the depth of the horror which is the consequence of this metaphysical, this cosmic, isolation and of this stiff-necked self-reliance of man. The political and moral decay of our days contributes much toward disclosing the absurdity and folly of such an attitude. Modern times have come to an end: the limit of the glory of man which characterized the spirit of modern times has been made manifest. This is the historical moment, it seems to me, when philosophy should "repent" and open the door to theology, so that a reconciliation between these hostile, and yet so closely related, sciences can be approached. Some religious existentialists have done a good deal to facilitate such a reconciliation in their own fashion.

Divine love demonstrates that man is not alone in the cosmos; that his own experience, his own burden and plight, his uneasiness and dread, not only are his but are shared by the Lord of the universe, by the Maker of all things. It further demonstrates that the recognition of his own limits, which is the essence of repentance, can finally free him in a manner in which he can never be freed by his own aspiration and ambition. The existential atheist is himself a mystic, after all; the nothingness which he regards as the "solution" of all problems is a mystical nothingness because it is all-embracing and absolute. The atheist comes to his negative mysticism because he repudiates and annihilates the religious articulation which culminates in the revelation of divine love. The atheist insists upon a rational, philosophic, and secular solution; therefore, he is punished by falling victim to a satanic mysticism.[14]

Freedom and Grace

FORGIVING love is the key that unlocks the ultimate mystery of reality by reconciling the world to God and God to man. The absolute community is a community of repentant sinners transformed into a community of lovers by the grace of God, as revealed in Christ. The Christian believer is both condemned and received by his Lord. He re-enters paradise by eating for a second time the fruit from the tree of the knowledge of good and evil; but this time he is not persuaded by the serpent but by his Maker himself, not by the tempter but by the Savior. And thus he is not again driven out from the state of harmony and peace, but, on the contrary, he is brought back into that state. This is a mysterious revelation indeed.

How can guilt be forgiven, if interpreted as sin against the Holy God? How can the Holy God pardon man's sin, even if repentance precedes pardon? Is not a deed something done that can never be undone? Is not the breach of trust and loyalty something that cannot be forgiven, even by a gracious, almighty, and loving Father? To be sure, a secular father's love can forgive a deed done by his son against himself, but only because the father is himself a finite creature who well knows that he, too, is not without sin and guilt and therefore that he is not entitled to harden his heart. The Heavenly Father is no such finite creature; he does

14. "I am the spirit that always negates," Mephistopheles says in Goethe's *Faust*, and a few lines later he identifies his realm with absolute nothingness. Cf. also the word of Friedrich H. Jacobi in his open *Letter to Fichte* (in *Gesamtausgabe* [Leipzig, 1812–25]), "God or—Nothing."

not live under human conditions, is never tempted, and is therefore prevented from sinning by his very nature. How can he pardon what is intrinsically unpardonable, man's self-disintegration, which foils any solution of the antinomy?

The Gospel says that God had to become man in order to accomplish this seemingly impossible victory; that he himself had to suffer from man's sin to the point of utter humiliation and destruction; and that love, being victorious under these circumstances, was able to restore man's integrity or to redeem him. I need not deal here with these christological problems. But I would like to discuss the problem of the relation between man's moral deficiency and God's saving grace under the philosophical (or pistological) point of view, which centers upon the question as to how the freedom of the will is compatible with faith in a power that leaves no room at all for freedom (God's "irresistible grace" in theological terms). Paul and after him Augustine and Luther strongly emphasized that man is "clay" in the hands of the Creator; and Barth has even gone so far as to declare that man is only a "hole" into which God pours his grace. How do doctrines like these fit into the scheme of thought set forth in this philosophy of faith?

It is certainly true that man, as compared with the Almighty, is like nothing, as Ecclesiastes, Job, and the Psalms so impressively point out. In the language of pistology, mystical reality articulated by biblical imagination represents the absolute "solution" of the antinomies of experience, so that the entire compass and contrast of world and ego is swallowed up and absorbed by it. The antinomies are as nothing when seen in the overwhelming light of this "solution." And yet Christian faith does not simply ignore the antagonism of God and world and does not simply disregard the existence of man as a self-dependent being but teaches that "God so loved the world. . . ." God therefore does not regard man as mere clay or as a "hole" but as created in God's own image and capable of doing good or evil, that is, as morally free. Only because man has this exceptional and central position does God descend to save him. Man is free enough even to reject Christ and to surrender to Satan. Without this freedom, grace would not be grace but a constraint or a merely physical act. Grace presupposes freedom

on the part of man. But it is also true that the contradiction between freedom and necessity is supposed to be abrogated by faith
in God, who is beyond this alternative because he is absolutely
free. How can God's unlimited freedom and man's limited freedom be combined?

Pistology need not consider this problem from the position of a
speculative or existential ontology but rather from the position of
religious faith alone. If faith were to renew the antagonism of
freedom and necessity presented in experience and if God were
simply to supplant the world in the contrast of world and ego,
faith would not fulfil its promise to solve the original conflict. Or,
to put it differently, faith would offer not an "ego-solution," but
an illusory "world-solution" like that of the Stoics or Spinoza.
The human ego would be completely crushed and man's relative
freedom would be replaced by an absolute lack of freedom, such
as Luther proposes in his writing against Erasmus. This is a form
of pantheistic theism. But the Christian faith gives an interpretation of the human situation in which man retains his freedom and
yet submits to the absolute power of God.

How is this possible? Can philosophy contribute anything to
the clarification of this intricate and subtle problem? Speculative
metaphysics is hopelessly ensnared if it tries to reconcile the opposites of freedom and necessity, whether it proceeds cosmologically or theistically. There is no honest way out, whether one philosophically conceives world or God as absolute reality. But faith is
not a speculative metaphysics, either pantheistic or theistic, or a
combination of the two. Faith is a personal attachment to the
living Father. Is this attachment conceivable without subjecting
man absolutely to the omnipotent will of God? Is not such surrender the very substance of faith?

It is. But it is a *surrender*. And a surrender presupposes that man
is free to surrender; otherwise his act is not human at all but merely the effect of an act of God. Now, in a way, it really is such an
effect. But again, in order to be an effect wrought upon man's will,
this will must be regarded as free. Otherwise the effect would be
merely physical, and this would indeed thwart the whole meaning
of grace. Divine grace, in contradistinction to physical causality,
can have an effect upon the recipient only if he understands what

he receives, and he must feel free, although overpowered. How can these extremes be brought into harmony? They can be only if man feels that it is his own deepest longing which is fulfilled in the overpowering effect of God's gracious and loving power. But this is the actual burden of the Christian faith.[15]

It is true that man gives up his moral freedom to reject the grace of God, if he surrenders. But in exchange he receives a higher spiritual freedom which makes him a fellow-laborer with God, so that he is able to participate in the divine power in which freedom and necessity are no longer opposed to each other because God is not opposed by the world or by any conditions not generated by himself, except the evil will of man. This evil will of man—the only power in creation which can and does resist his will actively —is broken by God's overwhelming grace and love. It is broken not by means of force or the stronger psychical energy but by means of love, which conquers from within the very soul of man, because it implies the unification of the human and the divine in the act of loving.

In the absolute community where there is no longer any schism between the head and the subjects, between the outer conduct and the inner motive, or between the poles of universality and individuality, no one is coerced, but neither is anyone free to do evil. Morality is transcended, as is the body politic. The absolute community is the community governed solely by love, and love is that desire which is in complete agreement with the law because the law is fulfilled in love. Kant is right: Love cannot be commanded, but not, as he thinks, because it is a "pathological" feeling, which in his language means a feeling dictated not by reason but by inclination. On the contrary, it cannot be commanded because it is both an inclination and an obligation or that obligation which man chooses to discharge, being impelled from within himself to that end. Therefore, the "ought" is transformed into impulse, and the impulse no longer resists the moral command.

In the community united by love, God, its head, does not impress his will upon the members from without. Rather, he lives

15. Cf. William Temple in *Nature, Man, and God* (London, 1934), p. 381, where he says that the relation of the divine and human wills involves "at once the denial of all human freedom over against God and the affirmation of a complete human freedom in submission to God."

within the heart of each individual, as Paul gives evidence when he says: "Christ lives in me." In so far as the believer lives by faith and acts according to his faith, he no longer lives in the world, and he and his neighbor are no longer in opposition. Therefore, God need not use force; the love of the believer is itself God's force, a force no longer distinguished from the human will. The inner split between will and desire disappears. Only thus are morality and the whole cultural sphere transcended and fulfilled by faith. And consequently freedom itself is not denied, but it, too, is transcended and fulfilled. This fulfilment continues in the direction of the will, since it determines itself and acts on its own accord in the moral field. For in morality, too, the will never acts merely as an individual will but always at the same time as a universal will, as Kant has clearly seen.

In the last analysis the human will is essentially moral because it always stands under the moral law. The moral will, obeying the law and willing the good, binds itself; and only by binding itself and acting in accordance with its obligation does the will act as will. In this sense Socrates was right to insist that man never does evil voluntarily. If he does evil, man acts against his own will, thereby contradicting himself.[16] This is the riddle of the evil will which is, and yet is not, a will. Paul agrees with Socrates when he exclaims, "For that which I do I allow not: for what I would, that do I not; but what I hate, that do I."[17] This is an accurate description of the phenomenon of evildoing. It illuminates the split which is simultaneously the origin and the consequence of this strange self-disintegration.

Moral action integrates man, but never entirely, since man can never act in complete agreement with his (good) will. Only in the Kingdom of God, where this agreement is guaranteed, is his full integration assured. To say that this effect is brought about at the expense of man's freedom is to pervert the truth and flatly deny faith altogether. Actually, faith carries through what is begun in moral life. It leads the will to the goal of its own striving and longing. It preserves freedom and consummates it by grace.

16. Cf. the author's *Primacy of Faith* (New York: Macmillan Co., 1943), chap. vi.
17. Rom. 7:15.

There is no difference between man's choosing the good and God's choosing man, for, inasmuch as man chooses the good, God has chosen him and is acting within him. The less man yields to merely individual, i.e., arbitrary ("fleshly") incentives, the more he obeys God. The less he is seduced by mere impulses which contradict his will, the more is he freed by grace, a genuine bondsman and companion of God and Christ. The more a man lives on the level of faith and acts accordingly, the more is his will both free and bound. But love alone fulfils the law; in the community of love, freedom and grace are no longer opposed to each other but are in perfect agreement. Grace, in fact, is not the adversary but rather the ally of freedom.

Culture is consummated by faith. But is the community of love actually real, so that the moral and political communities are replaced or ever replaceable by it? This question will be discussed in chapter viii.

Time, Conquered by Faith

THE human ego is not completely dominated by time as are the brute animals and all processes of nature. Man partly defeats time by his own resources. The ego is not merely an entity belonging to the world of space and time. Rather, it confronts this world as its counterpart; it is the ego or soul of the world and its very center; and it is superior to it in knowing it, for the world does not and cannot know the ego. This original contrast of experience is reflected in the relation between time and eternity, as we have seen. Because man is not subjugated to time, he can remember the past and anticipate the future. By virtue of this superiority over temporal transitoriness, he can act and react as a moral being. Because he is not merely a substance existing and changing in the time flux, he can be aware of this flux; and because of this superiority, he can take a stand outside and yet also within that flux and thus separate past, present, and future; time itself, in the last analysis, depends upon eternity (if we use this word as an expression of man's extra-temporality).

Natural time (symbolized by t in the equations of physics) is devoid of time dimensions because it is merely a measure of speed without relation to any definite present. The present is the temporal point in which the extra-temporal ego stands; and only because the ego as ego stands on the ground of eternity, does a present exist. But the present is the precondition of past and future, since the past is nothing but a remembered, and the future nothing but an anticipated, present and since both remembrance and anticipation need the present as the standpoint from which past and future can be seen. Nature therefore lacks both past and future in the proper sense, as long as man does not look at nature from his own vantage point. Nature exists and proceeds in that sort of time which Bergson calls *temps-espace;* this time is characterized by the categories of "before" and "after" and not by the three dimensions of past, present, and future.

Of course, man can reconstruct the past beyond the limit of his individual remembrance and even beyond the limit of the memory of mankind by means of vestiges, documents, monuments, and the like. But, even so, the standpoint of the present is the necessary precondition of any reconstruction of the past.[18] Dimensional time (and only dimensional time is time in the full sense of the word) and eternity are bound together, as are world and ego; neither is possible without its contrast, at least in so far as (secular) experience is concerned. On the other hand, as long as they remain together, they contradict each other. Time tends to swallow up eternity, and eternity tends to conquer time, as is clearly demonstrated by the virtues which, like loyalty and fidelity, defy transience and cling to what withstands change but are continuously threatened by the flux of time. Only in the realm of spiritual

18. In an interesting book, *History of Nature* (Chicago: University of Chicago Press, 1949), C. F. von Weizsäcker defends the thesis that nature is historical, since no reversal of its development is compatible with the second law of thermodynamics. He recognizes the mutual relation between nature as object and man as the subject of knowledge and is aware of the significance of man as the precondition of historical orientation. However, he gets into trouble when he speaks about the future, because he does not fully acknowledge that the time dimensions cannot be dissolved from man's time-consciousness. Thus he defines future events as being "possible" (i.e., expected, but not foreknown) and yet insists that "every future at one time becomes a present," which is true only if the future events are not only possible but necessary. This necessity abstracts from the element of expectation and conceives of time in the naturalistic sense in which all events are necessary; but in that sense events are not "future" any more, because there is no present from which they could be expected (cf. pp. 10–13).

imagination is eternity victorious; by faith we can "remember" the "first" day and anticipate the "last" day, as the biblical record does, in narrating the story of Creation and prophesying the "day of the Lord."

According to faith, God is absolutely extra-temporal and creates time as he creates the world and its order. Man lives by faith in knowing that time has a beginning and will have an end, although these terms, like all biblical terms, are not concepts but images of something that cannot be fully conceived, because it is essentially not rational (or intellectual) but spiritual and mystical and concerns not the events or data in this world but the relation between the ultimate ground of this world and all events or data in time. This relation is no longer temporal, of course, although spiritual imagination necessarily uses temporal metaphors in order to express it. Metaphorical language alone can articulate what is inexpressible in any rational language. It alone can make known the victory of eternity over time as it is experienced by the prophetic mind. In agreement with the "ego-solution" of faith, this victory is assured by the eternity of the living God, who reigns over the temporal world which he has created and which he sustains. The temporal world is not absolute, but it depends upon the absolute. Time has no power of its own to exist; it is rooted in the eternal ground of all existence.

Since religion transcends and consummates morality, the victory of eternity must appear as a moral victory over morality itself. This is exactly the meaning of God's defeating Satan and leading history to the end of man's final (and definitive) salvation. Inasmuch as the man of faith anticipates this end and feels assured of it, he already participates in the victory of the eternal and may enjoy "eternal life." The word "victory" indicates that time is needed to defeat time or that the temporal world is the very presupposition of the "solution" brought about by faith. Without the contrast of time and eternity—i.e., of world and ego—and of world and God, eternity could not be the conqueror of time, and faith would be destitute of any content.

Christ is the actual victor, inasmuch as he fulfils the promise of salvation. In that respect he ushers in the end of time, "realized eschatology," as Professor Dodd has called this momentous event.

Time is fulfilled in him; beginning and end meet; what was expected from the beginning and remembered by his people is now
present, the Kingdom of God, in which eternity reigns with no
encumbrances from the transience of the temporal.

Time is not, as Plato suggested, the image of eternity. Rather, it
is the image of disunity and manifoldness. It is the image of exter-
nality, especially in its mathematical aspect, which sets time on an
equal footing with space, as Bergson has so brilliantly shown.
Dimensional time already presumes a certain spiritualization, since
past and future are no longer so external to each other and to the
present as the before and after are in the mathematical scheme and
since they are bound together in the self by means of remembrance and anticipation and by means of loyalty and hope. Therefore, only dimensional time can be reconciled to eternity, as it is in
the Bible. Only when remembrance and expectation embrace the
temporal world as a whole can faith maintain an image of eternity
reigning over the destiny of mankind. Only the time scheme
which allows God to act can become the image of his purpose and
his dispensation.

Dimensional time alone is concrete or actual, i.e., the time in
which action can be intended and carried through by the self.
This time scheme is not merely general, like the t in the equations,
a merely quantitive factor in the physical order of a process, but it
is individual, qualitative, and a factor in a spiritual order of action
and reaction, of doing and suffering, of defeat and victory. One
might be tempted to think of eternity in a contemplative way,
since contemplation is not involved in temporal action but looks
at the world with detachment. Especially does artistic contemplation seem to elevate us completely over the turmoil and ever imperfect scene of human strife and to lift us up into the celestial
sphere, where time is conquered by eternity.[19] But this aesthetic
temptation is destroyed by reflection on the limits of the contemplative sphere and of contemplation itself.

Mystics indulge in the illusory calm of a pseudo-aesthetic vision
which they interpret as exalted over world and time. But such an
aesthetic articulation of mystical experience, tempting though it
is, forgets that the visionary must return to the temporal realm of

19. This contemplation is the origin of Plato's definition.

conflict and perplexity. It forgets that nothing short of faith in the final victory of the eternal will and purpose can generate that absolute trust which delivers the self from its contradictions, making it whole. Active love, far more than contemplative rapture, can dare to interpret "the silence of eternity." St. Bernard knew this truth better than Aristotle and Thomas Aquinas did. And the whole drama of the gospel is one great confirmation; otherwise it would not be a drama, i.e., an action of the son of God, to be imitated by everyone who dares to follow him. Only this active faith can unite what is disunited in time; only this faith can make man superior to the vicissitudes and chances of the ever changing scene of life and history. Only this faith can "glory o'er the wrecks of time."

This active faith triumphs over the horror of an infinite and spiritually empty time process which the Greeks were compelled to assume because of their mythological and speculative, i.e., exclusively contemplative, attitude. The cyclical conception of time events is but a consequence of this basic view and does not improve its dire implications but rather throws them into relief. The idea of temporal infinity springs from the nature of number, which prevents the intellect from embracing the world by means of mathematics and mathematical physics. Contemplation, as we have seen, can attain to a world-image only in the realm of art, not in that of scientific method. The idea of an infinite time process is derived from this impossibility; it merely expresses the impotency of the intellect adequately to depict spiritual infinity, which is concerned with the ultimate synthesis of universality and individuality. The temporal infinity of nature is a product of a scientific imagination that tries vainly to grasp this synthesis with an insufficient method.

Or, to put it in a different way, the intellect, urged to find the totality of the world, refuses (rightly) to discover it within any finite time and thus comes to the conclusion that there is, in reality, no such end. The infinity of space and time mirrors in a negative fashion the infinity of the spirit, as the speculation of Giordano Bruno illustrates with so revealing an enthusiasm. But the result is only negative; the positive thesis is illusory, since the intellect is unable to arrive at any positive solution. Speculative intellection is doomed to failure; it produces only an intellectual myth, the least satisfying and least adequate sort of myth. The thesis that the world has no beginning and no end in time is such a myth of the scientific understanding; but this understanding has no competence in the realm of myth, it loses all its prerogative and power when it tries to give an answer to the ultimate question. Of all kinds of eschatology, the intellectual is the most inane.

Spiritual, as compared with intellectual imagination, can truly be called "realistic," since it is the adequate medium through which the eyes of faith see ultimate reality. This imagination offers the only possible positive version of the negative intellectual thesis by insisting that time is not infinite but is bounded by the infinite spirit, i.e., by God. God is the beginning and God is the end. This faith is "realistic" because it destroys the illusory myth of intellectual speculation and imagination and "solves" the ultimate task, which faith alone can discharge. The beginning and the end of time point to the "really real," which is the mystically real.[20]

Time is the image of disunity, it is the sign of that original split which experience encounters in the duality of world and ego and in the contradictions of the polarities of consciousness. This consciousness is, as the antinomies indicate, not ultimate. It experiences the truth in a broken, somewhat distorted, way, in the way of secularity, which means, literally, temporality. Ultimate truth is not secular, for secular truth is "unreal" in the ultimate sense. Faith, supported by spiritual imagination, is alone "realistic"; it is the only possible form by which human eyes can see ultimate truth.

The philosophy of faith thus, in a way, confirms the earliest attempt of man at the knowledge of the ultimate, the attempt of Parmenides whose greatest disciple is Plato. Both teach that this world of ours is not the real world; that time and change and movement and manifoldness are "phenomenal" only; that the "really real" is eternal, unchangeable oneness. But the difference between this oldest and boldest trend of thought and the Christian faith is that the Greek thinkers believed in the possibility of fath-

20. Cf. the author's address "The Mystery of Time in the Mirror of Faith," *Anglican Theological Review*, XXV (April, 1943), 204 ff.

oming what is "really real" and thus fell victims to the temptation of a contemplative and intellectual solution, while biblical wisdom recognizes the insufficiency of such an enterprise. Greek speculation isolates the eternity of truth from temporal change and historical development. Biblical revelation, on the contrary, centers in the relation between the eternal and the temporal and thus succeeds in letting the eternal prevail over the temporal. Biblical faith is more "realistic" and more "logical" in this respect than Greek philosophy.

Culture is transcended and consummated by faith. The conflict between world and ego is finally quelled by the conquest of time. However, this conquest, though assured by faith, is not perfect as long as we live in time. And just so long the conflict between world and ego is not entirely abated. There is a tension between culture and faith which is not removed by the thesis of a consummation of culture through faith. Culture is not consummated in time, nor is it replaced by faith. Time is not fully conquered by eternity as long as it persists. Christ is the end of time, but time did not end with and in and through him. "Realized eschatology" is contested by the events that followed the great outburst of faith. Can the philosophy of faith say something about this remaining tension?

CHAPTER VIII
Remaining Tensions

The Tension between Biblical Faith and Civilization

FAITH consummates culture, it integrates man and provides him with the means whereby he can overcome secular self-contradiction. The antinomies of experience are thus solved not intellectually, but spiritually. However, this "solution" paradoxically generates a new tension, the tension between faith and the entire enterprise of culture. Because faith transcends the whole cultural horizon and surpasses the very meaning and function of cultural potentialities, the value of culture is endangered. Not only does faith triumph over all the cultural realms by consummating them, but it makes civilization, as such, questionable. If faith alone succeeds in attaining that goal toward which the activity of culture moves without final success, what validity can this activity or its results claim? Are they not obliterated by the triumphant power of God? Is not everything man can create or organize condemned to dwindle to total insignificance as compared with this power? Is not every relative solution overshadowed and even annulled when the absolute solution is reached? Can there still be any place, any function, for civilization beside the all-fulfilling revelation of God? This question displays the full depth of the problem to which this entire book is addressed: the problem concerning the relation between culture and faith.

When God reveals himself, man, together with all his works and institutions, seems to fade into nothingness. Secularity seems to lose its power—indeed, its very existence—when the glory and splendor of eternity appear, just as opinion or assumption grow dim when the sun of truth rises. In its brilliant light science and art, politics and morality, economics and technology, take on a shadowy life, a life that depends upon that supreme and omnipotent light and borrows its own strength and creativity from the highest source of creation and of life itself. Scientific truth cannot retain its isolated character after the all-embracing truth is revealed. No artistic work can keep its self-dependence apart from the self-revelation of the master-artist whose work is the whole world, including man. The state and the community of moral beings appear as insufficient and helpless attempts to bring about that perfect peace and justice which Christ could pronounce and create.

No wonder, then, that the Roman Catholic church claimed full power over state and individual, that science and art were regarded by her as realms of her own empire, that the whole of civilization was drawn into the orbit of the Christian faith. In the Middle Ages, culture seemed to be Christian and Christianity the sole and sufficient author and critic of civilization. Medieval culture was totalitarian because it was Christian through and through, at least as to its standards and norms. The pope in Rome was the supreme judge in all things human, the supreme sovereign, not only in matters of faith but in all matters of civilization. He was the vicar of Christ and of God on earth. He owned the political and spiritual power to crush all trends of thought and taste, of manners and legislation, which he regarded as un-Christian. The heritage of antiquity was submitted to his administration and jurisdiction.

But all this was but appearance, and even the appearance was not totally undisturbed; the struggle between church and state, the attempts at an independent scientific investigation and theory, the revolt against the moral standards of the church in many camps, and the emancipation of the arts disclose a rift. Greek thought was appeased, but not really subdued, as the Thomistic victory shows. It was a Pyrrhic victory, since the church thereby abandoned important positions and subsequently lost its power over men's minds. The contrast between the monastic and the "secular" clergy manifests the undercurrent of tension within the church itself; and the increasing strength of independent thought and feeling, which finally issued in the Renaissance, manifests the undercurrent of tension between a "secular" and a Christian tendency. This tension has come out into the open in modern times. It was already obvious in the antagonism of Renaissance and Reformation and widened in the course of the centuries, until it assumed the dangerous dimensions of today.

In this tension the antinomy between world and ego is in a way resuscitated. The claim of faith to have reconciled the world to God led to the medieval synthesis of culture and faith, but eventually it turned out to be illusory. The world regained its own independent strength and the organized community of faith split into the two communities of the Roman Catholics and the Protestants, the one upholding the old claim but deprived of its old power, the other maintaining that the medieval synthesis did not represent the true relation between culture and faith; that a certain independence of science, art, state, and morality must be allowed; that the church on earth and the Kingdom of God are not identical—in other words, that there is a final and inevitable tension between culture and faith which will last as long as history persists and time is not entirely swallowed up by eternity.

However, this new tension must not be confused with the original antinomy of experience. It is a tension between the realm in which this antinomy is not solved and the Christian "solution," which is a "solution," in spite of the fact that it generates new tensions between itself and secular culture, which cannot be absorbed by organized faith, although culture is completed and consummated by faith. The very completion and consummation are opposed to the incomplete and relatively independent realms of cultural activity. Faith completes and consummates culture not on its own level and within its own limits but by surpassing the horizon of secularity. A certain resistance against the completing and consummating power on the part of culture is therefore to be expected. In order to maintain its own significance, methods, and achievements, secular culture has to reject the "solution" offered by faith. If this tension were fully dissolved, culture would lose its vitality, its creativity, and its self-confidence. This happened in the earlier centuries of the Middle Ages, which are therefore called "dark." Only in the course of its gradual emancipation from the absolute sway of faith did culture gradually increase in strength and autonomy. But this very growth was destructive of the medieval or "Christian" civilization, as achieved in the Roman Catholic system of organized faith.

There is an ineradicable tension between secular self-contradiction persisting in the cultural spheres and its "solution" by faith. If this solution disregards the tension and tries to overpower secularity altogether, not only does culture suffer, but faith suffers also, since the suppressed power takes its vengeance by encroaching upon the realm of faith. Thus a process of secularization went on within the religious domain during the centuries in which ecclesiastical authority and power seemed most victorious. The very See of Rome became the seat of high culture but of low faith, until the storm broke loose in the little town of Wittenberg.

"The Christian faith does not promise to overcome the fragmentary and contradictory aspects of man's historic existence," Reinhold Niebuhr says.[1] Faith articulates mystical experience, but it does not obliterate the distinction between secular and mystical experience. If it did, mystical experience would no longer be mystical but would be transformed into secular expression, which is what always happens when the claim of faith is exaggerated and the nature of faith is thereby falsified. There is and remains a tension between secular and mystical experience as well as between secular culture and religious faith, at least on the level of Christianity.

In the Old Testament this tension is less obvious, partly because secular culture was relatively undeveloped during the period of its genesis and partly because faith itself was not yet so spiritual and separated from culture as it is in the New Testament. The word of Jesus concerning the separation of the things that belong to God from those that belong to Caesar can be applied to the whole tension between culture and faith.

There is a continuous "cold war" between these two powers. But this war is won from the start by God and by faith in God. "Man talks of the triumph of mind over matter, of the power of culture, of the elasticity of civilization; but God has natural

1. *Faith and History* (New York: Charles Scribner's Sons, 1949), p. 135.

powers, to which all these are as the worm beneath the hoof of
the horse: and if moral need arises, He will call His brute forces
into requisition. 'Howl ye, for the day of Jehovah is near, as destruction from the Destructive does it come' (Isaiah 14). There
may be periods in man's history when to man's unholy art and
godless civilization, God can reveal Himself only as destruction."[2] Sometimes this inborn tension between man's civilization
and God's holy will is overemphasized, as if no relation whatever
existed between the two.[3] If that were true, Unamuno would be
the last one who could state it, since the struggle between culture
and faith is very pointed in his thought and since he conceives
of faith through a philosophy which is certainly influenced by
his own cultural position. But if it were true, tension could not
arise between faith and culture, for tension presupposes that
there is a close relation, though not merely a friendly one.

Not only does faith consummate culture, it also judges it, and
no merely secular achievement can ever escape condemnation
on the part of this highest court. This condemnation is assured
because of conflict between secular and mystical experience and
spheres of reconciliation. The merely temporal solution can
never match the eternal, the merely human can never vie with
the divine. Although God may suffer man's own efforts in dis-
covering truth and creating beauty and in establishing institutions and laws, he can never fully approve of them, since they
must all stop short of the goal and since all of them lack the
ultimacy which characterizes truth, beauty, and goodness.[4]

On the other hand, faith in God produces no substitute for
science, art, state, and law; culture is indispensable as long as man
remains imperfect and continues to live under historical circumstances and the conditions of natural growth and decay. Sanctifi-
cation can never become universal among men as long as guilt
and sin are not radically effaced. So long will the tension between culture and faith persist. The classical period of Italian art
was the period in which faith degenerated, and during that time
the triumph of modern science set in. The democratic state is

2. G. Adam Smith, *The Book of Isaiah* (1889), I, 409 f.
3. Miguel de Unamuno says in *The Agony of Christianity*, trans. P. Loving
(1928), p. 106: "Christianity has nothing to do with civilization or culture."
4. The story of the Tower of Babel symbolizes this truth.

certainly more in agreement with Christian standards than the feudal system was; but only after the emancipation of the state from ecclesiastical fetters was this improvement achieved. All this points to the basic tension between cultural vitality and religious ultimacy. Without this insight, we cannot understand how the Greeks could accomplish the greatest glory in their cultural works despite their inferior religion. The perfection of their art is connected with the mythological character of their religion, while the holiness of the Old Testament God is bound up with a certain hostility against "graven images." There is an iconoclastic feature in Christianity because it recognizes the idolatry in image-worshiping.

The solution of faith is therefore to be qualified; it is not without a certain limitation, which can be traced back to the contrast between faith and religion, previously discussed. Although this contrast is itself only relative, since the two aspects partly overlap, nevertheless it has an important consequence. Faith transcends all civilization, but religion has a place within civilization and thereby clashes with the other realms. Or, to put it differently, religion has two roots, one mystical, the other cultural. Faith is more in line with mystical experience, while religion as distinguished from faith has a cultural lineage.

Biblical religion, as contrasted with paganism, has its place in the system of civilization on the higher level of active life and community organization, while mythological religion is closely attached to artistic imagination, although, of course, it, too, belongs to the sphere of active life. Biblical religion, therefore, is involved in the tension between the contemplative and the active spheres of civilization. This special tension heightens and increases the general tension between faith and culture; it gives this tension a special touch which is very significant in an age of science and scientism. The scientific form of totalitarianism is particularly unbearable because it totally ignores the active character of faith and tends to try to fulfil all man's spiritual needs by means of contemplation, even on the lower level of contemplative reconciliation by means of subordination. The frequent clashes between science and Christianity can easily be deduced from this tension.

The Tension between Morality and Faith

THE tension between culture and faith assumes its most subtle and hidden form as tension between (secular) morality and Christian ethics. Since morality is the transition from outer legality to inner self-determination and self-control, it is also the transition from culture to the realm of faith in which self-determination and self-control are transformed into obedience to God. This transition is subtle, since the will of God in a specific situation of life is not revealed in Scripture but has to be discovered from case to case and since moral reason is involved in that discovery. And one might think that moral reason cannot be neglected or eliminated from the decision about the question of what God wills me to do or not to do in a given situation. However, tension obtains between the two codes of morality, the one dictated by moral reason, the other commanded by the holy will, because morality is still a code of general rules, while the Christian faith implies a "code of love," which is always concrete and unique in each constellation of life and destiny. The "code of love" might easily conflict with moral rules.

In his profound "dialectical lyric," *Fear and Trembling*, published under the pseudonym of Johannes de Silentio, Kierkegaard discusses the contrast between the moral command of fatherly love and the divine command which required from Abraham the sacrifice of his only son, Isaac. Kierkegaard sees no reason why "the same thing might not have taken place on a barren heath in Denmark." The story of Abraham illuminates the universal conflict between ethical ideas and the unconditional and unfathomable will of God. Actually, this conflict is not confined to any special command but is universal because moral reason concerns the relation between human persons alone, while God commands us to follow him, whatever the effect may be in terms of social or family relations. Since all secular morality takes into account the fallen state of man, it is itself inevitably insufficient in the eyes of God, who demands that we should be as perfect as he himself is, and, according to its very essence, it is an imperfect morality concerning imperfect circumstances, duties, and obligations. Secular morality reckons with a separation of man from man which, in the eyes of God, is unholy and an outcome of sin. Charity does away with this separation absolutely. Therefore, duties and obligations simply disappear before the highest command; they are barriers to that complete and unrestricted relationship which results from complete and unrestricted love of one's neighbor. Morality, though infinitely superior to the code of civil law, still preserves a certain legality, as we have seen. The perfection which God commands is beyond all commandments because love is the fulfilment of the law. But, for this very reason, faith conflicts with the law on its moral level, and it is this conflict which the story of Abraham and Isaac illustrates.

This conflict, though it is most acute on the level of Christian love, nevertheless exists even in pre-Christian religions. Greek tragedy deals with similar tensions in many forms. Orestes has to murder his mother in order to carry out the command of Apollo, who wants him to take vengeance for the murder of Agamemnon. But his filial feelings contradict this command, and the deed, furthermore, provokes the Eumenides to persecute him. Antigone buries her brother out of a religious devotion, while Creon, her uncle, representing the civil law, executes her for this burial, which he has forbidden.

The conflict is most drastically expressed in the harsh words of Jesus, according to the Gospel of Luke: "If any man come to me, and hate not his father, and mother, and wife, and children, and brethren, and sisters, yea, and his own life also, he cannot be my disciple."[5]

Similar words are spoken by Jesus, when a disciple asks him to let him bury his father first, before following him: "Follow me; and let the dead bury their dead."[6] Any moral obligation toward family members has to be denied when a conflict arises between faith and morality, between loyalty to God and loyalty to a relative. And such a conflict may arise at any time, as long as the Kingdom of Heaven is "at hand" but is not yet the only realm in which men live. The contrast between the lower level of civil and moral action and the higher level of absolute and exclusive devotion to God cannot be avoided; man belongs to both

5. 14:26.   6. Matt. 8:22.

realms of morality, the secular and the spiritual, the relative and the absolute, the temporal and the eternal. Although it is evident which of the two has the ascendancy, still the tension between them is real, and only Christ himself was permitted to ignore the lower level. But even Christ advises the taxpayer to fulfil his civil duty. The Sermon on the Mount depicts the ideal, the regulative, morality which is in conflict with the other. Only a hypocrite can dismiss this conflict.

Dietrich Bonhoeffer, who suffered martyrdom under the mad tyranny of the Nero of our times, was fully aware of this inescapable tension when he took sides with Christ. In his stirring account of his faith,[7] he gives a deeply impressive picture of his soul. "When Christ calls a man, He bids him come and die. The Christian is committed to a daily warfare against the world, the flesh and the devil. At the very moment of their call, men find that they have already broken with all natural ties of life. Between father and son, husband and wife, the individual and the community, stands Christ the Mediator." No one can doubt that these utterances ring true. They display the formidable tension between "natural" duties and the mystical call of Christ during the Nazi period in which every Christian was confronted by these alternatives. But in "normal" times the same alternatives always lurk behind the deceptive façade of peace between the two sets of loyalties. It is hard to love one's enemy when the enemy is also the enemy of God, and it may even be doubtful whether we are permitted or commanded to love him. Christ himself certainly did not love the Pharisee.

This tension is particularly stringent with regard to the question of whether the Christian should serve as a soldier in war. It is a bitter conflict indeed, and no partisan position can be easily defended. The conscientious objector, as well as the man who believes it his duty to serve, represents a powerful position. Does the word of Jesus, "Render to Caesar . . . ," apply here also? Or must the Christian soldier follow Christ alone, even when he does not follow him exclusively in other fields, like marriage, civil rights, and so on? I would not dare to give an answer valid for

7. *The Cost of Discipleship*, trans. R. H. Fuller (New York: Macmillan Co., 1949).

each and every one; I only point to the tension between these alternatives. Again it seems clear which of the two calls is the higher one, but this does not solve the conflict.

Reinhold Niebuhr makes this tension the very nerve of his theology. As Christians, he says, we are never permitted to have an easy conscience because we have to live our lives between opposite sets of imperatives, and, although we know that one of them is the only absolute one, we can never feel satisfied with our decisions as long as we do not suffer martyrdom. In the early centuries of Christianity this knowledge was alive in every believer, and without it the Christian faith would not have survived.

A friend of mine, the Russian poet, philosopher, and religious writer, Fedor Stepun, speaks somewhere of the "duty to sin." What he means is the duty to obey civil and moral laws which contradict the religious conscience—the commandment of God, Christian love. As a man who had to endure the first years of the Bolshevik regime, until he was expelled from Russia and took refuge in Germany, he had ample possibilities to find illustrations of that "duty" and that inner discord which ensue from the ungodly conditions created by the enemies of God. But everyone under all circumstances will find himself in a situation in which he has to undergo the trial of this conflict, if he is a sincere believer but also a "natural" man living in a state and in a family and fulfilling professional duties.

Niebuhr speaks in his Gifford Lectures of the tension between the facts of life and the principle of faith. "In principle" we are members of the kingdom of love, inasmuch as we are Christians, but "in fact" we are sinners against the holy will of God, and therefore repentance is the only way in which we can ease our consciences. The contrast between fact and faith is hard and severe indeed.

The Tension between Fact and Faith

FAITH would not be faith if there were no tension between fact and faith, for the object of faith is not a fact and facts are not objects of faith but objects of secular experience or knowledge. Even those facts or events which are regarded as fundamental to faith are objects of faith not in so far as they are facts or events but in so far as they evoked faith in the first Christians. Pilate may have known the same facts, but they did not evoke faith in him; they were merely facts for him, as they were also merely facts for those Jews who did not follow Christ. Facts can be observed and classified by the secular mind; indeed, only if they can be observed and classified by this mind are they facts, while the religious meaning transcends the factual as such. Faith is the articulation of mystical experience, which is concerned with the original unity of world and ego; therefore, it is impossible, by definition, for facts as such to become objects of faith; they may become such objects, but only if they evoke religious faith, i.e., on account of their meaning.

If facts assume a religious significance, they are no longer merely factual but carry with them a meaning which makes them, as it were, transparent to the religious mind that sees in them the expression of God's acts and power. They cease to be mere facts and become images of the divine, pronouncing ultimate truth and revealing the mystery in which we live and move and have our being. Therefore, the religious mind is always allied with that spiritual imagination which alone can grasp ultimate truth and which is called "Holy Spirit" in the imaginative language of faith.

The contents of faith are never mere facts but are always meanings, and often not facts at all. Creation is not a fact, and, taken as a fact, it is simply not true. Its truth is deeper, more fundamental, than all the facts taken together. The original fall of Adam and Eve as reported in Genesis is certainly not a fact, either of prehistoric or of biological relevance; but it is more relevant to human life than all prehistoric and biological facts can possibly be. The burning bush, the rain of manna, the appearance of God on Mount Sinai, and all the great events recorded in the Bible are no mere facts, in so far as they are related to God; they are meaningful, and their meaning can be understood only by spiritual imagination.

But an even deeper and sterner break between facts and faith shows itself when we consider the ideal or absolute community founded by Christ. This community has a certain factual existence in or as the church, and yet this existence does not exhaust the meaning of the ideal. On the contrary, it is remote from the true and real meaning, inasmuch as it is but a humanly fallible and frail copy of the original as it existed in the mind of Jesus. Only spiritual imagination is capable of comprehending this original; the actual communities are more or less distorted copies, sometimes even the reversal of what they are supposed to be. The real Kingdom of God is not real as a fact but as a content of faith and a goal of action inspired and guided by faith. There is a tension between fact and faith which disturbs the mind of the believer, making his conscience uneasy.

The reality of the Kingdom of God is imaginative, not factual. But this certainly does not mean that it is less real than facts are. On the contrary, what lives in the soul of man as the content of faith and the goal of action is far more real than all facts because it is, or may be, the source of future facts. God shapes the world not only through facts but more directly and specifically through faith, inasmuch as the world is the human world in which the destiny of man is at stake and inasmuch as God is the judge and redeemer of men and not merely the creator of nature. For this reason the imaginative character of the contents of faith is by no means a deficiency, as compared with the factual character of the contents of perception and observation. On the contrary, it is the sign of an infinite superiority and of a unique significance which is bound up with real power, greater than that of the state or any other human institution. The imaginative character ennobles and elevates the contents of faith; all facts grow pale in comparison with this imaginative reality. The final destiny of man does not depend upon the ingenuity of statesmen or of the "infallible" decrees of popes; it depends solely upon the strength, purity, and sincerity of faith in the breast of the believer.[8]

But, although the tension between fact and faith is not an indication of any weakness in faith, it is nevertheless a tension which

8. Subsequently I found the following passage in a superb book on Shakespeare: "The imagination is not a faculty for the creation of illusion; it is the faculty by which alone man apprehends reality. The 'illusion turns out to be the truth.' Let faith oust fact, as Starbuck says in *Moby Dick*. It is only our absurd 'scientific' prejudice that reality must be physical" (Harold C. Goddard, *The Meaning of Shakespeare* [Chicago: University of Chicago Press, 1951], p. 553).

causes grief and sorrow in the hearts of those who long for the Kingdom of God and who suffer from the defects which impede its coming. It is true that spiritual imagination cannot conceive what life would be like or what man would be like if the tension between fact and faith did not exist; if faith were not impaired; if man were able to enjoy the glory and peace of the Kingdom in an undisturbed continuity, an unchanging eternity. So mysterious is the content of faith that this idea of a community which would be both absolute and also a fact cannot be fully comprehended. It seems as if the tension were necessary to inflame the heart with the holy images and to kindle in man's breast the eternal fire of devotion and inspired action.

The content of faith, however, is not only a "principle" over against facts, as the contradistinction of Niebuhr seems to suggest. Faith is a reality, of all realities by far the greatest and the most powerful, for it is God himself who unfolds his own power through faith. How powerful faith is, one feels nowhere more than in listening to a sermon by Niebuhr. It is not only a "principle" which is operative in his mind and words but the Spirit of God, challenging the sad facts of finite life, precisely because he contrasts them so powerfully with the reality of his own faith, illuminating the weakness of fallen man. Although man has only imaginative expression for the articulation of the ultimate mystery of reality, this expression can arouse the most ardent flame of hope and courage and thereby enkindle those actions which make faith itself a fact in a world of facts.

Principles, like notions and concepts, belong to the realm of thought. As soon as faith is formulated by theology, it evaporates into these thin and nebulous entities. Therefore, faith is most strongly expressed in prophetic pronouncement, not in a system of thought. As in the sphere of contemplation and contemplative creation art is much more powerful than science because it does not interpolate abstract notions between the extremes of experience but co-ordinates the extremes themselves by intuition and imagination, so also in the sphere of action the prophet is the most powerful and the most effective reformer of human life because his imagination is not controlled by facts, as the intellectual planning and action of the statesman have to be, but instead it controls the facts of life and challenges them and thereby indirectly changes history more deeply than politics can do. Only the "man of the world" would think of prophetic vision as a powerless dream and of the prophet as an impractical enthusiast.

Art and religion have this in common: they look at facts from the point of view of the totality of facts, either contemplated as an image-world or anticipated as the goal of action, i.e., as the Kingdom, the head of which is God. Only for science and politics, for technology and economics, do facts in the proper sense exist. Art and faith transcend the sphere of facts because they do not subordinate the particular to the general but co-ordinate the individual and the universal; facts are the particulars subordinated to the general, while religious and artistic events are individual and yet express the universal. They are "symbolical" or imaginative.[9] In spite of the immense difference between artistic and religious imagination and creativity, they are alike in surmounting the sphere of facts by means of imaginative vision. Consequently, art and religion are not "realistic" in the sense of science and politics (or morality). But they are "realistic" in a higher sense because they express the reality of the ideal, while the lower realms grasp only the reality of facts. The "realism"

9. I prefer the term "imaginative" to "symbolical" for two reasons:

1. A symbol represents something that is known directly in an unsymbolical way, e.g., *t* in physical equations symbolizes the time of natural processes which we can directly observe. The religious image, on the contrary, is the only form in which we know and can know what is imaged. A merely intellectual or speculative definition, e.g., of "creation" or "resurrection" can only circumscribe certain aspects and fragmentary connotations of the imaginative word but can never exhaust its content and may often falsify it.

2. A symbol does not resemble the thing symbolized, e.g., *t* does not resemble time as observed, nor does the American flag resemble the United States, whereas images like "creation" and "resurrection" do resemble what is imaged in them, as do metaphors or figures of speech in poetry. All religious insight or "knowledge" is parabolical; therefore, the parables of Christ are the classical illustration of how spiritual imagination operates.

Cf. Amos Niven Wilder, *Eschatology and Ethics in the Teaching of Jesus* (New York: Harper & Bros., 1939): "We call attention to the double sense of the word symbol with the conscious knowledge that they are only symbols for the purpose of illuminating readily identifiable realities. It is another thing for a person in dealing with realities that are beyond express identification or characterization, i.e., ineffable, to use *imaginative* conceptions to suggest them. It is in this latter sense that we can speak of the eschatology of Jesus as 'symbolical' " (italics are mine; p. 54; see also p. 161).

of science and politics is also bound up with the "real," that is, the animal, nature of man, inasmuch as science serves technology and politics is connected with economics. Art and religion completely surpass this lower "realism" because they penetrate into ultimate reality: art, as it were, ascending from facts, faith descending to them.

The Tension within Faith

THE tension between culture, or facts, and faith has its analogy even within faith. Faith mirrors and interprets the tension from its own perspective. Since faith is not a contemplative, but a living and active, attitude, tension is inevitably present in it. Life without tension would not be life; at any rate, it would not be the life of faith. Although faith, as Clement rightly remarks, is not a form of conjecture or assumption but a loyal adherence to and a firm confidence in God, still an element of adventure is immanent in it, in contrast to the certainty of mathematical knowledge. Indeed, such a certainty could never serve life, since life is not a mathematical equation but an undertaking, an enterprise, aiming at the goal of self-realization and self-reconciliation —in short, at the solution of the antinomies of experience. Faith assures us that this goal is reached in God, but human life is not itself in the goal; faith expresses this tension between man's own activity of self-realization and God's completion of this activity through his redeeming love and saving grace in the story of the original Fall and man's state of sinfulness. It is true that this tension is relaxed by faith, inasmuch as the sinner believes in the redeeming work of God; but, nevertheless, sin is a barrier between man and God as long as man lives on earth, trusting that God will redeem him, hoping that God will save him, but continuously threatened from within himself by his sinful inclination and his actual sinful willing and doing.

Paul gives touching expression to this inner tension: "I delight in the law of God after the inward man: but I see another law in my members, warring against the law of my mind and bringing me into captivity to the law of sin which is in my members.

O wretched man that I am!"[10] If a saint like Paul confesses this tension, how much more must an ordinary Christian confess the same! Man can never be sure that God will eventually accept him, that he will pass in the final judgment, that his repentance is strong and sincere enough, that his faith and hope will persevere to the end. Man hovers between heaven and hell. If nothing else, this opposition alone would witness to the inner tension of faith. The Christian, according to Paul, must incessantly work for his salvation: "Take unto you the whole armour of God, that ye may be able to withstand in the evil day, and having done all, to stand. Stand therefore having your loins girt about with truth . . . taking the shield of faith wherewith ye shall be able to quench all the fiery darts of the wicked. And take the helmet of salvation and the sword of the Spirit. . . ."[11] Faith is a shield which we need in the battle of life, salvation is a helmet that will protect us against the power of hell.

Faith is a dynamic, not a stable, attitude, a battlecry, in the campaign against Satan, the tempter who is always ready to entice us into the camp of the enemy. The tension within faith culminates in the vision of the struggle between God and the adversary. It is true that this struggle is resolved from eternity; it is not a struggle between equals, for Satan is inferior—indeed, he is only instrumental to God's own will and power; and yet it would not be a struggle at all, it would not possess the grave and dramatic dimensions, if it were merely fictitious. On the part of man it is, on the contrary, of deadly significance. God fights for me in this struggle. He wants to help me, but he can help me only if I stand fast and unswervingly beside him. Thus the tension between God and Satan is very real with respect to my own issue of salvation or condemnation. "Put on the whole armour of God, that ye may be able to stand against the wiles of the devil. For we wrestle not against flesh and blood, but against principalities, against powers, against the rulers of the darkness of this world, against spiritual wickedness in heaven itself."[12]

The Bible thus answers the objections raised against the stern monism of the creation "out of nothing." There is a duality within creation; there is a tension not only within faith as an attitude of man but within the very content of faith, a tension

10. Rom. 18:22–24.   11. Eph. 6:9, 13–17.   12. *Ibid.*, vss. 11–12.

between the living God and his adversary. However we may understand this tension "in heaven," however we may try to combine it with the omnipotence and omniscience of the Lord, one thing is undeniable: biblical faith accounts for the duality of good and evil by tracing it back to the very constitution of the Creation. A certain tension is, from the outset, immanent in the record of Creation. In the beginning God creates the duality of heaven and earth, of light and darkness, of day and night. Whether this antagonism already foreshadows the moral antagonism is not said. But it is noticeable that later the contrast between light and darkness does signify the contrast between good and evil. The Bible is as "monistic" as it is "dualistic," but, of course, it is neither the one nor the other because it is not a philosophical system but the Word of God.

An ultimate duality is involved in the imaginative idea of the living God, since the life of God would not be life at all if man did not introduce tension into the will and mind of the creator. Since God creates man as a free agent who assumes the responsibility for his own deeds, he creates the possibility of man's sinfulness; he wants man, not as a machine which functions according to its mechanical necessity, not even as a mere organism which always acts according to its instincts and organic ends, but as a free will that itself decides upon its own ends and thereby turns to the good or the bad of its own accord. Such a being is not dependent on God's will alone. In creating man, God created a potential adversary. Does God want the fight between good and evil in man's breast? Does he want a being who can "work for his own salvation"? Does he want a being who is tempted to do wrong and is able to resist or to yield to that temptation? Because God created man, the answer can only be: "Yes, he does." Goethe has God say (in the "Prologue in Heaven" in *Faust*) to Mephistopheles:

> The like of thee have never moved My hate.
> Of all the bold, denying Spirits,
> The waggish knave least trouble doth create.
> Man's active nature, flagging, seeks too soon the level;
> Unqualified repose he learns to crave;
> Whence, willingly, the comrade him I gave,
> Who works, excites and must create, as Devil.

Is Goethe perhaps right?

God wants the struggle between good and evil within the moral life of man, for this struggle makes man's life human and makes it, at the same time, significant to God. God is interested in man only because man is a moral agent involved in the moral issue of his self-realization which ensues from his freedom. This freedom makes man the "image of God"; or, more correctly, man is created in this image, inasmuch as he is free to choose or to reject the good, to obey or to disobey the divine will. The life of God as depicted in the Bible is a consequence of the relation between God and man. The dramatic element is introduced into the life of God through man's Fall, through his expulsion from paradise, through his longing for reconciliation, and through all God's subsequent acts which aim at the final work of salvation. God wants this whole dispensation from the beginning, as far as man can understand his mind and will. Only because God wants this development does he rejoice "over one sinner that repenteth, more than over ninety and nine just persons which need no repentance."[13] Here it is said clearly and bluntly that God prefers repentance to the attitude of a man who feels he does not need to repent.

But the most intense and ostensible display of the tension between God and Satan is the imaginative idea of eternal punishments in hell as depicted so graphically by Dante but as uttered by Jesus himself: "He that shall blaspheme against the Holy Ghost has never forgiveness, but is in danger of eternal damnation."[14] Origen could not abide this idea and taught that, in the end, even the devil would be reconciled to God and God would be "all in all." I think the gospel is more "realistic" in this respect, as in every other respect. Eternal hell-fire makes the very tension eternal. However, this view has to be qualified. Satan is not on a par with God ultimately; but in time the struggle between them goes on indefinitely. In eternity Satan has no place. Only if we conceive of time as being infinite will we arrive at a "time-eternity" or, better, sempiternity, to which the eternal punishments are ascribed. In the ultimate sense Origen is therefore right.

Someone has said that heaven and hell are, "in fact," the same

13. Luke 15:7.
14. Mark 3:29, and similar words in many other passages.

place, and only people differ in their attitudes to that place. Indeed, he who loves God more than himself may feel the eternal abode of God as heaven, while he who loves himself more than God may feel it as hell. God is one and the same, only we are many, and Satan, too, is legion. "In my father's house are many mansions."[15] Each of us has his own perspective toward the absolute ego that heads the absolute community, but God's love to each of us is a fatherly love. If the child loves his father, he will enjoy the father's love for him; if he does not care, this love might become an unendurable burden.

In the Crucifixion the tension between culture and faith as mirrored by faith reaches its climax. This central mystery, this mysterious center, of the Christian faith reveals the tension as that between the sinful world of man and the sacrificial love of Christ, who disregards and disavows the special religious rites and habits of his own people or of their most powerful class. So he falls victim to their vengeance. A pharisaically moralistic council and an imperialistic state, failing to recognize the power of the living God, join to crush him.[16] Faith inspired by this experience rises to the zenith of its historical development and refuses to accept this victory of the world over God as final and ultimate; it interprets its meaning in the reverse sense as the final and ultimate victory of the eternal over the temporal and exalts Christ to the throne of God the Father. The mystical and spiritual truth concerning the rank of culture above faith and of time above eternity is thus articulated in the most powerful religious experience and expressed in the most impressive imaginative language, so that the kingdom which Jesus wanted to establish on earth really comes into existence as his church.

In this most sublime and momentous hour of mankind, all the spiritual hopes and expectations of biblical prophecy seem fulfilled. The tension within faith is completely relaxed, so that the present seems to be the point of time in which the reconciliation between historical time and the eternal kingdom is finally enacted. The Messiah has come; but he will come again "on the

15. John 14:2.

16. Cf. the profound and eloquent discussion in Henry Sloane Coffin, *The Meaning of the Cross* (New York: Charles Scribner's Sons, 1942).

clouds of heaven." The end of time has drawn near, but a new time, a new era, has set in. The hopes and expectations of the centuries are fulfilled, but they reappear on a higher level. The tensions remain—nay, they increase—since the new faith is more exalted over the level of the temporal and the cultural than the old faith was; they are aggravated also because under the Old Covenant one particular nation was chosen to be the people of the Lord, so that its entire culture, all its customs and habits, all its institutions and laws, all its songs and melodies, all its thoughts and aspirations, were molded by this basic religious consciousness in spite of the disobedience and disloyalty of the Israelites throughout their history. But now a most marvelous, indeed, the greatest, civilization that ever existed on earth has been inherited by the Christians, a civilization at bottom and in its heart pagan and averse to the new faith. What else could arise under these circumstances than the most intense renewal of the tension between culture and faith? It did arise in full strength, endangering the inner unity of the individual believer and of Christendom as a whole. One of the symptoms of this new tension appeared in the emergence of Christian dogmatics, pretending to interpret the faith authoritatively and to take the place of Greek philosophical speculation.

The Tension between Faith and Dogma

DOGMA is the content of faith arranged in the form of propositions which claim to express its most important and central points. Dogma was first fixed as a result of the struggle to uphold biblical truth against falsifications or heretical views. The heretics are older than orthodoxy. "There must be heresies among you, that they which are approved may be made manifest among you."[17] Dogma is an intellectualized content of faith and sprang indirectly from Greek philosophy. It was impossible to defend faith against the assault of philosophers without entering the arena of philosophy and thus intellectualizing the content of faith. The first heretics were the Gnostics, those who thought it possible so to transform the Christian faith that, rather

17. I Cor. 11:19.

than the merciful action of God's redemption, a system of quasi-metaphysical insights might become the instrument of salvation. Or, to put it differently, faith in God's forgiving love as revealed by Christ was replaced by the Greek idea of salvation through knowledge. Gnosticism was victoriously combated by the early Fathers, but the very combat generated the necessity of expressing the right view in an authoritative form; so that, in the end, faith itself was no longer primarily understood as faith in God, in his grace and love, in his justice and power, in his will and deeds, but rather as an assent to those propositions which the church regarded as right doctrine. In this indirect way the intention of gnosticism was taken over by the church, and Greek intellectualism defeated the faith of the original community.

But not only did this historical development create the tension between faith and dogma; it is also a new manifestation of the tension between culture and faith, now emerging within the church and within the Christian life of the period; this tension was released only by the historical circumstances. Judaism could do without dogma because, in the first place, its faith was the only source of its cultural activity and, second, because it was inseparably connected with the existence of a nation, while the Christian faith was, from the outset, opposed to the surrounding pagan civilization and was not confined to any definite nation, with its habits, history, hopes, and expectations. It had to defend itself by producing forms of life and thought which would be exclusively religious; however, these forms were partly influenced by those cultural achievements against which faith had to fight. Thus not only did dogma arise as a strange outcome of the battle between faith and philosophy, but also dogmatics arose as a new philosophy, based upon faith and aiming at the systematic arrangement of the content of faith. In a similar way ancient art in all its ramifications was transformed into Christian art, Roman jurisdiction into canonical law, and Roman imperialism into the imperialism of the Roman See.

Dogma belongs to religion, not to faith. The struggle of many "liberals" against dogma is not so much a struggle against the content as it is against the intellectualistic form in which the content of faith is expressed or into which it is pressed. They often fight orthodoxy not because they are less firmly convinced that the content of faith is to be found in the Bible but, on the contrary, because they are more deeply convinced that it is to be found there alone and that its intellectualistic pronouncement means an estrangement from its original context and form. In Scripture the content of faith has a definitely nonintellectualistic form because spiritual imagination is operative in prophetic and evangelistic speaking. Spiritual imagination alone does justice to the mystical roots and meaning of every word used in Scripture in order to express the inexpressible, whereas intellectual statements are inadequate for this purpose because they generate the false impression that the intellect can formulate what imagination alone can grasp.

Dogma reduces faith to a kind of pseudo-scientific doctrine. Thereby it adulterates the real character of faith by substituting the "method" of subordination for that of co-ordination or by exchanging the higher level of imagination for the lower level of intellection. Only the erroneous belief in the superiority of rational methods as compared with those of faith can indulge in such a mistake; only the erroneous pretension that truth is more adequately expressed by logical means than it is by the creative vision of the prophet, by the parabolical language of Jesus, and by the paradoxical argumentation of Paul can lead to the emphasis laid on dogma. This pretension, however, eventually leaves the believer unsatisfied because it neither stirs his imagination nor really imparts knowledge in the scientific sense. In the end it generates a longing for a more satisfying, namely, a more rational, comprehension of things divine: for "natural" theology or for a speculative theology like that of Plato or Aristotle.

It was systematically consistent that Thomism issued in a speculation freed from the "fetters" of the Christian faith and that, in modern times, philosophy cut the tie with Christian theology. The primary blame for this trend must be laid upon scholasticism, which furthered it by producing the false claim of a "scientific" comprehension in the realm in which faith alone can reign. Augustine was much nearer to the truth than was Thomas Aquinas. But he, too, was fascinated by the philosophical desire for logical knowledge and too much a child of antiquity to understand the limits of thought and the superiority of biblical imagination. He bluntly says: "I impatiently desire not only to believe in what is true, but also to comprehend it."[18]

Faith understands very well the imaginative expression "Son of God." But if this expression is transformed into the dogma of the Logos who dwells beyond space and time but still is conceived as (or should I say "called"?) the "first begotten son of God" or "the second God," as this was done by Philo even before the rise of Christianity, when he tried to combine Platonic or Stoic speculation with the living God of the Bible, then the question may be put as to whether such a quasi-concept has any logical meaning. Certainly, it has no meaning for faith, in which only Jesus the Christ has this title. After all, "son" applied to the relation between Jesus and God is a highly imaginative term, which loses its imaginative significance when applied to logical knowledge, be it ontological or theological speculation. But it does not gain any logical significance when it suffers this loss, and in the end neither any imaginative nor any logical value remains.

Christological speculation is no more valid and true than any other speculation which tries to enlarge the realm of science beyond the limit of science and thereby to reconcile science and faith or to translate the religious language into a scientific one. This is most evident in the history of dogma, which is a history of frustrated and tortuous attempts at such a reconciliation. When the Cappadocians arrived at the conclusion that God, Christ, and the Holy Spirit are three persons but one substance, the Greek terms were most artificially imposed upon the mystical relation between those religious figures. The terms are meaningful only in the context of Platonic metaphysics in which *substantia* means Idea, while *persona* is the Latin translation of the Greek *hypostasis*, the term used to indicate the rational being, i.e., man in contradistinction to all beings whose Idea or form is not rationality.

Now one can easily understand the application of those terms when one thinks of the plurality of human beings, each of whom "participates" in the universal "rationality." But, if transferred to the sphere of the relation between the "persons" of the "deity," the odd conclusion is implied that an analogous participation in the

18. *Contra acad.* iii. 43.

divine region is valid, i.e., that the persons are divine beings because they participate in the universal "deity." This is correct
Greek metaphysical thinking, but it has nothing whatever to do
with revelation and Christian faith. On the contrary, in this religious sphere the Greek concepts are not only insufficient but outright blasphemous. They presuppose that there is a universal Idea
or form which makes God God, whereas the living God of the
Bible is what he is, precisely because he is not subject to any ideal
realm like that of the Platonic Ideas but is absolutely independent
and sovereign. The living God does not participate in a prior *Idea*
of divinity but negates such an Idea by his very being. To think of
"instances" of this Idea, as the persons would represent them, is as
unbiblical as possible; it is Platonic. There is no universal genus or
species called "divinity," which would be the universal (or rather
the general) concept and to which the "persons" would be subordinated as the particular is subordinated to the general. If the
living God were to be conceived that way, then his very deity
would only be borrowed from an Idea higher than himself. But
this is evidently nonsense.

The early Christian Fathers like Irenaeus were much more careful and more in agreement with the spirit and the letter of the
Bible when they conceived of the relation between God and
Christ in the "modalistic" way, whereby the Logos is the Word
spoken by God—God's mind or wisdom or will in distinction from
God himself. In this modalistic Christology the mystical relation
between God and Logos, God and Christ, is much more loyally
preserved than it is in the Cappadocian formula. Perhaps Karl
Barth was induced to prefer the modalist conception for this same
reason.

The Platonic Christology suggests that an Idea lies beyond and
behind the Trinity of the living God, his Son, and his Holy Spirit.
But since, in the system of Plato, the Idea is the really real, while
the instances or individuals belong only to the phenomenal realm,
the conclusion would be correct that Father, Son, and Spirit also
belong only to the phenomenal world, while the Idea of the deity
alone is really real. This conclusion was actually drawn by some
Christian mystics. They insisted that God as he is in himself is not
the Father or the Son or the Spirit but rather the incomprehensible

Being behind and beyond the revealed "persons." Since this mystical conclusion agrees in a way with the Bible, which speaks of God's hiddenness, the Platonic and the mystical interpretation joined in a powerful alliance. Of course, in mystical theology the incomprehensible deity is no longer a Platonic Idea but rather a "superessential" being that can be comprehended only in negative terms.[19]

Dogmatics is unavoidable in a world in which the tension between culture and faith, and especially between science and faith, exists. For in such a world a safeguard must be created which defends faith against attack by secular science and theory. However, the tragic consequence of this necessity is the immediate danger that dogmatics itself falls victim to the tension and produces a doctrine which is more scientific than biblical and more rational than mystical. No system of dogmatics seems possible which could entirely escape this danger. Karl Barth tries hard in his system to preserve the contact with biblical revelation; but even he cannot help transforming imaginative into logical conceptions and rationalizing the mystical content so that one is continuously puzzled by the question of whether he succeeds better in making the incomprehensible comprehensible or the comprehensible incomprehensible. In both respects he really achieves more than any of his predecessors. But, on the whole, such a tightrope feat is not a very pleasant spectacle, and I prefer to its ambiguous display the outright rational dialectic of Hegel, which is frequently approached by Barth but without the speculative vigor and consistency of the great heretic.

The one who dogmatizes is easily tempted to think of his system as being the truth and of the Bible as revealing only fragments of the truth in a more or less unsystematic and therefore inadequate fashion. Exactly the contrary takes place, however. By systematizing the content of revelation, he presents the truth not in a more, but in a less, adequate—namely, in a less mystical—form. What makes the Bible a religious book is just its mystical and (what is inseparable from the mystical root) its imaginative, i.e., nonration-

19. There is, however, a model for this nonconceptual concept even in Plato, when he conceives of the Idea of the Good as lying "beyond the substance" (*Rep.* 509B) and when he speaks of this Idea in mystical and enthusiastic fashion as the origin of all knowledge and of all being.

al, nonmethodical, nonsystematic, way of presenting it. Dogmatics tries to convert the religious truth, which is a living truth and a truth which gives us life, into a dead truth, which is scientific and for that very reason no longer what it is in the context of revelation.

This is a tragic outcome of the tension between the contemplative and the active spheres, between the lower (science) and the higher realm, and, finally and especially, between the secular and the mystical. Although dogmatics attempts to preserve the character of the mystical by transforming the holy mysteries into theological concepts, still it subtly secularizes the mystical. In the last analysis, dogmatics is the work and thought of man, whereas the Bible is the Book of God. However strongly dogmatics may emphasize this infinite contrast, the very undertaking of writing a system of dogma runs counter to it and humanizes to a certain degree what is not human—makes contemplative or scientific what is the content of an active faith.

The moment that this is done, the antinomies of experience return in all the unabated strength which they show in the cultural realm, since the content of faith is now converted into a content of human thought and thus surrendered to human logic. Faith does not solve the logical contradictions in a logical fashion; on the contrary, it solves the living self-contradiction in a living fashion by articulating imaginatively mystical experience and by interpreting events in the light of spiritual devotion. If this "method" is abandoned and the method of logical thinking is used instead, the "solution" of faith is given over to a sphere in which it necessarily loses its peculiar power because the task of logical understanding and systematic comprehension thrusts itself forward. A strange twilight between the consciousness of mystery and the ardor for lighting it up by means of systematization ensues from this task.

I will give only one example of this tension. Barth tries to demonstrate that the holiness of God demands the triumph of his mercy over all human sin; but this triumph is made possible only by God's judgment over sin. The logical consequence is that sin is the presupposition of God's revelation. However, such a conclusion, inescapable though it is, leads to the fallacy that God wants sin in order to have an occasion for triumphing over it. Indeed, this fallacy is evident to every believer because it destroys the very meaning of sin and of forgiving grace; but in the context of dogmatics it is nevertheless logically demanded. Thus Barth is trapped by his own logic, which is the logic of thought and not of faith, and he finds only one escape from this trap: he insists that God's mercy and grace are unfathomable. But why, then, does he argue at all? Why does he pretend to know that, for example, Saul "is necessary on behalf of the holiness of God's grace[?]. If no Saul existed with evil spirit sent to him from God . . . David could not exist either, the right king of Israel . . ."?[20] This is poor logic, which fails to illuminate what no human mind will ever be able to understand.

The Tension between Faith and Philosophy

THERE is a deep-rooted contrast and conflict between faith and knowledge, or reason. This conflict had already set in when the earliest Greek thinkers were beginning to criticize the religious faith of their nation and to replace it by philosophic speculation. It lasted throughout the development of Greek thought. Socrates was a victim of this struggle. In the latest period of Greek philosophy, thought became more and more religious. Stoicism is a philosophic faith. In the period of Christian philosophy the two opponents were reconciled in various ways. In modern times they seemed to live in peace, but only because they were ignoring each other, each believing itself to be the only access to ultimate truth. Finally, in Hegel a new kind of reconciliation was created; philosophy was identified with true Christian theology. After the historical collapse of Hegelianism the strife between the two world powers was renewed in one way or another, until the theology of Karl Barth. He firmly repudiated philosophy's claim to know God and to rival the Christian faith, while some of the existentialists today stress this claim with the utmost vigor, asserting that there is a philosophic faith[21] which

20. *Die Kirchliche Dogmatik*, Vol. II: *Die Lehre von Gott*, II. Halbband, II. Auflage (Zurich: Evang. Verlag A. G. Zollikon, 1946), p. 410.
21. Cf. *Der philosophische Glaube* by Karl Jaspers (Munich: A. Piper & Co., 1947).

is more satisfying than religious faith because it is universal and based not on mystical experience and historical events but on reason and thought. So the circle of ancient development seems to repeat itself once more.

Is there really a philosophic faith? If we take philosophy to be the attempt made by man to understand his experience, his cultural activity, and his faith, we must admit that Karl Barth is more right than the existentialists. Only pre-Christian philosophy could aim at a philosophic faith, as Socrates and Plato did. Christian philosophy relied upon Christian faith, while modern philosophy boasts that it can and does find the truth by merely secular investigation and speculation, without needing the support or the guidance of any faith. The failure of Christian philosophy was its belief that reason and thought could arrive at the knowledge of the same God who reveals himself in the Bible. This fundamental error gave rise to the dogmatic speculation of Philo and of his successors up to Thomas Aquinas. The consequence was that natural or rational or metaphysical theology grew within this new speculation from century to century, until in the end it emancipated itself entirely from revealed theology. This happened not only in the Renaissance but earlier in the thought of Albertus Magnus and Thomas Aquinas. They bluntly declared that secular and sacred theology are to be distinguished and that secular or natural theology is able to demonstrate the existence of God and to know the essence of God, although certain mysteries, like the Trinity, the Incarnation, and the Resurrection, are known by revelation alone.

It is almost incomprehensible that Thomas Aquinas failed to realize the illusion of his whole undertaking. How could he have so profoundly deceived himself? How could he have fancied that the notion of the god whose existence he proved by the human light comprehends the living God, who reveals himself, when the former is the god of pagan philosophizing while the latter is the God of biblical faith? It is appalling to see how deeply he was taken in by his master Aristotle, who completely distrained his intellect, while his heart was still in the bondage of Christ and the church. Augustine was naïve in his identification of Plato and the gospel, but Thomas Aquinas was not naïve in his application of Aristotle. He had realized that the equation of reason and revelation is not so perfect and so simple as it had seemed to be to Origen and Augustine. He had learned that philosophy has its own right and its own precinct. But, since he admired and venerated Aristotle as the perfect pattern of a philosopher, he fell victim to the illusion that the theology of this great pagan thinker could be adopted by a Christian theologian.[22]

Since Kant, we have known that all the proofs of God are so many fallacies. It is regrettable that Kant is called an "agnostic" because of his rejection of those proofs. He should, on the contrary, be called a Protestant philosopher (which the Germans call him), since he protested against any natural theology, as Luther had protested against scholasticism and for the same reason. Indeed, Kant is much more in agreement with the gospel than is Thomas Aquinas, since the gospel allows no doubt about the impossibility of philosophic knowledge of the living God, the Father of Jesus Christ. The "natural light," as we have seen earlier, is not bright enough to enlighten our understanding about the mystery of God. Faith alone, the illumination by the Holy Spirit, lights up this darkness.

Philosophy is a secular undertaking, based upon secular experience and secular thought, and therefore barred from the throne of the Highest, who reveals himself through the mouths of his prophets and of his Son. Philosophy is reflective self-understanding of man, while faith is a gift of God's grace, awakening loyalty and confidence and leading mankind toward the goal of the Kingdom, in which love reigns and governs heart and will.

But if this chasm thus separates philosophy and faith in the Christian sense, how could we dare to comprehend the nature and the function of faith by means of a philosophy of faith? If such a tension exists between the two attitudes or activities, how could we attain to any insight into faith at all? How could we, specifically, venture to determine a place for faith in the system

22. I cannot explicitly expound here the scope of intellectualism which characterizes the natural theology of the *Summa*. I must confine myself to only one quotation, which obviously shows how far this trend leads. In Question 14, Art. 12, the author defines the divine intellect as "intellect knowing itself alone." This definition, of course, is in full agreement with Aristotle, but it only makes it evident that the Aristotelian god is by no means the Lord and loving Father of the Old and New Testaments, whose "intellect" certainly does not merely know itself but is engaged in planning how to redeem and to save mankind.

of culture, although faith does not belong there but partly consummates and partly judges, or completely abnegates, the value of culture?

We have seen that philosophy is, indeed, in a precarious situation if it deals with faith. In a sense, it transgresses its own limit and enters a realm which it prohibits itself from entering! A "philosophy of religion" is a very difficult enterprise indeed if the philosopher understands himself and thereby understands his faith. Thus the necessity arose of speaking about "mystical" experience, although from the point of view of secularity such an experience cannot be regarded as authentic and trustworthy and its articulation by religious experts, called "prophets," cannot be taken as valid. Furthermore, the philosopher is coerced into speaking of "ultimate reality" or of "original unity" or of an "absolute solution" of the antinomies of experience, although all these expressions are highly objectionable, if not entirely devoid of meaning, as long as I strictly keep within the boundaries of secular experience and secular thought, which, as a philosopher, I am obliged to do. In all these respects the tension between faith and the philosophy of faith comes to the fore and makes its weight felt disturbingly.

However, this tension would not even be conceivable as a tension without the philosophy of faith. Only by advancing into the territory of faith, only by building a philosophy of faith, can the tension between faith and such a philosophy be detected. And the whole enterprise is by no means an arbitrary and ambitious invasion of a foreign country. On the contrary, if the task of philosophy is the self-comprehension of man, then it is its undeniable and indispensable duty to comprehend faith too, since faith is an attitude of man, after all, though an attitude toward something that transcends the horizon of man's comprehension. The tension between faith and philosophy does not annul this duty; it does not destroy the validity of the philosophy of faith, although the tension has to be taken into account and itself comprehended. It characterizes as much the limit of thought as the peculiar essence of faith.

Philosophy as a secular enterprise is limited because secular experience is limited, as the antinomies of experience and the impossibility of solving them by cultural activities demonstrate. Hegel has said that to know the limit is to transcend it. This is true in a qualified way, although Hegel has drawn extravagant consequences from his thesis. It is not true that the acknowledgment of the limit allows me to penetrate into the realm beyond by a limitless conquest; it is not true that I can know the infinite, merely because I know that the finite is limited. But it is true that the very concept of the finite at least enables me to know that there is something beyond it or that the finite is limited by the infinite. Only because the infinite exists in whatever mode of existence does the finite itself exist as itself. Indeed, we must be able to transcend the limit if we can know that there is a limit.

Therefore, philosophy in this definite sense transcends its own limit in knowing that it is limited. The land beyond its limits cannot be conquered, however; it can only be visited, as it were, and abandoned again with the consciousness that it always will be a foreign land, impenetrable and unfathomable as a whole. So it is with faith. Faith is as mysterious as is its "object" and its basis, i.e., mystical experience and religious articulation. Philosophy can visit this mysterious sphere, since faith is my faith and since philosophy is my self-comprehension. But, in spite of this my ownership, the land of faith remains a foreign country beyond the reach of my self-comprehension, and I can never make it quite my own.

That there is such a foreign country philosophy learns first, though only negatively, from the antinomies which are as inevitable as they are insoluble by human activity and human thought. Contradiction cannot be the last word of reason because it destroys reason; if reason cannot get rid of contradiction by its own logical means, it has to "postulate" a power stronger than itself which inflicts contradiction upon thought but which also conceals its solution. Mystical experience fills this empty space in its own silent and yet eloquent fashion. It assures me that my inability to solve the antinomies by cultural and secular activity is not a mere defect or a fault on the part of man and reason but is well founded in the nature of the infinite as the transcendent. It manifests this nature in the way in which world and ego also manifest themselves: in the way of immediate experience. To that degree faith is in agreement with reason and thought.

In the last analysis the distinction between secular and mystical experience is altogether relative. After all, experience itself is a mysterious thing, never completely to be illuminated or comprehended. It simply occurs. That we experience world and ego as an ultimate duality is known by experience, but it cannot be derived from anything else by means of reasoning or logical deduction, as Fichte and Hegel thought it could. Experience is the ultimate source of knowledge, as it is the ultimate source of culture, and to that degree it is mysterious itself. Indeed, secular and mystical, cultural and religious, experience interpenetrate and mutually influence one another so thoroughly that in the last analysis it is impossible actually to separate them. All culture is the culture of the faith which guides and inspires it, and all faith is the faith of its culture, which contributes to its religious exposition and exhibition.

Consequently, the philosophy of experience, culture, and faith might eventually be replaced by Christian theology. The duality of world and ego might be interpreted in the light of faith as the outcome of man's Fall, and the antinomies of secular experience and the entire sphere of secularity as punishment, to be traced back to the banishment from paradise, in which Adam and Eve enjoyed a permanent harmony with each other, with nature, and with God. They did not yet know the distinction between the secular and the sacred because they lived in the state of original unity in which world and ego were still united in God; in which, therefore, culture was not needed; and in which all experience was mystical, precisely because the distinction between world and ego did not yet exist for them.

But such a theological philosophy is, of course, as imaginative as is the content of faith and therefore does not perform what secular philosophy must perform. Only after philosophy has done its job, can it yield to the superior and mysterious interpretation of its content by the queen of all sciences—sacred theology. However, even theology does not solve the tension between philosophy and faith; it only transforms it into that between rational and imaginative thought. A theological philosophy of culture and experience is opposed to the secular philosophy of faith, as expounded here, and to that degree it manifests the tension by this very opposition. Although secular and mystical, cultural and religious, experience and thought are only relatively separated from each other, being inwardly united, nevertheless a tension between these opposites does exist and gives rise to secular philosophy as separated from sacred theology. Neither a philosophical theology nor a theological philosophy can remove this remaining tension.

The Limits of Thought

ALL the remaining tensions point to the incomprehensibility of the ultimate. Neither secular philosophy nor sacred theology can alter this ultimate verdict. Philosophy has to acknowledge and respect ultimate reality as a fortress which can be neither stormed nor taken by siege in any measurable time. Theology admits that the God of biblical faith is a hidden God and that he will never reveal himself completely as long as we live on earth. Knowledge and thought are limited, as humanity is limited. Even revelation does not eliminate this human limitation, since God can reveal himself only inasmuch as the comprehension of man is able to receive his revelation. Although mystical and religious experience enlarges the scope of comprehension significantly, a certain limitation persists, and the remaining tensions disclose it.

It is not necessary to assume that the limit of thought is the limit of our human thought only. True, the biblical word, "My thoughts are not your thoughts," spoken by God, seems to suggest that the thoughts of God excel ours. But this word, of course, like all biblical words, reveals God and things divine in an imaginative and figurative language and may simply mean that the distance between God and man is immeasurably great, so that man can never hope to understand God by means of thought. It may mean not that our thought but that thought by its very nature is no adequate instrument for the comprehension of the Lord. Perhaps thought is a human way of comprehending, as Paul seems to intimate when he exalts the power of love over knowledge and prophecy, over hope, and even over faith. The ultimate may be incomprehensible by thought, just because only love can embrace it, since love itself is incomprehensible in its power and infinite in its effect.

Thought is not a stable set of propositions but an ever moving, ever striving, ever unfinished, action of the thinking mind. This action, like all action, presupposes a certain tension between opposites. Thought cannot move and strive without the tension between problem and solution, between question and answer, between a point of departure and a goal to be reached. Only this tension moves the mind and produces results, which, however, are not final but contain new tensions which demand a new exertion. Thought, in other words, is, like all human undertakings, finite and therefore limited. This is the reason why there is a history of thought and why thought always kindles the flame of new thinking but also of hostile rejection and refutation. Thought never comes to its end; its endlessness is the signal of its finiteness, the manifestation of its intrinsic limit. The inner tension of thought can never be overcome. There is no rest, no finality, in thought, as there is no finality in life either.

The original antagonism between universality and individuality, between unity and manifoldness, between freedom and necessity, and between time and eternity is thought's own inner antagonism, which is resuscitated in the antagonism between the world- and the ego-aspect of the thinking mind and of its achievements. The world-aspect makes thought a historical process in which a vast multiplicity of individual ideas emerge and submerge, appear and reappear, fight one another, triumph, and are vanquished. The ego-aspect of thought represents the universality of truth, the unity of all the aspects and relations of experience, the result of man's freedom, and the knowledge of eternal reality. Since this antagonism is a necessary ferment of the movement and life of thought, it can never be neutralized by thought. Only the philosophy of faith can indirectly overcome it by pointing to the solution of faith itself; it is faith which underlies and inspirits this philosophy, after all.

But even the philosophy of faith, inasmuch as it is a product of the thinking mind, is not immune to the inner limitations of thought. In so far as it is the product of the thinking mind and not only of faith, it is exposed to the same conflict to which all thought is subject. The philosophy of faith can move and breathe only in the medium of contrasts which never disappear. The ultimate as

the ground of all the contrasts and conflicts can never be conquered by thought. When philosophy or theology, or both in unison, try to think out what faith presents as ultimate truth, it necessarily fails and falls back to the antinomies of experience.

The very idea of the ultimate or of ultimate reality leads into
this impasse. Hegel is perfectly right in concluding that the absolute is the opposite of itself. This, indeed, is the only valid definition of the ultimate, if thought is induced to define it. But this
definition only confirms the impossibility of thinking out what,
in truth, transcends all thought. When Barth argues that sinful
Saul was necessary to pave the road for David and that David was
necessary as the precursor of Jesus, he falls victim to exactly the
same kind of logic which he abhors in Hegel. He, no less than the
great architect of the dialectical system of Mind or Spirit, dares
to think out what essentially cannot be thought out because the
ultimate ground of the duality of good and evil is altogether beyond the limit of thought. Whether it is the speculative panlogist
or the dogmatic theologian of the church who transgresses the
boundary line of thought and logic does not matter, since both
commit the same blunder: the pretense that dialectical thinking
is able to solve the problem of how the opposition can be reconciled to the absolute unity. Hegel says that the absolute unity is
opposed to itself; Barth says that God allows evil in order to defeat evil. At bottom both are the same.

Thought is always stretched between polarities and therefore
can never arrive at an ultimate one or oneness. Parmenides
thought he had made the impossible possible by declaring that
being alone is, while nonbeing is not. But he had to admit in the
end that this is only one aspect of thought and that there is a
second one which deals with what is not. This duality was like a
thorn in his side. Although he protested that the second aspect
is an aspect not of truth but of illusion, even so the problem re-
mained as to how illusion can spring from truth, if truth alone
"is" while illusion "is not." How can the duality of truth and error
be accounted for? After all, truth has to account for its own adversary. This is the same ultimate problem with which Hegel and
Barth struggled in vain, because it transcends all possible thought.
There is a limit of thought which no human being, not even the

most sagacious dialectical thinker, can violate with impunity. Thought has to admit this barrier; only thus can it escape frustration; and, what is more important, only thus does it maintain respect for the limitations of humanity.

Faith Unlimited

ALTHOUGH faith is involved in tensions of several kinds and although it is as dynamic as thought, yet it is not limited in the way thought is. While the thinking mind never reaches its goal, faith is always at the end, for which it is destined. This fundamental difference is derived from the fact that thought is an enterprise of the human mind, whereas faith is the response to the divine call. Or, in other words, thought is based upon secular logic, faith on mystical experience and religious prophecy. It is the nature of secular experience and logic never to come to an end; but it is the nature of mystical and religious experience to contact the ultimate and to trust its revelation. Faith is therefore not limited by an insurmountable barrier. On the contrary, it is the only human activity which surmounts all the barriers of secular experience and secular culture. In this sense faith has no limits. It stretches out toward the infinite, and there it rests: "Restless is our heart, until it rests, O God, in Thee." Faith is the only course that leads beyond the limits of humanity; it is the meeting ground of man and God and in a mysterious way lets man share the eternal joy of heaven.

Faith articulates the "eternal Yes" of life, which transcends the sphere in which every Yes is challenged by a hostile and opposing No. It articulates that absolute oneness which can never be thought out. It is deeper than thought can be because it is not limited by the oppositions necessary to make thought move. Indeed, it is the depth itself which is behind and beyond every thought—the depth in which all secular experience is rooted without ever revealing it. In faith this depth comes to the fore; it takes on a certain imaginative expression which enables us to touch upon it and to feel touched by it. Faith is therefore all-embracing and all-penetrating. It is not limited by the boundaries of time and

history or of knowledge and human power. It can "move mountains"; it can, what is more, move the heart of God.

It is true, though, that the tension which is within faith somewhat strains its content. The opposition between God and Satan,
between the Lord of glory and the prince of this world, between
heaven and hell, between his holiness and our sinfulness, between
his eternity and our temporality, mirrors all the oppositions which
limit us in our own existence, which cause tragedy and frustration, conflict and affliction; in short, it mirrors the antinomies of
experience. But, even so, faith triumphs over these tensions, and
it is just this victory which more than anything else gives joy to
the heart of the faithful and the peace that "passes all understanding."

It is also true that the duality of faith and religion somehow disturbs, or interferes with, the ineffable joy and inspiration which
the believer feels in moments of ecstasy. Faith is nearer to mystical experience, religion nearer to cultural articulation. Faith is the
inner side of religion, religion is the outer expression of faith.
Religion is the world-aspect of faith; faith is the ego-aspect of religion. In religion the antinomies recur because the world-aspect
of faith alienates faith from its source and true meaning. Seen
from within, faith is both universal and individual—my faith and
yet also the faith of all the believers in Christ; faith reconciles the
opposition of (moral) freedom and (historical) necessity on the
basis of freedom; it reconciles the opposition of time and eternity
on the basis of eternity. Religion, on the contrary, challenges this
reconciliation because it belongs to history and is conditioned
by historical necessity and temporality; there are many religions
partly hostile to one another, all claiming universality and yet dependent upon individual founders and civilizations. Faith is unlimited, religion is humanly limited.

It is the very essence of faith that this contrast is overcome by
faith itself. To the faithful, Christianity is not a religion but the
rock on which he builds his life. It can be this rock only inasmuch
as the limits of culture and history and of necessity and time are
no longer obstructions; the faithful lives beyond their barriers;
his faith passes them as it passes contradiction. Although the two

aspects demand and supplement each other, to the faithful the world-aspect is merely a veil through which "the eyes of faith" pierce into the true substance of religion.

The religion of the New Testament differs from all religions, in that it knows the duality of the two aspects and proclaims the ascendancy of the inner one. Jesus, in attacking the Pharisees and in stressing that man was not made for the Sabbath but the Sabbath for man,[23] reversed the order of the Old Covenant and, indeed, of all religions by pronouncing the primacy of faith or, what is essentially the same thing, the primacy of the spirit in its contest with the letter. The spirit does not know any limits at all; it "searcheth all things";[24] it "giveth life";[25] "where the Spirit of the Lord is, there is liberty."[26] God himself is spirit. Spiritual faith is unlimited; and especially it is not limited by any literalism which would cling to the cultural appearance instead of penetrating into the innermost meaning of words, habits, symbols, and parables. The historical is no more than the temporal, and therefore an accidental and contingent articulation of the eternal.

The substance of the Christian faith is neither rational nor doctrinal, it is mystical and mysterious, ineffable and inexpressible. However, this basic truth should not be overstressed to that point at which faith would be reduced to mystical silence. Articulation is essential. Otherwise the substance might be in danger of being lost, and the community might be destroyed. But it is precisely the existence of the community which defeats the world and which is the fruit of the victory of faith. To communicate with one another implies the necessity of means of communication, i.e., the necessity of articulation. "We have this treasure in earthen vessels,"[27] but without any vessels we would not have the treasure at all. The spirit without the letter cannot be communicated and, indeed, would not be the spirit of God living in his community. Revelation is not pure spiritualism but an act of the living God, his decree, his command, his legislation, judgment, and execution, his active love and redeeming word. To be active and efficient, the spirit of God must appear on earth and take on the form of man; and that means that human language must become the

23. Mark 2:27.   25. II Cor. 3:6.   27. *Ibid.*, 4:7.
24. I Cor. 2:10.   26. *Ibid.*, vs. 17.

medium in which the spirit reveals itself. The letter is the religious aspect of faith, it is the outer body of its inner meaning; but, without that embodiment, faith would be without content—it would be no faith.

The content of faith is mysterious because it is transparent and cannot be exhausted by any dogma or doctrine whatever. It is always richer, always less definite, always less fixed and less capable of being fixed, than are logical propositions. It is imaginative and therefore alive and constantly changing as to meaning and function. It is unlimited. It is infinite, though always at its end. Mysteries are, of course, not merely things incomprehensible, even less things absurd; in that case they could not offer any "solution" of the ultimate problems of life and existence; they are mysteries because they cannot be replaced by scientific statements, be they philosophic and speculative or theological and dogmatic. It is their function to stir and to move the soul in the direction of the fulfilment of her deepest longing, in the direction of perfect peace and absolute truth. But they can only stir and move, they cannot be defined or conceived. Definition and conception would limit their infinite and indefinable, ever flexible, ever creative, meaning which makes them mysteries.

Of the two great mysterious events which have kindled faith in Jesus the Christ, the Crucifixion represents what is literally true, the Resurrection what can be apprehended only by the spirit. Of course, the Crucifixion has its own spiritual meaning, and the Resurrection has its own literal foundation. But, in spite of this, there is a difference between the two events which corresponds with the two aspects of faith, the outer and the inner. The Crucifixion is a historical event in a sense in which the Resurrection is not. The Crucifixion marks the victory of the world over the love of God; it is the victory of the cultural powers over the power of faith—the victory of Satan over God, the victory of fallen man over Christ. Therefore, the men of the world stood under the Cross, believing themselves to be superior to the Savior. "And the soldiers clothed him with purple, and platted a crown of thorns, and put it about his head, and began to salute him, Hail, King of the Jews!"[28] They mocked his mission and degraded his divine

28. Mark 15:17-18.

dignity and sublimity. They did not know what they did. This is the victory of blind necessity over providential freedom. This is the victory of the "killing" letter over the "quickening" spirit. This is the victory of the world over the Eternal Ego.

The Resurrection is the correction of this abysmal error; it reverses the meaning of the event by bringing out the truth that the letter is weaker than the spirit; that time cannot destroy what is eternal; that freedom and foresight are more powerful than necessity and ignorance; that the world can never defeat God and that Satan can never conquer mankind. In this sense the Resurrection is the true center of the Christian faith, its greatest manifestation and its most sacred mystery. It images the victory of faith over culture; it mirrors faith in its unlimited glory. "Behold the hour cometh, yea, is now come, that ye shall be scattered, every man to his own, and shall leave me alone: and yet I am not alone, because the Father is with me. These things I have spoken unto you, that in me ye might have peace. In the world ye shall have tribulation: but be of good cheer; I have overcome the world."[29]

29. John 16:32–33.